GUEST OF HONOR

GUEST
OF
HONOR

———◆———

Booker T. Washington,

Theodore Roosevelt,

and the White House Dinner

That Shocked a Nation

———◆———

DEBORAH DAVIS

ATRIA BOOKS

NEW YORK   LONDON   TORONTO   SYDNEY   NEW DELHI

ATRIA BOOKS

A Division of Simon & Schuster, Inc.
1230 Avenue of the Americas
New York, NY 10020

First Atria Books hardcover edition May 2012

ATRIA BOOKS and colophon are trademarks of Simon & Schuster, Inc.

For information about special discounts for bulk purchases,
please contact Simon & Schuster Special Sales at 1-866-506-1949
or business@simonandschuster.com.

The Simon & Schuster Speakers Bureau can bring authors to
your live event. For more information or to book an event,
contact the Simon & Schuster Speakers Bureau at 1-866-248-3049
or visit our website at www.simonspeakers.com.

Designed by Joseph Rutt/Level C Design

Manufactured in the United States of America

10   9   8   7   6   5   4   3   2   1

Library of Congress Cataloging-in-Publication Data
Davis, Deborah, date.
    Guest of honor : Booker T. Washington, Theodore Roosevelt, and the White House
dinner that shocked a nation / by Deborah Davis.—1st Atria Books hardcover ed.
        p.   cm.
1. Roosevelt, Theodore, 1858–1919.   2. Washington, Booker T., 1856–1915.
3. Presidents—United States—Biography.   4. African American educators—
United States—Biography.   5. United States—Social conditions—1865–1918.
6. United States—Race relations—History—20th century.   7. United States—
Politics and government—1901–1909.   I. Title.
    E757.D247 2012
    973.91'1092—dc23
    [B]   2012009045

ISBN 978-1-4391-6981-0
ISBN 978-1-4391-6983-4 (ebook)

For my husband, Mark Urman

A dinner invitation to the White House, it is said, is like a command. Etiquette rules that it cannot be declined.

—Gilson Willets,
Inside History of the White House

CONTENTS

———◆———

GUEST OF HONOR

INTRODUCTION

———•◆•———

C an a dinner change history?

On October 16, 1901, President Theodore Roosevelt invited Booker T. Washington, distinguished educator and renowned African American leader, to dine with the First Family at the White House. Washington accepted, and the two men, along with Mrs. Roosevelt and another guest, spent a convivial evening eating, drinking, and discussing politics. The meal seemed uneventful until the next morning, when news that a black man had dinner with the President sent shock waves through the nation. Though blacks had built the White House, worked for most of the presidents (including Roosevelt), performed at the chief executive's musical recitals, and held political office, not a single African American had ever been invited there to dine. The event, unprecedented in White House history, provoked inflammatory newspaper articles, political cartoons, fire-and-brimstone speeches, even vulgar songs. The scandal escalated to the point where this single dinner ignited a storm of controversy, divided the country, and threatened to topple two of America's greatest men.

It may have been headline news in 1901, but I had never heard of this particular "first," nor of its tumultuous aftermath, until presidential candidate John McCain mentioned it in his concession speech on election night, 2008. I was intrigued because I considered such unexplored moments in social history my specialty. In earlier books, I had told the little-known story of a controversial painting that almost destroyed the career of the great artist John Singer Sargent, and I'd chronicled the behind-the-scenes drama of Truman Capote's legendary Black and White Ball. As soon as I heard about it, I wondered if this scandalous White House dinner could be the inspiration for my next project.

At the age of forty-two, TR, as Theodore Roosevelt liked to be called (never "Teddy"), was America's youngest president, and he had amassed an astounding list of accomplishments during his four energetic decades. In addition to being an author, historian, naturalist, rancher, Republican Party dynamo, and founder of the fabled Rough Riders during the Spanish-American War, TR had served as police commissioner of New York City, assistant secretary of the navy, governor of New York, and vice president of the United States. Nineteen hundred and one was the year that a Japanese scientist isolated the powerful hormone adrenaline, and TR may have been the first official "adrenaline junkie." He was at his best when life was fast, risky, and challenging. As president, he successfully arm-wrestled with big business, was one of the founders of what we now call the "green" movement, and brought youth, vitality, and sheer testosterone to the White House.

In 1901, forty-five-year-old Booker T. Washington was the

country's most famous and respected African American. He had founded Alabama's Tuskegee Institute, an industrial school for blacks, wrote the bestselling autobiography *Up from Slavery*, dazzled audiences with his powerful speaking skills, and sipped tea with Queen Victoria at Windsor Palace. At the height of his illustrious career, Booker T., as I will usually refer to him, was dubbed the "Negro Moses," the man best equipped to lead his newly emancipated race into the twentieth century.

As I immersed myself in the wealth of historical material about TR and Booker T., including books, essays, and newspaper articles about them, as well as all the letters and memoirs that they had written, I was struck by the many similarities between their seemingly disparate lives. Like mirror images, they both pursued lofty goals in childhood, found love and suffered loss as young men, embraced public service throughout their careers, and emerged as leaders. Even the homes they built, TR's "Sagamore Hill" and Booker T.'s "The Oaks," were oddly similar. In a more enlightened time, they might have traded places, with TR heading a school and Booker T. entering the White House.

They were great men, but they weren't perfect, and it is those imperfections that I found most interesting about them. TR could be so reckless that fans and foes alike bemoaned his inability to control himself. Whether he was jumping head-first into battle (as he did during the Spanish-American War) or making the occasional ill-considered remark about race, sometimes he just didn't think, and his rash behavior undermined his good intentions.

Booker T., on the other hand, was accused of being overly cautious. He preached patience and moderation instead of activism, and, according to his detractors, he failed to hold the

South accountable for its attitudes and actions. In their disapproving eyes, he was an "Uncle Tom." I didn't see him that way. Booker T. may have tried too hard to please, and some of his ideas about uplift were a little simple (for example, be clean, industrious, and perform a job well, and the South will make a place for you). Nonetheless, he was the architect of a practical plan for blacks to become educated, enlightened, and self-sufficient. In his own way, he was the bridge between slavery and the civil rights movement. Even now, students at Tuskegee are inspired by him. "I like to call him Booker T.," a tour guide at the Oaks told me, explaining that he felt as if he knew him personally.

Every book has its surprises, and my biggest revelation in writing this one was the story's remarkable supporting cast of African American achievers. Many of them, like Booker T., had been born into slavery and faced seemingly insurmountable obstacles, yet they succeeded. I came across a fascinating roster of black politicians, poets, musicians, lawyers, professors, artists, writers, and experts on etiquette, as well as a famous socialite and a legendary football coach who modeled his gridiron plays on Napoleonic military maneuvers. Although many of these men and women have been forgotten by the general public, their histories remain fresh and enthralling sagas of accomplishment at a time when opportunity, advancement, and equality were seemingly within the grasp of black Americans for the first time.

Contrary to my initial impression, there was nothing at all musty about the year 1901, which provided a vibrant, many-layered backdrop for the Roosevelt-Washington story. Movies had just been born, so America entered the new century calling for lights! cameras! and action! The country converted from steam power to electricity, snapped photographs with the revolutionary and easy-to-operate Kodak "Brownie," and danced to the beat of an exciting new sound called "ragtime." The emphasis was on Progress with a capital *P*. Americans were racing forward, full tilt ahead. However, there were still reactionary stumbles along the way, and the conflagration surrounding this particular White House dinner was one of them.

When I was growing up in the 1960s, one of the most important frontiers in the civil rights movement was the lunch counter. All over the South, black (as well as white) activists protested segregation by staging sit-ins at restaurants where African Americans were denied service. In 1901, the White House dining room table was the precursor of those lunch counters. Booker T. sat with the President, fully aware of the risk, knowing that one way in which equality could be measured was by where an African American could—or could not—dine.

Can a dinner change history? I believe this one did. And, like every important dinner, it begins with a host, an invitation, and a guest of honor.

THE BIG HOUSE

———•◆•———

Hale's Ford, Virginia, was "about as near to nowhere as any locality gets to be." That's how Booker T. described the rural community in Franklin County where he was born in April 1856, or maybe '57 or '58—he was never sure of the year because the records kept by slaves were very sketchy. He wasn't sure about his father, either, although rumor had it that he was a white man from a nearby plantation, possibly the Hatcher farm or the Ferguson place. His mother, Jane, cooked for her owners, the Burroughs family, and lived with her three children, John, Booker T., and little Amanda, in a broken-down cabin on their property. The floor was dirt, the walls were cracked, and the centerpiece of the dilapidated one-room dwelling was a large pit where the Burroughses stored their sweet potatoes for the winter. There was also a swinging "cat" door for a house pet to use as an entrance and exit, something that always amused Booker T. because there were enough holes in the broken walls to provide full access for a whole litter of cats.

Jane had a husband, a slave named Washington Ferguson who belonged to the Ferguson family next door, but she saw him infrequently because he was hired out on jobs far from home. Whenever he visited, Wash proved to be a hard, unsentimental man with little patience for his two stepsons or his daughter, Amanda. During the Civil War he escaped to West Virginia, where he became a free man. Not that his new life was easy. Wash toiled in the salt mines of the Kanawha Valley and endured long separations from his wife back in Hale's Ford.

Although Booker T. always referred to the Burroughs home as the "big house," there was nothing big about it. The word *plantation* usually evoked images of stately white mansions with Roman columns and sweeping verandas, but Jones and Elizabeth Burroughs and, at various times, some or all of their fourteen children lived in a nondescript, five-room house made of logs. They were working farmers, not Southern aristocrats, and the ten slaves they owned were an investment as well as a source of labor. Each slave had a dollar value. Jane, who was getting on in years, was worth $250, while Booker T., who had a lifetime of work ahead of him, was assessed at $400.

Daily life for Booker T. was defined by what he didn't have and couldn't do. He and his siblings never slept in a bed or sat down at a table to share a meal. Instead they ate like "dumb animals," he later recalled, grabbing "a piece of bread here and a scrap of meat there." Even kernels of corn that had been overlooked by the pigs were fair game for a hungry boy. Having a mother who was a cook made things worse because she prepared the meals for the "big house" in her own fireplace, and the tantalizing scents of forbidden foods reminded the children of what they were missing. Occasionally Jane would see to it that a bootlegged chicken came their way but, more than anything, Booker T. coveted the ginger cakes he saw his young mistresses serve their visitors. He thought the delicacies, sweet with molasses and fragrant with the exotic scent of ginger, were "the most tempting and desirable things" he had ever seen. Freedom, in his childish imagination, was an unlimited supply of ginger cakes.

Booker T.'s dream was to learn to read. His favorite chore was to escort one of the Burroughs daughters to the Frog Pond Schoolhouse down the road. After she would go inside, he lingered and listened at the window, fascinated by the lessons and recitations he heard. He couldn't make much sense of it, just enough to know that he wanted to enter this "paradise" and learn more. This was out of the question because teaching a slave to read was against the law in Virginia and everywhere else in the South. Besides, his other chores beckoned. There was corn to deliver to the mill, water to distribute to the field hands, and plenty of cleaning and sweeping.

The job he enjoyed most was fanning the dining room while his owners ate their meals. It wasn't hard—all he had to do was work a pulley that operated a system of paper fans—and he could be privy to the family's conversations. They discussed news of the ongoing war between the South and the North, and the machinations of Abraham Lincoln, the man they deemed responsible for all their troubles.

In the slave quarters, however, Lincoln was a god. Booker T. was often awakened by the sound of his mother praying for Lincoln to win the war, so she and her children could be free. Other slaves shared her reverence for the Union leader and, according to Booker T., "all their dreams and hopes of freedom were in some way or other coupled with the name of Lincoln."

In April 1865, Lincoln's forces entered Richmond, Virginia,

and Union soldiers brought news of victory to slaves throughout the state. Jane, her children, and the rest of the slaves were
called to the big house. Assembled on the front porch, they listened excitedly as the Emancipation Proclamation was read to
them by a Union officer. The incredible truth that they were
free sank in.

As the Burroughses watched the rejoicing of their former
slaves, they seemed sad, not only because of the loss of their
property, Booker T. observed, but also because they would be
"parting with those who were in many ways very close to them."

Some slaves, especially the older ones, decided to stay with
the Burroughses because they could not imagine a life other
than the one they knew. But Jane made up her mind that the
only way to experience freedom was to leave the plantation.
The family jubilantly packed their belongings in a small cart and
set out to join Wash Ferguson in West Virginia. Booker T. and
his siblings had to walk and camp in the wilderness throughout
the two-hundred-mile trek to their new home. There were long
days, cold nights, and even a terrifying encounter with a giant
snake in an abandoned cabin. But their newly acquired freedom
made the band of travelers feel euphoric and invincible.

Casting a shadow over Booker T.'s happiness was the sad
news of Abraham Lincoln's assassination. The great leader was
fatally shot on April 14, 1865. Even as Booker T. celebrated his
own promising future, he mourned the death of his hero, who
had virtually transformed him from a piece of property into a
proud and independent citizen of the United States.

———•◆•———

FIVE HUNDRED MILES from the backwoods of Virginia, in
the heart of New York City, six-year-old Theodore Roosevelt

and his little brother, Elliott, solemnly stood at a second-floor window in the Union Square mansion owned by their wealthy grandfather, Cornelius Van Schaack Roosevelt. It was April 25, 1865, and the two young boys were enthralled by the sight of Abraham Lincoln's funeral procession passing directly in front of the house. The President's body, which had been on view in Washington, DC, was on its way to its final resting place in Springfield, Illinois, by way of Baltimore, Harrisburg, Philadelphia, Jersey City, and New York, where a significant tribute was in progress.

Theodore, who was born in New York City on October 27, 1858, worshipped Lincoln. But one of his earliest life lessons was that there were two sides—a North and a South—to every story. His mother, Martha Bulloch, was a Southern belle who grew up on a plantation in Roswell, Georgia, while his father, Theodore Roosevelt Sr., was a philanthropic Northerner from one of New York's original aristocratic Dutch families. "Mittie," as Martha was called, and "Thee" adored each other and their four children: Anna ("Bamie"), Theodore (sometimes called "Teedie" in his youth, and later TR), Elliott, and Corinne.

The family enjoyed a genteel existence in their five-story brownstone at 28 East Twentieth Street. Mittie, who always dressed in white, was considered one of the most beautiful women in the city, and Thee was so involved in his children's lives that they called him "Greatheart," after the hero in John Bunyan's allegory *The Pilgrim's Progress.* Money was plentiful— Thee's father owned a successful glass business—and his fortune enabled his sons to make fortunes of their own.

The Roosevelt children were a smart, energetic, and good-natured bunch. They were educated at home by their mother's sister, Anna Bulloch, and fussed over by their grandmother

Bulloch, who moved in with them after her husband died. Surrounded by doting relatives, they enjoyed a secure and privileged life, from the bountiful meals served in the family's parlor floor dining room, to the toys and comfortable beds that awaited them in their upstairs nursery. The children had a few complaints—the horsehair furniture in the parlor was prickly, they suffered the occasional punishment for misbehavior, and TR's recurring bouts of asthma sent the whole household into a panic, usually in the middle of the night. But, for the most part, the Roosevelts' familial universe was a tranquil one until 1861, when the outbreak of the Civil War created understandable tension in a household torn by divided loyalties.

Mittie's brothers, James and Irvine Bulloch, were conscientious Southern gentlemen who eagerly enlisted in the Confederate Army, and Mittie, her mother, and her sister shared their enthusiasm for the cause. Thee, on the other hand, was a staunch supporter of Lincoln and the Union Army. Knowing that his wife was terrified that he and her brothers might come face-to-face on the battlefield, Thee paid a thousand dollars to a surrogate to fight in his place, a common practice at the time. Not that he shirked his wartime responsibilities. The ever-diligent Roosevelt was the architect of the country's first payroll savings program for soldiers, which enabled military men to put aside money for their families while they were off fighting the war.

TR honored his Southern roots when he helped his mother surreptitiously send care packages to her relatives in Georgia. And he paid homage to his father when he theatrically prayed aloud for the Union Army to "grind the Southern troops to powder," something he did when he wanted to annoy his mother. Mittie and Thee maintained their relationship and their sense of humor, however, and managed to navigate these challenging wartime years.

The Roosevelts set aside their conflicting loyalties to pay tribute to Abraham Lincoln on the occasion of his funeral. The entire city was in mourning, its businesses closed and its silent buildings swathed in black, with crowds lining the streets, jockeying for the best vantage points. Lincoln's hearse was drawn by sixteen gray horses and followed by a procession of fifty thousand mourners. The cortege was so big, and moved so slowly, that it took four hours to pass by the Roosevelts' window. The boys had the best view in town when the procession stopped in Union Square for a memorial service. There were speeches, prayers, and a reading of poet William Cullen Bryant's "Funeral Ode to Abraham Lincoln." Despite the record number of spectators, the city was eerily silent. "New York showed its grief at Lincoln's death amply and elegantly," praised the *New York Times.*

There was one unfortunate backstage drama that almost spoiled the tribute. Inexplicably, the New York City planning committee refused to allow African Americans to march in the cortege, a shocking decision considering that Lincoln was responsible for freeing the slaves. If the dead man's horse could follow him, why not "the men for whom President Lincoln fought and worked, and died," incredulous members of the black community asked.

Ultimately, it took an irate telegram from the secretary of war to resolve the issue. "It is the desire of the Secretary of War that no discrimination respecting color should be exercised in admitting persons to the funeral procession in New York tomorrow," snapped the official communiqué. Grieving blacks were permitted to join their white counterparts in the procession, where they could "drop a tear to the memory of their messiah and redeemer." A journalist covering the story noted sarcastically, "That ended the war of the races."

STRIVE AND SUCCEED

————•◆•————

In the late 1860s, TR and Booker T. were young boys filled with energy, enthusiasm, and boundless curiosity: they embodied the new, postbellum spirit of America. The feeling was that *anything* could be accomplished with a little pluck and luck. This was the capitalist gospel preached by author Horatio Alger Jr. in his popular motivational novels, with such apt titles as *Paddle Your Own Canoe; Sink, or Swim;* and *Strive and Succeed.*

Ironically, Alger's real-life story was not the lively and uplifting stuff of his fiction. As a young man, he aspired to be a writer and enjoyed some success with his short stories for juveniles. But his overbearing father, an old-school Unitarian minister, insisted his son follow in his footsteps. After dutifully graduating from divinity school in 1864, Alger accepted a position with a small congregation on Cape Cod. His career came to an abrupt end when two boys accused the young minister of sexual improprieties and the horrified church elders quickly sent him packing.

Alger moved to New York City, where he became fascinated with the lost boys—the homeless "newsies," bootblacks, and street musicians who seemed to be everywhere after the Civil War. These vagabond children lived on the streets, supporting themselves as best they could. In 1854 they received a helping hand from the Children's Aid Society, which opened the first Newsboys' Lodging House, a refuge where a homeless boy could find a bed and a hot meal. One of the charity's most active and enthusiastic patrons was Theodore Roosevelt Sr., who visited every Sunday and brought TR with him.

Alger was also a frequent visitor, and the boys he met at the Lodging House were the inspiration for "Ragged Dick," "Paul the Peddler," "Phil the Fiddler," and dozens of other characters who became cultural icons for generations of admiring young readers. One of the writer's biggest fans was seven-year-old TR, who enthusiastically read Alger's short story "How Johnny Bought a Sewing-Machine" in his favorite children's magazine, *Our Young Folks*.

TR recognized Johnny as a kindred spirit and embraced the idea that hard work, discipline, and courage could transform any boy into a hero, and any life into an adventure. The problem was that everyday survival was not an issue for the moneyed Roosevelts, so TR had to create his own adventures. Many of his ideas came from books. He was an enthusiastic reader who started working his way through the family library at such an early age that sometimes the oversized volumes were bigger than he was. TR was drawn to stories about great explorers, from Dr. Livingstone in the jungle to Natty Bumppo in the American West, to mythic heroes, such as Longfellow's King Olaf, and to academic texts about science and natural history.

TR's favorite roles were those of scientist and explorer, and he took them very seriously. He collected animals and insects for his "Roosevelt Museum of Natural History," mimicking his father, who was one of the founders of the American Museum of Natural History in New York City. When writing about his bug collection, the young naturalist noted, "Now and then a friend has told me something about them but mostly I have gained their habbits from ofservation." He even taught himself how to dissect and preserve specimens, and dramatically bemoaned the great "loss to science" when his mother threw away a stash of dead mice he had stored in the kitchen.

TR was bright, curious, daring, and wise beyond his years, but his quick mind and exuberant personality were trapped in a sickly body that held him back from the audacious life he imagined for himself. He was, in fact, the classic weakling who was always at the mercy of bullies. He was thin and gangly, and suffered from frequent debilitating bouts of asthma that left him gasping for breath and had his terrified parents administering coffee, cigars, bursts of cold air, and other desperate remedies meant to shock his lungs into working properly. "I was sick of the Asthma last night," he wrote repeatedly in his diary. He also had attacks of cholera morbus, a form of gastroenteritis that caused diarrhea and vomiting.

Theodore Sr. was convinced that his son's physical debilities would stand in his way, so he did what any good Victorian father would do—he urged TR to find a way to overcome them. "Theodore, you have the mind, but you don't have the body," he said. "Without the help of the body, the mind cannot go as far as it should. You must make your body," he urged. It was a loving challenge, but a challenge nonetheless. Adolescence brought TR to a crossroads. If he wanted to realize his potential, he had to act on his father's advice.

TR started exercising at John Wood's gymnasium on East Twenty-Eighth Street. Wood's advertisement in the *New York Times* suggested that "all young men of sedentary habits" should be coming to his gym for classes. Society families like the Roosevelts sent their pampered sons to train there much as they enrolled them in dancing school. TR's mother sat on the sidelines, watching her boy lift weights, pound the punching bag, and struggle at the chest machine. Mittie was so impressed by her son's dedication to his regime that she commissioned Wood to turn the screened porch outside the Roosevelt nursery, or the piazza, as the family called it, into a private gym. (She sometimes regretted the impulse whenever the boys did something really daring, such as hoisting a plank over the edge of the second-story wall to use as a "balance bar.")

TR worked out faithfully but did not see immediate results. The scrawny teenager was still bait for bullies, as he discovered on a trip to Maine, when he encountered two rowdy boys who teased him mercilessly because they sensed he was, as he himself put it, a "predestined victim." TR wasn't hurt but he was frustrated and embarrassed by his inability to defend himself. With his father's encouragement, he signed up for boxing lessons with John Long, a former prize-fighter. TR was slow and awkward at first, but he persevered. When Long staged "championship" matches among his students, TR gave his all. One thrilling day, he defeated his opponents—boys he described as being even scrawnier than he was—and won first prize, a pewter cup. To TR, that small, inexpensive trophy instantly became his most prized possession because it symbolized his newfound ability to *win*.

His self-improvement campaign received a big boost when his father gave him a twelve-gauge shotgun. TR was enthusiastic about hunting but discovered that his targets always seemed to elude him. It turned out that the problem was poor eyesight, and the solution was spectacles. "I had no idea how beautiful the world was," he marveled, once he donned his first pair of glasses. They literally gave him a new outlook on life, and his toned body made him feel stronger, healthier, and more in control.

In the fall of 1872, the Roosevelts embarked on a trip abroad that included a long voyage up the Nile on an exotic *dahabeah*, a luxurious private boat. The *Aboo Erdan* was a floating palace, outfitted with every convenience. On this expedition, the sickly boy was replaced by an energetic and intrepid adolescent who galloped through each day, hunting, shooting, riding, collecting specimens, and exploring ruins, just like the scientists and adventurers he admired.

———•◆•———

THE JOURNEY NINE-YEAR-OLD Booker T. began with such excitement in April 1865 ended unhappily ten days later in Malden, West Virginia, where he discovered that Wash Ferguson lived in an ugly little shanty in a slum, a place far less appealing than the old Burroughs cabin. At the nearby salt mines, giant coal-fueled furnaces pumped black smoke into the air, covering everything with layers of filth. And it wasn't just the air that was unwholesome. "Some of our neighbors were coloured people and some were the poorest and most degraded white people. . . . Drinking, gambling, quarrels, fights, and shockingly immoral practices were frequent," Booker T. later recalled.

Wash wasted no time in announcing that he was counting on his stepsons to help support the family. That meant they had to work beside him in the salt mines, leaving no time for school. An unhappy Booker T. realized that he had traded one kind of slavery for another. His mother saw his disappointment and managed to get hold of a dog-eared copy of *Webster's Spelling Primer* for beginning readers. Thrilled to own his first book, Booker T. studied the alphabet in his spare time, until the strange squiggles started to make sense. He also took lessons at night from a young black teacher who had moved to Malden to run the local school.

A little bit of knowledge made him want more and, eventually, he persuaded Wash to let him attend school during the day. There was one catch: Booker T. would have to work the early shift at the mine before racing off to class, and waiting for the shift to end meant missing the beginning of lessons. He came up with the clever solution of setting the mine's clock a half hour ahead so he could leave in time to make the start of classes. Of course, there was hell to pay when his bosses figured out what he had done. They reset the clock and locked it away from his prying hands.

At school, Booker T. noticed that all of the children had at least two or three names. Throughout the South, newly emancipated slaves selected their own surnames to assert their independence from their former masters. When his teacher asked, "What is *your* name?" he thought carefully before replying. For as long as he could remember, he was always called Booker—just Booker—and he never imagined being more than that. Now, in a powerful moment of self-creation, he answered "Washington, Booker Washington." He selected Washington because it was synonymous with history, freedom, and greatness. It no longer mattered that he'd never known his biological father. For the first time, he had a name and an identity all his own. The initial *T* came when he learned that his mother had given him a middle name, Taliaferro (pronounced "Tolliver").

Thanks to his lessons, Booker T.'s mind was expanding, but his world seemed to be shrinking. Wash hired him out to work at the local coal mine, a dirty and dangerous place that he despised. Another opportunity came his way, but it had drawbacks of its own. Mrs. Viola Ruffner, the wife of the mine owner, was looking for a houseboy and someone recommended Booker T. for the job. Mrs. Ruffner was an exacting Yankee who went through servants at a rapid rate because no one could meet her standards. Booker T. was frustrated in his efforts to please her, until he decided to treat the Ruffner household as if it, too, were a classroom. Whether the lesson involved sweeping a floor or sewing on a button, Booker T. was an attentive pupil who seized the chance to observe his "betters" and emulate them. Mrs. Ruffner had an air of the schoolmarm about her so she encouraged Booker T. to improve himself. "He was always ready for his books," she said in praise. Her library inspired him to assemble one of his own. His bookcase was an old dry-goods crate housing a few cast-off volumes, but he was proud of it.

By the time he was fifteen years old, he was curious about everything, including politics. He joined the local chapter of the Republican Party, and his mastery of reading and writing won him the job of secretary, an accomplishment he never imagined possible when he was a slave. But Booker T. still had higher ambitions, and longed to see the world beyond Malden. One day he overheard two miners talking about a school in Virginia, the Hampton Normal and Agricultural Institute. According to them, it had been established for colored students, some of whom were permitted to work on campus to cover the cost of their tuition. Booker T. didn't know where the school was located, or how he could possibly get there, but he thought about it day and night. "I was on fire constantly with one ambition," he said, "and that was to go to Hampton."

Even Booker T.'s mother, always his staunchest supporter, thought this dream was impossible. However, her son was so persistent that ultimately, albeit reluctantly, she gave him her blessing, and helped him pack his small satchel for his journey to Hampton, nearly four hundred miles away. His brother, John, contributed some hard-earned money to the cause, and friends offered pennies, nickels, and quarters—whatever they could spare—to the boy who was going off to "boarding school."

In the fall of 1872, well-wishers waved as Booker T. left Malden in high style, on a stagecoach, but early on in the trip he ran out of funds and had to walk and hitchhike the rest of the way. Each day brought new challenges and hardships. Money, or the lack of it, was always his problem, but there were other unanticipated ones. When the coach stopped at a small hotel in the mountains, Booker T. thought he could persuade the owner to give him shelter for the night, despite his empty pockets, because that's what people back home did for one another. The man turned him away without even asking if he had money, and Booker T. was surprised to learn that black people were not welcome at the establishment, simply because they were black.

In all likelihood, the proprietor of the Virginia hotel was a solid Southerner who was expressing his mounting resentment about the federal government's Reconstruction Acts. They chafed when Congress carved the former Confederacy into five zones and imposed military control. The stern message from Washington was that if Virginia, the Carolinas, Georgia, Alabama, Florida, Arkansas, Mississippi, Texas, and Louisiana refused to protect the rights of their newly liberated African American citizens, federal troops would do the job for them.

The real insult to Southern sensibilities was the idea of *social* equality. "Obedience and even the semblance of affection were the first requirements of slave conduct," according to historian Bertram Wyatt-Brown, and a good slave supported the illusion that the "master" was a superior being. After emancipation, that "clear vertical hierarchy" was eliminated and white Southerners had to divide space "horizontally, albeit unequally." Suddenly it was important to institute a new unwritten code, a sort of racial etiquette, to keep that division intact. Don't look a white person in the eye; don't take up too much room on the sidewalk; don't enter a house through the front door; don't be too assertive—enforced deference was the new slavery, and there were serious consequences for breaking the rules.

"This was my first experience in finding out what the colour of my skin meant," Booker T. said about the incident at the hotel. The realities of the road dimmed his enthusiasm, but not his determination.

Three hundred miles later, he arrived in Richmond, Virginia, a victory of sorts because he was only about eighty miles from his final destination. Still, he was penniless, and everywhere he looked, food stands heaped high with fried chicken, apple pies and all manner of delicacies taunted him. Surrounded by prosperity and plenty, he was tired, hungry, dirty, and lonely. His bed that night was a patch of bare ground under an elevated sidewalk, his battered satchel serving as his pillow.

The next morning, Booker T. found a job as a stevedore and managed to work a few days to earn enough money to finish the trip to Hampton. Sometime in October, he finally found himself standing in front of Academic Hall. The place he'd imagined as a grand palace of learning was, in reality, a modest redbrick building. But it was the gateway to opportunity. It marked the end of one quest and the beginning of another, because, while Booker T. had made it to Hampton, he still had to persuade the school to accept him.

Mary F. Mackie, Hampton's head teacher, took one look at the bedraggled sixteen-year-old and dismissed him as a tramp. Booker T. didn't blame her for thinking he was unworthy—he *was* a sorry sight after so many days on the road—but he knew he could impress her, if only she would give him a chance. That chance came when Miss Mackie asked him to sweep one of the recitation rooms. Thanks to his training with Mrs. Ruffner, no one cleaned as thoroughly as Booker T. He swept the room once, and then did it again and again, until the old floorboards gleamed. He dusted the furniture four times, as if his future depended on it. In fact, it did.

When Miss Mackie examined his work, she announced, "I guess you will do to enter this institution." She hired him as janitor, which enabled him to pay the ten-dollar monthly fee the school charged for board. His tuition, seventy dollars a year, was deferred. His mission accomplished, Booker T. was, in his own words, "one of the happiest souls on earth."

THE FORCE THAT WINS

———•◆•———

When Booker T. started classes at Hampton he discovered that his academic schedule was far more demanding than anything he had experienced at the plantation, or in the mines, for that matter. The school day began at 5:00 AM and the pace was brisk for the next twelve hours, as he studied arithmetic, grammar, geography, bookkeeping, spelling, writing, elocution, and other subjects. There were small pockets of time for recess, meals, and prayers, followed by bedtime at 9:30 PM.

Being away at school presented lifestyle challenges Booker T. never anticipated. His dormitory bed was baffling because it had two sheets—something he had never seen before. The first night he slept on top of them, and the second he squeezed himself under both, until finally he watched his dorm mates and followed their example. Hampton meals were served at regular hours, with tablecloths and napkins, and students were expected to know how to use the cutlery. They were also required to bathe and brush their teeth every day, and to wash their own clothes. The bath was a revelation to Booker T., who discovered that being clean made him feel healthy, even virtuous, and did wonders for his self-respect. As long as there was water, whether from a faucet or a backwoods stream, he put it to good use. Maintaining his wardrobe was trickier because he didn't own much more than the clothing on his back. Most nights he had to scrub his only pair of socks and hope they would be dry by morning, or else his feet would be cold and damp the rest of the day.

Fortunately, Booker T. had a mentor to guide him through this strange new world of curriculum, manners, and hygiene. General Samuel Chapman Armstrong, Hampton's founder, was the son of a Presbyterian missionary who had transplanted his family to Hawaii, where his children grew up among the natives. Observing the islanders' struggle to become "civilized," young Armstrong concluded that industry and morality went hand in hand—a busy native was a good native. His prior experience with "savages" (which is how the Hawaiians were viewed by mainlanders) earned him a special position in the Union Army during the Civil War—he was placed in charge of a troop of African American soldiers. After a series of promotions, the young general emerged from the military as a social crusader. Armstrong hatched a postwar plan to help newly emancipated slaves help themselves. The Hampton Institute, his brainchild, was the place where they would do it.

Booker T. called Armstrong "the noblest, rarest human being that it has ever been my privilege to meet." He wanted to be just like Armstrong—altruistic, hardworking, principled, and, above all, a gentleman.

He thrived under Armstrong's tutelage and took advantage of all that Hampton had to offer, seizing every opportunity for self-improvement. When he noticed a twenty-minute gap between dinner and study hall each night, he organized a group of debaters who called themselves the "After Supper Club," and they used the time to perfect their skills. Debating led to lessons in oratory, and he practiced public speaking with a fellow student who came from New England so that his own words would sound less "plantation" and more refined. Next he studied the speeches of Abraham Lincoln, hoping to emulate his powerful ideas, verbal clarity, and homespun humor. From Lincoln, Booker T. learned that a modest demeanor and a well-timed anecdote or joke could charm the most difficult audience, a lesson that would serve him well all his life. Even though he was the youngest member of his class, he became its leader. "You literally took the school by storm," a classmate told him almost twenty years later.

Hampton wasn't all about intellectual pursuits and polish. General Armstrong stressed the practical importance of an industrial education and encouraged his students to recognize that there was dignity, not shame, in manual labor. Booker T. continued to work as the school janitor while he studied and, during the summer months, he supplemented his income by returning to the mines in Malden or waiting on tables at a resort in Connecticut. In 1875, his final year at Hampton, Booker T. was asked to participate in a part of the graduation ceremony that consisted of a public debate regarding the United States' annexation of Cuba. His persuasive argument against it (if the country doesn't know what to do with its four hundred thousand newly emancipated blacks, he wisely pointed out, how could it take responsibility for an influx of uneducated Cubans?) won high praise from a visiting *New York Times* reporter, who said that Booker T. "presented with vigor" and "carried the whole audience, both white and black."

He was an exemplary graduate with a seemingly bright future, but like so many young people fresh out of school, Booker T. couldn't decide what he wanted to do, or where he wanted to go. He drifted for the next two years while attempting to make up his mind. He taught in Malden, considered becoming a lawyer, and even entertained the notion of going into politics. In 1878, his strong oratorical skills led him to enroll in the Wayland Baptist Seminary in Washington, DC, to study for the ministry. Booker T. had not experienced a "call to preach"—a religious epiphany that struck some African American churchgoers with such intensity at the time that it prompted them to fall dramatically to the floor in a trance. But he did know that preaching was one of the most popular and accessible professions for blacks during Reconstruction, so he decided to try it.

Eighteen seventy-eight was an exciting time for Booker T. to move to Washington to begin his religious studies. For one thing, the capital's $18 million renovation had just been completed and the city never looked better. Old Washington had been a "miserable mockery of a metropolis," according to one critic, especially immediately following the Civil War. The streets, where they existed, were uneven, unpaved, and bordered by cheap stores, dilapidated buildings, and unsightly tent cities inhabited by soldiers and emancipated slaves. A stagnant canal emitted foul odors and bred pestilence. There was mud everywhere, except in the areas that were small Saharas of dust. Even the Washington Monument was a blight on the landscape. America's marble tribute to its first president was abandoned in 1856 when the project ran out of funds so, for years, an unsightly fragment sat on an empty lot. The city looked so run-down that there was serious talk of moving the U.S. capital to another, more attractive part of the country. St. Louis was one of the locations under consideration.

Washington needed a major face-lift, and Alexander Shepherd was the enterprising man who tackled the job. In 1871, Shepherd had been appointed vice chair of the Board of Public Works. People called him the American Haussmann, evoking the work of Baron Georges-Eugène Haussmann, the visionary French city planner who had recently transformed Paris from a medieval warren of decrepit buildings to the beautiful "City of Light." Shepherd wanted to perform the same kind of alchemy in Washington, so he called for 180 miles of paving, 200 miles of sidewalks, and 25,000 shade trees. He filled the canal, covered the swamps, drained the mud, tore down old buildings, and built spacious drives and parks throughout the city.

The new Washington was beautiful, but Booker T. was a country boy at heart, and he had an ingrained suspicion that cities were unwholesome places where people succumbed to bad influences. He disapproved of the fast living he witnessed in the capital and was especially critical of the young blacks who migrated to Washington during Reconstruction. Many obtained low-level government jobs but wasted their wages on frivolities and dressed up in overpriced finery they could ill afford. Sometimes they spent half a week's salary to hire a carriage for a few hours so they could pretend to be society folk. They were imitating wealthy Washingtonians in the hope of fitting in, but their efforts often made them the butt of ridicule, and they were called "Bon-tons" by their detractors.

Booker T. criticized blacks who worked and squandered their wages, but he was even more disapproving of those who *didn't* work at all. After the war, many slaves left their rural homes for the nearest big city, and the District of Columbia was a choice destination because it was relatively hospitable. The Freedmen's Bureau established a refugee camp that provided food, schools, and hospitals. "A large proportion of these people had been drawn to Washington because they felt that they could lead a life of ease there," Booker T. observed, but he concluded that "there seemed to be a dependence on the government for every conceivable thing." The word *dependence* was not in Booker T.'s vocabulary. He believed that the best kind of help was *self*-help.

At the opposite end of the social scale were the politicians, professors, doctors, lawyers, businessmen, and bankers who constituted the rarefied social world of the capital's black aristocracy, and they kept their distance from ordinary "coloreds." They lived in beautiful houses maintained by servants, their children attended good schools, and they vacationed at expensive resorts. Some affluent black families, such as the Wormleys, dated back to the city's earliest times. James Wormley was born "free" in 1819. His father owned a thriving livery business, so the family enjoyed financial security. Young Wormley tried his hand at various jobs—he worked as a steward on a riverboat, a driver, and he even set out in search of gold with the 49ers. Eventually he traveled to England in the service of an American diplomat and dazzled the Court of St. James's with his preparation of terrapin, a special dish featuring Chesapeake turtle.

When he returned to Washington, the star chef convinced a congressman to back Wormley's Hotel, an establishment that became popular with politicians and visiting dignitaries. Wormley was known as "the most polite gentleman in Wash-

ington" and his beautiful hotel was "First Class in every re-
spect," as his advertisement in the *Washington Post* promised.
It featured a bar, a barbershop, a restaurant that showcased
Wormley's considerable culinary talents, and a skilled African
American staff trained to anticipate every need.

The hotel was close to the White House, so it was the meeting
place of choice in 1876 when a group of Democrats and Republicans gathered secretly to solve a national problem. They were
attempting to find a solution to the disputed presidential election that had just taken place. Governor Samuel Tilden, a New
York Democrat, had walked away with the popular vote and
was likely to score a majority of electoral votes as well. But supporters of Republican candidate Rutherford B. Hayes contested
the votes in Louisiana, Florida, and South Carolina, hoping
for a recount in their party's favor. The Democrats controlled
the House but the Republicans controlled the Senate and were
represented by President Ulysses S. Grant. There was corruption on both sides, a filibuster was in the works, and the nasty
controversy threatened to divide the country, until Southern
Democrats proposed a backroom compromise.

They wanted an immediate end to Reconstruction and the
removal of federal troops from Louisiana, Florida, and South
Carolina. Once the soldiers are gone, *we'll* take care of black
rights, they promised. In exchange they offered an uncontested
presidency for Hayes. The deal was made, Hayes became president, and Southerners regained control of the South, which
was very bad news for African Americans. Ironically, the deal
that jeopardized the future of Southern blacks (later called the
Wormley Compromise) was brokered at a hotel owned by a
prominent black man.

President Hayes tried to repair his damaged relations with

the black community by naming Frederick Douglass the new marshal of the District of Columbia. Douglass, who was born a slave in the 1820s, was the most visible and respected African American in the land. After running away from his abusive owner and settling in the North, he became an abolitionist, a great orator, an acclaimed writer, a champion of women's rights, and a famous statesman. During the Civil War, he advised President Lincoln on issues of race, and after Emancipation served as president of the Freedman's Bank, an institution founded during Reconstruction to manage the savings accounts of ex-slaves and African American veterans. The bank failed in the shaky postbellum economy, but Douglass remained a beloved black leader.

The prestige of his new appointment was undermined when President Hayes rewrote the federal Marshal job description. Unlike his predecessors, Douglass was *not* invited to present guests to the President at White House receptions because that would have involved having *him* in attendance at social events. Douglass diplomatically claimed that he did not perceive this as a slight and defended Hayes, but his African American friends saw the demotion for what it was.

In 1878, the same year Booker T. first came to town, Washington was not only home to a black hotelier, a famous black statesman, and various black professionals, but it also boasted the country's first black socialite. Josephine Beall Wilson Bruce was the beautiful, twenty-five-year old bride of Blanche Bruce, the first emancipated slave elected to a full term in the U.S. Senate. He was born a house slave on a Virginia plantation in 1841 and, after the war, worked as a printer, a porter on a riverboat, and a schoolteacher, before using his savings to buy an abandoned cotton plantation in Mississippi. A political career

followed, and Bruce served as sheriff, tax collector, and superintendent of schools in Mississippi before winning his Senate
seat in 1875.

His first day on Capitol Hill was tense. On that occasion,
Bruce stood alone as he waited to take his oath, painfully aware
of the fact that the other junior senators were lining up with the
"seniors" from their home states. James Alcorn, the senior senator from Mississippi, refused to acknowledge his black associ-
ate and no one else had the nerve to do so, until Senator Roscoe
Conkling of New York approached and graciously offered his
arm. "Excuse me, Mr. Bruce," he said. "Allow me the pleasure
of presenting you." Bruce accepted his magnanimous gesture
and the two men became friends. Other Washingtonians followed Conkling's lead and, eventually, Bruce developed a
reputation for being smart, dedicated, and affable. Within three
years he was a respected politician and power broker in the
new Washington.

When it came time to select a wife, Bruce courted Josephine
Wilson, the daughter of an affluent African American dentist
and his pianist wife. With her curls, finely arched brows, delicate nose, and fair skin, Josephine was a classic beauty who was
often compared to a "Spanish lady." But she wasn't just lovely
to look at, she was smart, charming, and cultivated, and she
moved in the highest social circles in her native Ohio. Given
her pedigree, everyone wondered what would happen after
she set up housekeeping in Washington. "There is some social
agitation here with regard to the manner in which Mrs. Bruce
will be received by the 'swells' of Washington," reported the
New York Graphic. "Ought we to visit her?" the columnist asked,
pointing out that Josephine was, perhaps, "better educated
than most of the women who intended to snub her."

"Washington is all ablaze to see you," the smitten senator wrote to his fiancée shortly before their wedding, sidestepping the reason *why* capital dwellers were so curious. In any event, Josephine's debut was delayed because the Bruces sailed off for a four-month honeymoon in Europe immediately after the wedding. Gossip columns reported the details of her going-away outfit, from her plum-colored silk dress to the charming feather on her "jaunty chip hat." Josephine was a bona fide fashion plate.

In Paris, the senator visited with former president Ulysses S. Grant while his bride shopped for a new wardrobe at the exclusive House of Worth. Bruce spared no expense in outfitting his wife—she had to maintain her reputation as a trendsetter—and he saw to it that the residence awaiting her in Washington was fit for a queen. Their fourteen-room house on M Street was staffed with servants, including a cook and a personal maid; when the time came, there would also be a proper nanny for their son. The Bruces wholeheartedly embraced the concept of upward mobility and they chose not to see color as an obstacle to their ascent.

Their reception in the capital fell along predictable lines. The Bruces shot to the top of the city's black aristocracy. Republicans, including President Hayes's wife and the wives of cabinet members, accepted them with varying degrees of enthusiasm, but they were roundly snubbed by offended Democrats, especially those who hailed from the South. Senator Allen Thurman, a Democrat from Ohio, quickly denied a rumor that his wife had called on Josephine Bruce. Despite the fact that they were left off the occasional guest list, the Bruces never lacked for invitations.

High-profile achievers such as Blanche Bruce, Frederick Douglass, and James Wormley were living proof that a black man could make it in Washington, but Booker T. struggled during the year he spent there. He felt out of place because the Wayland students, unlike his hardworking companions at Hampton, were a little spoiled and dependent. "They knew more about Latin and Greek when they left school, but they seemed to know less about life," he later wrote. He also realized that, without the motivation of a calling, studying ministry was just an "easy way to make a living," and Booker T. was never one to take the easy way out. He abandoned the ministry and resumed his quest for the right profession.

A significant opportunity presented itself in 1879, when General Armstrong asked him to speak at Hampton's commencement. "The idea is to . . . show what clear heads & common sense colored graduates of this school have attained, and to win the respect of all by a generous noble manly spirit," Armstrong wrote to his former pupil. Booker T. was honored to accept, and delivered a speech titled "The Force That Wins," emphasizing the importance of patience and hard work. He was so eloquent and dignified at the podium that the *Congregationalist* of Boston reported "there are some graduates of Yale or Harvard . . . who can write a better address than his, but they are not very many." Armstrong's plan to promote Booker T. as an example of a Hampton high achiever worked: the *Congregationalist* went on to say, "The institute that can develop such a man . . . may well take credit to itself for doing good work."

Subsequently, Armstrong paid Booker T. the highest compliment by asking him to join the faculty. Booker T. accepted and took charge of an incoming class of Native Americans and the Hampton night school, which he called "The Plucky Class" because the students worked all day yet somehow found the energy to study all evening.

Two years into Booker T.'s tenure, General Armstrong received a request from the town fathers in Tuskegee, Alabama. Could he recommend a white educator to serve as principal of the community's brand-new industrial school for "Negroes"? Inquiries such as this one came in frequently, and whenever they did, Booker T. and his fellow teachers resented the assumption that they were not qualified to be school principals. Apparently General Armstrong felt the same way, because he fired back a letter recommending Booker T. for the position. He called him "the best man we ever had here" and, to emphasize his point, he wrote "I know of no white man who could do better."

From Tuskegee came a rapid and somewhat surprising reply. "Booker T. Washington will suit us. Send him at once." That Sunday night, the general gathered Hampton's students and faculty in the chapel and read them the telegram from Tuskegee. The crowd was jubilant. Booker T.'s appointment was an accomplishment for him, for Hampton, and for blacks everywhere. The slave who dreamed of learning how to read was getting his very own school, and he would be the first African American in the South to have won this great honor . . . and great responsibility.

AN EXEMPLARY YOUNG GENTLEMAN

———— •◆• ————

In 1876, Harvard was the destination of the lanky seventeen-year-old Theodore Roosevelt—described as being all teeth and glasses. He was a little sad to leave his parents and siblings but eager to start his exciting new life as a college man. "Take care of your morals first, your health next, and finally your studies," his father advised. TR listened, then threw himself into his work with characteristic zeal. He was curious about everything and sometimes so vocal in class that one of his professors finally snapped, "Now look here, Roosevelt, let me talk. I'm running this course."

When he arrived at Harvard, TR was a bit of a snob. His circle in New York consisted primarily of old, socially established families, much like the Roosevelts, but in Cambridge many of his fellow students were strangers and hence a little suspect. "I most sincerely wish I knew something about the antecedents of my friends," he complained to his sister Corinne. Eventually he relaxed a little, and his letters included happy accounts of dinners, sleighing parties, and attending dances with his new chums.

In 1878, his sophomore year was suddenly and terribly blighted by the death of his beloved father. "He was everything to me," TR mourned, "father, companion, friend. I have lost the only human being to whom I told everything." He was profoundly affected by his loss, and dark days followed.

TR turned to his dearest friend, Edith Kermit Carow, for comfort. They were neighbors and constant playmates as children (three-year-old Edith was with TR and his brother on the solemn occasion of Lincoln's funeral, but the boys locked her in another room after she became frightened by the procession and started to cry). When ten-year-old TR traveled through Europe with his family, it was Edith, his "most faithful correspondent," he missed most. He carried a small picture of her and the sight of it always made him homesick.

Edith had grown up to be a remarkable young woman and a beloved member of the extended Roosevelt clan. She was smart, spunky, and opinionated, and she and TR spent a good deal of time together engaged in rigorous debates about books and current events. That summer, their long-standing friendship seemed to be budding into a teenage romance, but during Edith's annual visit to the Roosevelt vacation home in Oyster Bay, Long Island, there was an unexplained "incident" in the summerhouse that created a rift between them. Roosevelt insiders suggested that an impulsive TR proposed to his childhood friend, but he was rejected. Whatever caused the split, he and Edith separated and remained distant for years to come.

TR's spirits lifted at the start of his junior year at Harvard, when he was recruited by the school's most prestigious clubs, including Hasty Pudding and the Porcellian, a gentleman's home-away-from-home at Harvard since its founding in 1791. Porcellian's symbol was the pig, and its rousing motto was *Dum vivimus vivamus*, which meant "While we live, let's enjoy it!" TR put a lot of thought and effort into his appearance and, with a sizable inheritance of $125,000 from his father's estate, he could afford to dress like a "dude," a young man who was so fashionable that he set the trend. "Please send my silk hat at once," he commanded his mother in a letter, adding the annoyed postscript, "Why has it not come before?"

That same year, he was introduced to a dazzling young woman who won him over at first sight. She was seventeen-year-old Alice Hathaway Lee, a willowy blonde with a personality so radiant that her nickname was "Sunshine." TR was smitten with "pretty Alice" and soon forgot about Edith; he joyfully threw himself into the role of ardent suitor. He exhausted his horse Lightfoot by trotting him out on daily six-mile rides back and forth to Alice's home in Chestnut Hill. When the worn-out animal had to rest for a few weeks, TR traveled all the way there and back on foot. Alice's heart was a prize he was determined to win. "See that girl?" he confided to a friend. "I am going to marry her. She won't have me, but I am going to have her!"

Alice turned down his first proposal, but TR persisted, calling upon his mother and sisters to help him with his romance. She visited the Roosevelts in New York, where she saw TR in his impressive natural habitat, surrounded by the women who worshipped him. Finally, on January 25, 1880, Alice agreed to be his wife, and he considered her acceptance one of his greatest achievements. The couple planned an October wedding, leaving plenty of time for TR to graduate from Harvard in June and go off on a six-week hunting trip with his brother. He abandoned his childhood dream of a career in science or natural history for a more practical plan to study law in New York at Columbia.

After the wedding and a blissful honeymoon at the Roosevelt summer home in Oyster Bay, the young couple—she was eighteen, he was twenty-three—moved into the family manse on West Fifty-Seventh Street because Alice was considered too young and inexperienced to run her own household. This way she was able to spend her days with Mittie and her sisters-in-law while TR divided his time between law school and the ambitious undertaking of researching and writing his first book—a comprehensive history of the Naval War of 1812.

Most evenings, Alice and TR attended dinners, parties, and balls hosted by others in their exclusive social set. They turned up in all the best places, including Caroline Astor's famous ballroom, where they were among society's top "400." Alice was sometimes impatient with TR's tendency to overextend himself. "We're dining out in twenty minutes and Teddy's drawing little ships," she complained one evening when TR was fussing over a drawing for his book instead of getting dressed for yet another formal night out on the town.

TR was an exemplary young gentleman in all ways but one: he had developed a passion for politics. When he told his friends that he was interested in joining the local Republican association—the 21st District Club, as it was called—they warned him that politics were "low" and that he would find himself in the company of "saloonkeepers, horsecar conductors, and the like." *Gentlemen* in their set simply didn't do that. But TR had a mind of his own and decided to try it anyway. He attended Republican meetings once a month, walking a few blocks from the Roosevelt mansion to Morton Hall, a barnlike room outfitted with spittoons and dingy furniture, and located atop a working-class saloon.

Fortunately, TR was a good mixer and was able to talk to laborers as easily as he traded bon mots with socialites. Republican regulars were impressed by his energy and saw him as a vote-getter who would appeal to the moneyed friends of his family as well as to the younger college set. They proposed that he run for assemblyman in the 1881 election and he accepted (albeit a bit reluctantly). He demonstrated his good breeding with a discreet campaign letter soliciting support: "I would esteem it a compliment if you honor me with your vote and personal influence on Election Day," he wrote to potential voters, signing off, "Very Respectfully, Theodore Roosevelt."

TR won the election in November and headed for Albany in January. By the end of February he had introduced four bills, including one designed to "supply pure and wholesome water for the city of New York." He was a dynamo, inspiring journalists to use words such as *watchdog* and *reformer* when describing him. One admirer compared him to "a splendid breeze blowing through the legislative halls and making everyone feel brighter and better." Like his father, TR believed that men of privilege, blessed with wealth and education, had an obligation to serve, so he dedicated himself wholeheartedly to his new profession.

If he had any flaw, it was his impulsiveness. The *New York Herald* suggested "he has little tact and says and does many things that a calmer judgment would disapprove." But TR was also enthusiastic and committed to helping others help themselves. He worked so hard during his three terms in Albany that even his enemies credited him with invigorating New York state politics.

BRICK BY BRICK

———•◆•———

When Booker T. arrived in Tuskegee to take charge of his school he was surprised to discover that there was no school. Local officials had secured two thousand dollars from the federal government to pay for faculty, and they had recruited Booker T.—their only teacher. That was the extent of their preparation. The job of finding a building, obtaining supplies, and raising the money to pay for it all was left in the hands of Tuskegee's incredulous new principal. The truth was, no one really expected him to succeed.

The fact that he faced a seemingly impossible challenge made Booker T. work that much harder. Thirty students, men and women ranging in age from sixteen to forty, had enrolled and they were depending on him. He found an old, dilapidated church to use as a temporary classroom and pretended not to mind when rain poured in through the holes in the roof. On those inclement days, a student held an umbrella over his head while he taught. Eventually he heard about an abandoned plantation that would be a perfect location for the Tuskegee campus (and the irony of a former "big house" turning into a school for blacks did not escape him). The property came with a price tag of five hundred dollars. Booker T. borrowed the money, paid it back, and then immediately needed more for the expenses that mounted daily. He began to realize that fund-raising, not teaching, would occupy the better part of his time.

Tuskegee was attracting new applicants each month, so Booker T. needed help. He invited Olivia Davidson, an accomplished young African American teacher, to join him. Like Booker T., she had been born a slave in Virginia, and the paleness of her skin suggested that she was probably the daughter of a white man. After emancipation, her mother moved the family to Ohio, where young Olivia attended the Albany Enterprise Academy, a pioneering private school for black students. She also attended Hampton Institute and, in 1879, was one of the admiring graduates who listened raptly to Booker T.'s rousing commencement speech. Subsequently, Olivia continued her studies at a school in Framingham, Massachusetts, and started to make a life for herself in the North. However, when she received an imploring letter from Booker T. Washington, asking her to come to Tuskegee to help him start his school, Olivia agreed to become Tuskegee's first "lady principal" (many schools considered it proper to maintain separate principals for their male and female students). Eventually, two more teachers joined their growing faculty.

In August 1882, Booker T. married Fanny Norton Smith, his childhood sweetheart from Malden. They had been courting long-distance for several years while she was a student at Hampton and he was starting out in Alabama. Fanny was a beautiful young woman whose mother hoped for a more prosperous son-in-law than a struggling teacher with a make-shift school. But Fanny remained true to Booker T. despite her mother's objections. By the time the newlyweds set up house-keeping in Tuskegee, Fanny was twenty-four and Booker T. was twenty-six. Ever industrious, they rented a larger house than they needed so they could provide room and board for the other teachers. Fanny kept busy with her chores and taught a home economics class. By all accounts, she was a lovely and modest young woman who was content to stay in the back-ground while her husband occupied center stage at Tuskegee.

Luckily, Booker T. had the determination and the energy to be a one-man show. He was willing to do anything—build classrooms, clear fields, plant crops—whatever it took to keep Tuskegee going, and he expected his students to do the same. Self-help was the core of his philosophy, but not all of his pu-pils shared his do-it-yourself vision. After emancipation, many blacks thought that access to "big books" and "high-sound-ing subjects" such as Latin, Greek, and banking was the most expedient route to equality and a better life. They disdained programs that promoted technical or remedial courses, and public schools (even rural, one-room schoolhouses) offered a stripped-down, classical curriculum to former slaves who had barely learned to read.

Booker T. knew from experience that these fledgling stu-dents had to master more practical subjects first. He wanted to teach them the basics of personal hygiene that he had learned at Hampton. The most powerful weapon against ignorance was, he said, the toothbrush. The "Gospel of the Tooth-brush" was so important at Tuskegee that owning and using one was actually a condition of enrollment. Booker T.'s philosophy was that the man who brushed his teeth was more likely to succeed in life, and not just because he was clean. He understood the importance of image at a time when so many blacks were unfairly labeled "dirty" and "shiftless," and claimed that one of the saddest sights he ever saw was a young black man wearing unkempt clothes, in a filthy, untended cabin, studying a French grammar book. French wouldn't get him very far if he didn't know how to take care of himself, Booker T. pointed out. Booker T. viewed his students through the exacting eyes of Mrs. Ruffner and General Armstrong, constantly emphasizing the importance of manners, morals, and discipline.

He also required Tuskegee students to learn fundamental trades, such as construction and farming, because he wanted them to be self-supporting after they left school. When they objected to working with their hands (one indignant student protested that he was there "to be educated, not to work"), Booker T. would bring them around to his way of thinking by rolling up his sleeves and getting the job done. No task was beneath the school's principal. There were just as many chopping bees at Tuskegee as there were spelling bees, with Booker T. leading the way with an ax.

Booker T. was so single-minded in his pursuit of self-sufficiency that his efforts were sometimes comic. When Tuskegee needed a new building and there was not enough money to pay for one, Booker T. added brick making to the school curriculum. His plan was that students would make their own bricks, then use them to build their own building. Tuskegee's first homemade kiln produced about twenty-five thousand bricks. While they looked good, they crumbled and proved useless. Booker T. supervised the building of a second kiln, with equally disastrous results. The third kiln the students produced looked promising . . . until it collapsed.

A desperate Booker T. found himself with three useless kilns, no bricks, and no money. In a last-ditch attempt to finance a working kiln, he took the train to Mobile, Alabama, pawned his gold watch for fifteen dollars, and used the money to buy more materials and a train ticket home. This time the kiln worked and the bricks were just right. Tuskegee got its new building, the students saw that persistence led to results, and Booker T. learned to trust his instincts. When the dormitories needed mattresses, the students made those, too. At Tuskegee, whatever could be homemade was, because Booker T. knew that independence was the *real* key to freedom. Be clean, industrious, and perform a job really well, and the South will make a place for you. That was his strategy for success. Eventually he retrieved his gold watch, only to pawn it again and again whenever the need arose.

GREAT EXPECTATIONS

———— • ◆ • ————

In 1883, Booker T. and TR's professional achievements were crowned by happy developments in their personal lives. Both Fanny Washington and Alice Roosevelt were pregnant. Tuskegee's first baby, Portia Marshall Washington, was born in June and her proud father named her after the heroine of his favorite play, Shakespeare's *The Merchant of Venice*. The following February, Alice gave birth to her namesake, Alice Lee. TR was busy working in Albany the night his daughter entered the world—he routinely traveled back and forth between the state capital and New York City when the legislature was in session—and the first telegram he received was upbeat and congratulatory, the kind that prompts backslaps and cigars. While in the midst of celebrating, a second, more urgent telegram arrived, calling for his immediate return to New York City. The baby was fine, but his young wife was very ill and seemed to be failing fast.

Shaken by the news, a frantic TR jumped on a train and raced home to find unimaginable tragedy. Alice was dying of a previously undiagnosed kidney ailment called Bright's disease. At the same time, in the very same house, his mother was deathly ill with typhoid fever. TR ran from one sickroom to another, watching helplessly as the women he loved slipped away from him. Mittie died the morning of February 14. Eleven hours later, Alice passed away in her husband's arms. Baby Lee (no one could bring themselves to call her "Alice" so soon after her mother's death) was healthy and beautiful, but she did not make her father happy. Nothing could. In his diary, he marked that terrible Valentine's Day with a thick black X.

In Albany, Republicans and Democrats in the state assembly set aside their differences long enough to express condolences to their unfortunate young colleague, and even adjourned early in his honor, an unprecedented gesture of respect on their part. One of the speakers urged TR "to work bravely in the darkness" and to "know that God is just," words that the bereaved young man found oddly comforting.

A double funeral was set for Saturday, February 16, at the Fifth Avenue Presbyterian Church. According to newspaper reports, the service was "simple, but unusually touching," and the sight of the two rosewood coffins covered with flowers—one designated for "wife," and the other for "mother"—brought tears to the eyes of the society figures in attendance. As for TR, he was in a "dazed, stunned state," his old tutor, Arthur Cutler, observed. "He does not know what he does or says." Fearing that he would "go mad" if he were idle, TR rushed back to Albany and tried to concentrate on his work, only to find that the state capital was simply too familiar a setting to be an effective change of scenery. Everything reminded him of Alice.

A few months later, Booker T.'s family was cursed by a similar domestic tragedy. Fanny, who was always a little frail, fell from a wagon while on her way home from a school picnic. She never fully recovered from her injuries and died on May 4, 1884. Like TR, Booker T. was away from home during the crisis and had to interrupt a fund-raising tour in Philadelphia to race back to Tuskegee. Fannie's death left him sick with grief. He couldn't sleep most nights, so he walked up and down the campus roads until sunrise, and during the day, he seemed so distant and troubled that his friends feared they might lose him, too.

Overwhelmed by grief, both TR and Booker T. felt incapable of attending to their baby daughters, who were painful reminders of the wives they had lost. TR handed Baby Lee to his sister Bamie, justifying his actions with the excuse that "her aunt can take care of her a good deal better than I can. . . . She would be just as well off without me." Similarly bewildered by the thought of raising a child, Booker T. called in Fanny's mother, Celia Smith, to care for eleven-month-old Portia. Without a sweet wife to complete their vision of married happiness, the men wanted no part of the familial scene they had once embraced so eagerly. Home was a bleak and forbidding place, redolent of disappointment and loss. In the face of such tragedy, the only way to move forward was to move on.

Dressed in a somber black suit, Booker T. headed for any place where he might raise money for Tuskegee. Sometimes he was accompanied by the Tuskegee Singers, an audience-pleasing quartet who sang Negro spirituals such as "Old Black Joe" and "Swing Low, Sweet Chariot." Like a traveling salesman, Booker T. went from door to door, ringing bells in the hope of convincing ordinary folk to contribute. He also reached out to businessmen and philanthropists, never knowing if a day of fund-raising would yield five dollars or five thousand dollars—

but the amount didn't matter because Tuskegee needed every cent. There were days on the road when Booker T. had to hurry to the post office with freshly raised cash so he could send it to Alabama to pay bills.

After a few months, Portia's grandmother decided to return to her home in Virginia, and the child was left in the hands of various women who worked at Tuskegee. Booker T. was so concerned about his daughter, and the precarious financial status of his school, that the stress made him ill. In October 1885, his doctor ordered him to spend ten days in bed, an unprecedented interruption of his breakneck schedule. He seemed to be collapsing under the weight of his grief. His illness was a way of retreating from the problems at hand.

TR's retreat was more literal. He needed to immerse himself in a completely different way of life, so he answered the call of the wild—specifically the Dakota Territory, where he had invested in a cattle ranch. TR attended to his political obligations until the end of the legislative session in June 1884, four months after Alice and Mittie's funeral, then packed his bags and headed west to "Cowboy-land," America's exciting frontier.

TR loved everything about the wilderness—the stark landscape, the brutal beauty of the elements, and the exhilarating tests of manhood he experienced every day. The fashionable New Yorker commissioned a genuine buckskin suit, similar to the one Daniel Boone wore on his treks. Aside from finding it practical (buckskin was a neutral color and so soft that it made no noise in the brush), TR viewed the outfit as his connection to the noble hunters and explorers he had read about as a child.

Cowboys frequently made the mistake of dismissing TR as a city slicker because his spectacles made him appear weak and

sissified. "Four Eyes," one barroom bully called out to him de-
risively. TR jumped to his feet and confronted the man. "You're
talkin' like a fool," he said. "Shut up. Put up. Be friends, or
fight." A few seconds later, the fellow sheepishly extended his
hand, and TR won the battle without lifting a finger. On another occasion, he had to silence a big-mouth with a quick right
punch, and then a left. He preferred words, but wasn't afraid to
use fisticuffs if necessary.

Journalists were fascinated by the "gentleman cowboy."
They wondered how he got by without daily newspapers, the-
aters, restaurants, and the other "comforts of a refined civilization." But TR loved the rigorous cowboy lifestyle, riding his
horse thirteen hours a day, camping under the stars (and sometimes under a downpour), herding cattle, hunting elk, subsist-
ing on dry biscuits and water, and falling into the deepest of
sleeps after thrilling adventures on the trail.

Even with his punishing frontiersman schedule, there were
quiet moments when TR surrendered to sorrow. He channeled
these emotions into a heartfelt literary exercise, a forty-five-
page tribute to Alice and Mittie. *In memory of my darling wife
Alice Hathaway Roosevelt and of my beloved mother Martha Bulloch
Roosevelt who died in the same house and on the same day on February 14, 1884,* the booklet's dedication read. It contained newspaper accounts of the funeral, condolence speeches from friends
and government officials in Albany, and an impassioned elegy
to his sunny and saintly young wife. "And when my heart's
dearest died," he wrote, "the light went from my life forever."

LET ME KEEP LOVING

———•◆•———

A year after their wives' deaths, Booker T.'s health was deteriorating rapidly and TR's cattle ranch was burning through his inheritance at an alarming rate. Work and travel distracted them for a while, but what both men wanted and needed was a good woman. Fortunately, neither had to wait long. When they finally opened their eyes to the possibility of love, they found their sweethearts in their own backyards.

Booker T. and Olivia Davidson worked side by side for several years, but after Fanny died, their professional relationship took a romantic turn, and they married in 1885. The two educators had a lot in common, including similar backgrounds and a talent for fund-raising. Olivia traveled through the North appealing for money for Tuskegee, and, though she excelled at the job, her new priority was to make a real home for little Portia and to restore her husband's health. With this in mind, she enrolled Booker T. in a groundbreaking program at Harvard to educate physicians and teachers about the benefits of physical culture. The course was expensive—Olivia had to raise a hundred dollars to cover the costs—but she believed that Booker T.'s well-being was important enough to warrant the investment. In the summer of 1887, a pregnant Olivia accompanied Booker T. to Harvard. He learned all about physical fitness and nutrition and mastered a rigorous course of calisthenics, while she gave birth to their first son, Booker T. Washington Jr.

The family returned to Tuskegee, where a healthier, happier Booker T. resumed his busy schedule of fund-raising and lecturing. Olivia stayed home and concentrated on the children and her students. The Washingtons shared the belief that propriety would lead to racial uplift and Olivia was determined to give Tuskegee's young women a crash course in refinement. Many of her students were country girls who spent their days working in the fields and their nights in one-room cabins, where menfolk were often crude, and basic amenities, such as soap and water, were in scant supply. The city girls had it worse in some ways. They were surrounded by all manner of vice—snuff, alcohol, vulgar finery, and fast men—and if no one was there to tell them "Don't," they were likely to yield to temptation.

To help her girls make better choices, Olivia developed a curriculum that was part home economics and part charm school. Under her tutelage, they learned how to keep themselves neat and clean, how to dress modestly, and how to behave with decorum. There were practical lessons, too, in elocution, nutrition, and housekeeping. Olivia emphasized that even the simple act of setting a table could be a civilizing influence on a family. There was nothing frivolous about her instructions, although she delicately sidestepped the unspoken motivation for transforming her students into proper young ladies. In doing so, she was waging war against the most pervasive—and the most despicable—postbellum racial stereotype in the South, the black Jezebel.

It was common practice on plantations for slave owners to sexually exploit black women. They added insult to injury by perpetuating the myth that their victims were not victims at all, but hot-blooded "Jezebels" who couldn't control their own libidos. In a self-serving reversal of blame, this made the black woman responsible for leading the white master astray. In her quiet and efficient way, Olivia wanted to obliterate the specter of the wild and immoral temptress and replace her with the black gentlewoman. In this mission, she set a fine example for her students.

The Washingtons welcomed their third child, a son they named Ernest Davidson, in February 1889. Olivia was weak after the birth—she was always "delicate" in that Victorian, ladylike way, but her postpartum condition that winter was particularly fragile. Late one night, while Booker T. was away on a trip, a chimney caught fire in the Washington house and Olivia had to rush the children to safety. This terrifying experience pushed her over the edge and Olivia's health declined to the point where she hovered between life and death for several months. She died on May 9, 1889, leaving her devastated husband a widower for the second time. Unlike quiet and retiring Fanny, who lived and died within a small family circle, Olivia Davidson Washington had mourners everywhere. One distraught Northern philanthropist wrote, "She was one of the most intelligent and attractive Colored Women who have chanced to come within my ken."

When Booker T. took stock of his life, he realized he was in terrible straits. He had lost his muse and companion. Not only had Olivia helped him build and fund Tuskegee, but she had also inspired him to continue his own education, and he was a better person for her encouragement. Now he was alone with three children, two of whom were babies. And since Olivia's prolonged illness had forced him to abandon his fund-raising efforts, money was again a very pressing problem.

A month or so after Olivia's funeral, Booker T. attended commencement exercises at Fisk, a black college in Nashville, Tennessee. A subdued Booker T. was the guest of honor at a dinner for Fisk's graduates. Seated across from him was a remarkable young woman named Margaret James Murray. Undaunted by Booker T.'s reputation as a great educator, she boldly told him that she wanted a teaching position at Tuskegee. Booker T. was to learn that whatever Margaret Murray wanted, Margaret Murray got, and eventually, that included Booker T. himself. She was a force of nature, smart, strong, fearless, and outspoken.

Although she presented herself as a twenty-four-year-old girl, Margaret's official date of birth was in 1861, which made her a mature woman of twenty-eight. Like Booker T., she had faced seemingly insurmountable obstacles during her childhood because she was the mulatto daughter of a poor, black washerwoman and an unidentified white father. But Margaret grew up to be capable and ambitious. After one conversation with Booker T., she was hired to teach English at Tuskegee. Eventually she worked her way up to Olivia's former position of lady principal. Her insistence on high standards for her students won Booker T.'s respect; she also won his heart. He was charmed by her earthy, buxom beauty and her no-nonsense personality. Margaret was so different from the ethereal Olivia that he did not feel as if he was betraying his lost love. He thought about her constantly and even scribbled romantic musings in his notebook. One entry, titled "Maggie," hints at the depth of his emotions.

Maggie
1. *Poem*
2. *Last summer*
3. *Tell real feelings to Boys*
4. *What an institution I could make with her help*
   Let me keep loving.

Margaret brought order to the chaos of Tuskegee (even the male teachers feared her critical eye and sharp tongue), and Booker T. hoped that she would be equally effective on the home front. In 1891 he proposed. Margaret loved Booker T. but she was more interested in academia than domestic life. In fact, she didn't like children and wasn't afraid to say so. "Little folks," as she called them, generally left her cold. Worse still, she actively disliked eight-year-old Portia. "You have no idea how I feel because I cannot feel toward Portia as I should," she wrote to Booker T. while he was off on a fund-raising trip. "I somehow dread being thrown with her for a lifetime." Even Margaret acknowledged that this was a shocking admission for a stepmother-to-be, so she assured Booker T. she would understand if he wanted to walk away from their relationship. He must have assumed she would develop some maternal feelings for his motherless offspring because he went through with the marriage in the fall of 1892.

———•◆•———

LIKE BOOKER T., the widowed TR found happiness in his own backyard, or, more accurately, in his sister's front hallway.

Although he preferred his rugged, elemental way of life in the Dakota Territory, TR frequently returned to New York to spend time with his daughter and to keep his hand in Republican politics. During a visit in September 1885, he unexpectedly ran into Edith Carow, his childhood friend and former sweetheart, at Bamie's New York townhouse. They had not seen each other since the double Roosevelt funeral more than a year and a half ago, and life had not been very kind to Edith during that time. Like a tragic heroine in an Edith Wharton story, she was one of those unfortunate young women with a good family name but limited prospects. Her alcoholic father died and left his wife and daughters with a reduced income that forced them to contemplate a move to Europe, where they could stretch their dollars. Marriage was an unlikely option because Edith was twenty-four—practically an old maid—and everyone in her social set knew she had a mind of her own. She was not the sort of woman to settle for just *any* husband.

Edith may have given up her girlish notions of romance but they were resurrected by the sight of TR standing before her. The frontier had forged the bespectacled city slicker into a "titan," blond, bronzed, and hard as tempered steel—"hearty and strong enough to drive oxen." TR was equally enthralled by the sight of Edith. Her dark good looks were the opposite of Alice's golden, girlish beauty and her tempestuous personality seemed to have softened with time. Mutually charmed, they set aside their differences and quietly embarked on a new and more mature relationship. By November they were engaged, although they kept their "understanding" a secret until the following September, when a New York gossip column ran an unauthorized announcement of their upcoming nuptials. TR was so afraid that the sudden news would upset his older sister that he wrote her a conciliatory letter, even offering to let her keep little Alice. Nonsense, said Edith. She was never Alice Hathaway Lee's biggest fan, but she would not punish her rival's daughter by keeping the child from her father.

TR and Edith were married in London on December 2, 1886. The marriage certificate listed twenty-five-year-old Edith as a "spinster," and twenty-eight-year-old TR as a widower and "ranchman." TR embraced the future with his new wife and young daughter, who would be living with him for the very first time. If he thought about his first bride, he kept those memories to himself. In fact, TR never again mentioned his lost love, not even to his child. It was as if the lovely Alice—the woman he once called the light of his life—had never existed.

Now TR's world revolved around "Darling Edie," and they wasted no time in having children, Theodore Jr. in 1887 and Kermit in 1889. TR believed that upper-class families had an obligation to produce as many offspring as possible. If pressed, he would offer lofty theories about propagation and social responsibility, but the truth was he enjoyed being part of a lively gang of playmates and wanted to re-create the happy camaraderie he had shared with his siblings and Edith during *their* childhood. Edith, departing from the Victorian stereotype, actually enjoyed having an intimate relationship with her husband, and welcomed the pregnancies that followed.

The expanding family wintered in New York and summered at Sagamore Hill, a country house TR built in Oyster Bay, where he had spent his boyhood summers. With its sizable front porch and dark, paneled interior, the twenty-two-room Roosevelt place looked old, solid, and traditional even when it was brand-new. The splendid natural setting—a hill overlooking Long Island Sound, surrounded by fields and woods—was an idyll for the Roosevelts, who enjoyed long, pleasant days of rowing, horseback riding, woodchopping, and exploring. Edith's only complaint was that she often found herself alone with the children while TR went off on his travels.

In 1888, TR campaigned for Benjamin Harrison during the presidential election, and the job of civil service commissioner was his reward. The position—he was supposed to uphold the spoils system method of filling government jobs with loyal Republicans—seemed a little dull and bureaucratic for the man who thrived on adventure. Complicating matters was the fact that TR was an incurable crusader who enthusiastically expressed his opposition to blind political patronage. "The spoils-monger and the spoils-seeker invariably bred the bribe-taker and bribe-giver, the embezzler of public funds, and the corrupter of voters," he protested. For the next six years he waged war on civil service corruption, and he wasn't afraid to criticize President Harrison for failing to improve the system. During his watch, the sleepy civil service office became such a hotbed of activity that his coworkers couldn't wait to come to work to see the daily fireworks. "Every day I went to the office it was as to an entertainment," one fellow commissioner later recalled.

In Washington, the Roosevelts had two more children—Ethel in 1891 and Archibald in 1894. The popular couple befriended prominent capital insiders, including two famous Henrys—Adams and Cabot Lodge—and they enjoyed living in a cozy little rented house where they entertained the city's intelligentsia. Washington was a "very pleasant big village," TR quipped. He was so effective in his post that incoming president Grover Cleveland, though a Democrat, invited him to continue working for his administration. TR accepted.

MOVING UP

———————•◆•———————

In 1893, Booker T. accepted an invitation to address the Conference of Christian Workers at their annual meeting in Atlanta. It was a risky proposition because he had scheduled speaking engagements in Boston immediately before and after the Atlanta event, and traveling between the two locations in such a short period of time seemed impossible. Determined to find a way, Booker T. studied the train schedules until he came up with a backbreaking itinerary that landed him in Atlanta a half hour before his speech and required him to depart for Boston only one hour later.

"Two thousand miles for a five-minute speech," was the way a weary Booker T. described the experience. However, his brief address turned out to be the prelude to an exciting new chapter in his life. Some important white Atlanta businessmen were in the audience that night, and those five minutes convinced them that they needed Booker T.'s help on a very special project.

The World's Columbian Exposition in Chicago, a fair famously called the "White City" because of its classical white buildings and blazing display of incandescent light, was the envy of America that year. It attracted twenty-seven million visitors and, more important, their valuable tourist dollars. In addition to boosting revenue, the Columbian Exposition proclaimed to the world that Chicago was a vital, forward-thinking showcase for technology and culture, and a great place to have a good time.

That very sort of self-promoting spectacle was what the city of Atlanta wanted. Thirty years had passed since the city went up in flames and the vanquished Confederacy promised that "the South will rise again." Local businessmen believed that the time had come to shine a light on progress and prosperity in the *new* South, and they wanted to do it with their very own World's Fair—the Cotton States and International Exposition. They planned to fill eleven acres with buildings and exhibits celebrating all that Dixie had to offer, including a steam-powered textile mill and a theater showing those newfangled "moving pictures." Their big plans came with a big price tag—$2 million—so the Cotton States needed all the help they could get, including financial support from the federal government.

The exposition's promoters contacted Booker T., asking if he would accompany the delegation to Washington to appeal for funds. It was a wise move on Atlanta's part because there was some controversy as to whether blacks had been treated fairly at the Columbian Exposition in Chicago. Apparently they were excluded from the fair's planning board, and prospective black exhibits were subject to review—and rejection—by white judges. Problems continued once the fair was up and running because blacks were portrayed as eye-rolling, spear-waving savages in kitschy Midway shows. An angry Frederick Douglass joined forces with antilynching crusader Ida Wells to write a pamphlet titled *The Reason Why the Colored American Is Not in the World's Columbian Exposition.* In it they exposed racism in the "White City," where "White" *really* meant white.

Atlantans wanted to avoid making the same mistake, and were sensitive to postbellum scrutiny from the North because they were eager for those government dollars. Booker T. accompanied the delegation to Washington and endorsed the fair before a congressional committee, saying he believed it would give his people an opportunity to show how far they had come. His words carried weight, and the delegation won a $200,000 appropriation. There would be a "Negro Building" showcasing "Negro" exhibitions (some blacks considered this a hollow victory because they believed every exhibit should be integrated). But the most significant indication of the black man's progress had nothing to do with a pavilion or a diorama. It was the fair's invitation to Booker T. Washington to speak at its Opening Day ceremony on September 18, 1895.

Years of lecturing had honed Booker T. into a powerful speaker who was popular on both sides of the Mason-Dixon Line. He had the ability to make philanthropic Northerners and reactionary Southerners feel good about supporting Tuskegee, and it was that talent that won him a place onstage at the opening. It was, in fact, the first time that a black person was asked to address a mixed audience in the South. An honor, yes . . . but in Booker T.'s mind, the invitation was also a loaded gun. What could he possibly say to a roomful of whites and blacks, Southerners and Northerners, without offending *someone*?

Booker T. fretted for weeks. He was always very careful about what he said and how he said it, and he even wrote stage directions in the margins of his speeches, noting when he should emphasize a word, or pause for impact. He rehearsed over and over again for Margaret and members of the Tuskegee faculty, but his preparations did nothing to ease his mind.

On the morning of September 17, the day before the ceremony, Booker T. and his family boarded a train to Atlanta. He felt like a man on his way to the gallows, and it didn't make him any happier to know that other people shared his concern. At the station, a sympathetic white farmer summed up his situation this way. "With Northern whites, the Southern whites, and the Negroes, all together . . . I am afraid that you have gotten yourself into a tight place." But there was no turning back.

Booker T. spent a sleepless night in Atlanta. The next morning, he assumed his position in the Opening Day procession. The city was so crowded that the parade took three hours to advance to the exposition grounds. Spending so much time under a hot sun made him feel anxious and exhausted. In his weakened state, failure seemed inevitable. One of Booker T.'s friends was so nervous that he couldn't bring himself to enter the lecture hall. A thousand people, mostly Southerners, crowded into the room, and there was no reason to believe they would be warm and welcoming to the black man from Tuskegee.

Booker T. sat on the stage, dreading the moment when his name would be called. If he failed, he would fail big, and he was afraid of the consequences for his race. Other speakers droned, the room became unbearably hot, and finally, it was his turn to take the podium. The band played the "Star-Spangled Banner," then "Dixie," which prompted the audience to cheer. When the music changed to "Yankee Doodle," their enthusiasm waned. Booker T. stepped forward to a smattering of applause from the African Americans in the audience. He was momentarily blinded by the blazing sunlight coming through the windows, but quickly composed himself and stood "straight as a Sioux chief," gripping a pencil in his hand like a talisman. Bending his body toward the audience in a folksy, conversational way that called to mind the casual style of Abraham Lincoln, he began speaking. "One third of the population of the South is of the Negro race," he said in strong, measured tones.

One third . . . a number to be reckoned with. Was it a threat? According to Booker T., that depended on how blacks were treated by their countrymen. They could constitute "one-third and more of the ignorance and crime of the South, or one-third of its intelligence and progress." Either way, he reminded his audience, the black population was a force. Booker T.'s real objective that day was to open doors, not alienate potential supporters. He argued eloquently for education and employment opportunities for his people, urging blacks and whites to "cast down your bucket where you are." For blacks, this meant helping themselves and pursuing attainable goals in the South. For whites, it meant supporting, encouraging, and employing the very blacks they once owned and exploited.

Then Booker T. diplomatically addressed the ultimate question: social equality. "In all things that are purely social we can be as separate as the fingers, yet one as the hand in all things essential to mutual progress," he promised reassuringly, holding up his hand to demonstrate his point. He invited all men to work together to make their "beloved South a new heaven and a new Earth."

His gospel of reconciliation prompted the audience to jump to its feet with a roar of enthusiasm. They were expecting angry recriminations, not talk of mutual support, and they liked what they heard. Most of the blacks in the room were moved to tears, overwhelmed by feelings of pride and hope. Booker T. entered the Exposition Hall an educator but left a superstar. He was called "magnetic" and "divine," and whites and blacks alike crowded around him to offer their congratulations. Later, President Grover Cleveland praised him, writing, "Your words cannot fail to delight and encourage all who wish well for your race." But for Booker T., the highest compliment came from a Bostonian who said his speech was "worthy to rank with Lincoln's 'Gettysburg' in eloquence, elevation, and far-reaching influence."

Booker T.'s speech was a stunning success. Interestingly, its "cast down your bucket where you are" message was familiar to much of the audience because it was a variation on Russell Herman Conwell's "Acres of Diamonds," an inspirational talk that had been popular on the lecture circuit for more than thirty years. Conwell, a lawyer, journalist, and Baptist minister, was well-known for this colorful motivational speech, which he delivered for the first time in 1861. It told the story of Ali Hafed, an ancient Persian who left his home to travel the world in search of diamonds. He never found them, and ultimately died without fulfilling his lifelong dream. Ironically, the man who bought the house Ali Hafed abandoned found a treasure trove of diamonds and other precious gems on his property. Conwell's point was that there could be acres of diamonds— or resources—in a man's backyard or, metaphorically, within himself. Americans were so enthusiastic about "Acres of Diamonds" that Conwell gave the speech more than six thousand times, made a fortune, and ultimately used the money to found Temple University.

Booker T.'s message of self-reliance and progress may have been recycled, but the twist was that it was now delivered by a black man of rare eloquence. Just as the Cotton States Exposition founders had hoped, his appearance heralded the birth of the new South and "the burial forever of the old South and negro slavery," an accomplishment a journalist at *Century Magazine* viewed as "great cause for national rejoicing." The jubilant writer may have gotten a little carried away, for the "negro problem" in the South was far from solved. But thanks to Booker T.'s performance in Atlanta, the cause had a dynamic new spokesperson. He was hailed as "the Moses of his race," and "the new Frederick Douglass."

It was a perfect moment to identify a "new" Frederick Douglass because the original had died of a heart attack in February, at the age of seventy-eight. The famous abolitionist was less active in his final years and had lost some of his followers when he married a white feminist in 1884. But he had been his race's official spokesperson for most of the nineteenth century, and there were big shoes to fill when Booker T. gracefully took his place.

After the Atlanta lecture, invitations poured in from liberal-minded Northerners who were eager to hear Booker T. speak. In December 1895, he was the guest lecturer at the Hamilton Club in Chicago. A month later, he celebrated Lincoln's birthday with the Union League Club in Brooklyn, and soon there were also trips to Boston, Buffalo, Cincinnati, St. Paul, and Washington, DC, Audiences appreciated the fact that Booker T. always leavened his speeches with a seemingly endless repertoire of amusing anecdotes. He told funny stories about blacks, frequently using dialect to make the tales more colorful. One of his favorites involved an old man who was trying to catch a train. According to Booker T., the man hailed a driver, who happened to be white: "Hurry up an' take me to the station,

I's gotta get the 4:32 train!" To which the white hack driver replied: "I ain't never drove a nigger in my hack yit an' I ain't
goin' ter begin now. You can git a nigger driver ter take ye
down!" The colored man thought for a moment and said, "All
right, my frien', we won't have no misunderstanding or trouble; I'll tell you how we'll settle it: you jest hop in on der back
seat an' do der ridin' and I'll set in front an' do der drivin'."
The driver agreed and the old man caught his train. The moral
of Booker T.'s story—and there was always a moral—was that
practicality was more important than protocol. Arriving at
one's destination was the real goal.

When he traveled to new places to give speeches, Booker T.
always visited the black neighborhoods. He'd walk into a
business—a grocery store or a barbershop—to ask questions
and offer advice. He was so modest and unassuming that few
people realized that the gentleman proffering practical business tips was the famous Booker T. Washington. Emmett Jay
Scott, the young man whom Booker T. later hired to be his
private secretary, walked right by him the first time they were
scheduled to meet. "[S]omehow I was expecting to see a big
man, with a tall hat, and perhaps gold spectacles, and a general
air of fame," he explained.

Booker T. may not have looked famous, but thanks to his
speech in Atlanta he was fast becoming so, and his name became synonymous with racial uplift. Recognition was never
important to him, but there was one accolade that had more
significance to him than any other. In the spring of 1896, he
was sitting on his porch at Tuskegee when he received a letter postmarked Cambridge, Massachusetts. "My dear Sir," it
began, "Harvard University desires to confer on you at the ap-
proaching Commencement an honorary degree." Booker T.'s

eyes filled with tears as he recalled images of his younger self—
the boy slave, the adolescent coal miner, the eager fledgling
student. From bondage, ignorance, and poverty to *this*, a master's degree from the oldest and most renowned university in
America.

On June 24, Booker T. traveled to Harvard, where he stood
with his fellow honorees, including Alexander Graham Bell and
Major General Nelson A. Miles, the commander of the United
States Army. It was a day of historic "firsts"—the first time
in the school's history that commencement was conducted in
English instead of Latin (so guests could actually understand
what was being said) and the first time an honorary degree was
conferred on a black man. Booker T. received an enthusiastic
welcome from the crowd when his name was called, and as
he stepped up to the podium, President Charles William Eliot
greeted him with the words "Teacher, wise helper of his race;
good servant of God and country."

Later that day, he spoke at the annual alumni dinner and
instantly won over the audience with his appealing blend of
humor and sagacity. "I feel like a huckleberry in a bowl of
milk," he said drolly as he surveyed the roomful of white faces.
That got a laugh. Then he boasted that the Negro race must be
stronger than any other because one little drop of African blood
in a man's veins caused him to "fall to our pile on the counter,
and we claim him at once, and you can't get him away from
us." Loud laughter followed this observation, too, and the audience was ready to listen to anything he had to say.

Booker T. chose this moment to deliver a message from his
people. "We are coming. We are crawling up, working up, yea,
bursting up. Often through oppression, unjust discrimination, and prejudice, but through them all we are coming up,

and with proper habits, intelligence, and property, there is no power on earth that can permanently stay our progress!"

Every journalist commented on the eloquence of his words. "The colored man carried off the oratorical honours," reported the *New York Times*. The *Chicago Daily Tribune* recognized the larger import of Booker T.'s triumph. "Harvard has honored the race and no less honored itself by naming Booker T. Washington Master of Arts. *Master* he is," the writer continued, "no longer serf." "Is he the Negro Moses?" asked T. Thomas Fortune, owner and editor of the influential African American newspaper the *New York Age*. The answer was yes. By virtue of his accomplishments, his dedication, and to no small effect, his visibility, Booker T. had become the undisputed leader of his race.

ROUGH RIDING

————— •◆• —————

While Booker T. was rising, TR was more or less stuck. In fact, he had the crushing feeling that he was on his way down instead of up. He had made a serious career fumble that was proving difficult, if not impossible, to correct. In 1894, the Republican Party approached him about running for mayor of New York City. TR was uncertain about accepting, but the larger, insurmountable, obstacle was Edith. She wanted to stay in Washington and was dead set against a risky political undertaking. Ultimately, TR turned down the offer and, when the candidate who replaced him was elected, he realized the victory could have been his. "It was the one golden chance which never returns," he lamented to a friend. He doubted that another opportunity would come his way, a suspicion that was reinforced when the incoming mayor offered him the lowly position of commissioner of street cleaning, which he perceived as an insult. TR declined politely and resigned himself to staying with the Civil Service Commission. He was visibly depressed, and Edith, who held herself responsible for his unhappiness, worried that there was friction between them for the very first time.

There seemed to be no solution, until TR had a wild thought. What if he asked to become one of New York City's police commissioners? (There were four, two Republicans and two Democrats.) Normally, it wasn't a high-visibility position, but in TR's mind, crime-busting had real appeal, and he was thrilled when he won the appointment.

In 1895, he reported to Police Headquarters and immediately launched what the city newspapers called a "Reign of Terror." TR realized that there was corruption—"gangrene," he said— "from top to bottom" in the department and he was eager to cure it. New Yorkers, he decided, needed to be protected from the very men who were supposed to protect them. He took to the streets in the middle of the night to walk the beat and check up on his force. More often than not, he'd find the officer on duty asleep or loafing in a saloon, and that's if he found him at all. When confronted, the slackers were usually belligerent, until someone pointed out that the man with the large, flashing white teeth and spectacles was none other than Police Commissioner Roosevelt himself. A run-in with TR—or the threat of one, because his nocturnal prowls were publicized in the newspapers—inspired lawmen to take their jobs more seriously. The city became a safer place.

TR's crusade to reform the Police Department made him popular with New Yorkers, until he mounted a campaign to enforce a long-standing but rarely observed law prohibiting the sale of alcohol on Sunday. Saloon owners protested because they lost a significant amount of their weekly revenue each Sunday they were forced to be "dry." However, the real victims—and opponents—of TR's hardnosed support of the unpopular Sunday blue laws were workingmen. Wealthy people could drink any day of the week: the Sabbath was usually the *only* day laborers could indulge. Inventive proprietors found loopholes that sidestepped the law; the hour between 12 AM on Sunday and 1 AM on Monday was not covered by the code, for example, so bars could be open for sixty minutes in the middle of the night. Saloons that served food—a sandwich, a pickled egg, or even a pretzel—could sell alcohol. And, according to the new Raines Law, any building that maintained a dining room and ten bedrooms could be classified as a "small hotel" where Sunday drinking was permissible. This odd ordinance prompted bars to carve out makeshift "sleeping" areas so they could win "small hotel" status and offer their customers food, alcohol, and a special, added attraction, on-site prostitutes in those handy new bedrooms.

It was a messy and discouraging situation for TR, an idealist who imagined there would be more public support for a right-minded crusader. "I have not one New York City newspaper or one New York City politician on my side," he confessed to his friend Henry Cabot Lodge. After a year of enduring dirty politics and assaults on his character, he concluded that the thankless job of police commissioner wasn't for him.

He plotted an exit strategy with a specific Washington appointment in mind. The man who was fascinated by all things naval (and who once happily occupied himself by drawing little ships) wanted to be the assistant secretary of the navy—a post that would give him the opportunity to play with real ships. TR volunteered to campaign on behalf of William McKinley, the Republican candidate for president in the upcoming 1896 election. Marcus "Mark" Hanna, the chairman of the party and

McKinley's staunchest supporter, accepted his offer, although he and McKinley were wary of TR's involvement in their campaign because he was thought by many to be outspoken, unpredictable, and reckless.

TR traveled cross-country, speaking on behalf of McKinley and against his Democrat opponent for the presidency, William Jennings Bryan. The Republicans won the White House, but when the time came for TR to receive his reward, there was nail-biting suspense as McKinley pondered his final decision. Ultimately, TR received the appointment he coveted, partly because New York Republicans wanted the unmanageable reformer out of their hair. He happily moved back to Washington to serve under Secretary of the Navy John D. Long.

Not long after taking the job, TR found that the country faced a pressing issue on the international front. Spain was waging a bloody campaign to retain its colony, Cuba. Even though the battle was right off America's shores, President McKinley took an isolationist stand and insisted upon staying out of it. TR promised he would uphold the party line, but, typically, he had his own ideas about how to handle Spain, and neutrality wasn't one of them. "Cowardice in a race, as in an individual, is the unpardonable sin," he said, "and a willful failure to prepare for danger may in its effects be as bad as cowardice." He'd learned the importance of fighting the "good" fight when he was a boy, and later as a young man in the Dakotas. Sometimes a man had to use his fists. TR firmly believed that his country should prepare its navy for a righteous war against Spain, and he never passed up an opportunity to say so. He urged McKinley to strengthen the American fleet and send it to Cuba. On February 16, 1898, the U.S. battleship *Maine* was blown up while it was anchored in Havana Harbor. It was unclear at the

time whether Spain was responsible, but the incident turned
TR into a "jingo," an out-and-out war enthusiast.

Secretary Long, a mild-mannered man who enjoyed his days
off, made the mistake of staying home from work on February 25, a week after the *Maine* incident. He warned his impulsive assistant secretary not to do anything important "without
consulting the President or me." But TR chose this fortuitous
moment to do something very important . . . and very rash. He
virtually seized control of the navy and spent the entire day
sending out orders that carried one message: prepare for war.
"Keep full of coal," he cabled Commodore George Dewey,
and be ready to mount "offensive operations" in the Philip-
pine Islands "in the event of declaration war." It was a bold
and insubordinate move. Secretary Long was shocked when he
learned of his assistant's recklessness. "[T]he best fellow in the
world—and with splendid capacities—is worse than no use if
he lacks a cool head and discrimination," was his analysis of
TR's behavior. But there was no point in countermanding the
orders because, at this point, war with Spain was inevitable.

President McKinley declared war on April 11. TR was ec-
static. Not only was he enthusiastic about the idea of war, but he
was actually going to Cuba to fight in it. He submitted his res-
ignation and organized a volunteer cavalry regiment that came
to be known as the Rough Riders. TR's adventurous friends,
ardent admirers, lawmakers, and lawbreakers lined up to fight
in his unit. The group included Harvard football player Dud-
ley Dean, polo star Joe Stevens, four New York City policemen
who had served under TR, Civil War heroes, cowboys, Indian
fighters and Indians from the Southwest (Cherokees, Chicka-
saws, Choctaws, and Creeks), and even the occasional outlaw
(including one named "Tennessee," a gaunt, taciturn man who

later confessed to being a murderer). "All—Easterners and Westerners, Northerners and Southerners, officers and men, cow-boys and college graduates, wherever they came from, and whatever their social position—possessed in common the traits of hardihood and a thirst for adventure," TR said proudly of his colorful band of volunteers.

Lieutenant Colonel Roosevelt rush-ordered a custom-made uniform from Brooks Brothers and sailed with his regiment to Cuba. Despite punishing conditions—a shortage of supplies, poor sanitation, disease, brutally hot weather, and unfamiliar jungle terrain—TR flourished and led his band to victory on San Juan Hill. He said the dangerous battle was the greatest moment of his life. The United States won the war and, on August 14, 1898, after a 133-day odyssey, the colonel and his surviving Rough Riders came home to a hero's welcome.

The soldiers were quarantined for a month at Camp Wikoff in Montauk, New York, but as the restrictions eased, important visitors, including President McKinley, came to pay their respects. Congratulations poured in and the valiant TR, exuding health, power, and vitality, became the face of what was called "a splendid little war."

RISING STARS

———•◆•———

While America was celebrating its victory over Spain, Booker T. expressed public concern for Cuba and its people. He believed it was his country's responsibility "to follow the work of destruction in Cuba with *construction*," so he proposed creating scholarships at Tuskegee for Cuban blacks and mulattos who could use the skills they learned to open industrial schools at home. He also wanted the black soldiers who fought in the Spanish-American War, commonly known as the Buffalo Soldiers, to be recognized for their valuable contribution to the victory.

Sometime during the last week in August, Booker T. had the opportunity to speak to TR about this very subject. According to Max Bennett Thrasher, a journalist traveling with the Washingtons during a lecture tour of the Carolinas, the two men met in New York, presumably in Montauk, where the Rough Riders were billeted. On this occasion, TR and Booker T. talked about the war and "the bravery of the colored soldiers," for whom

Colonel Roosevelt had the highest praise. Thrasher supplied the barest details about the encounter in a column he penned for the *New York Tribune*. But he suggested that on that September day, the Black Moses and the Most Popular Man in America discovered that they had a great deal in common.

There was an historical precedent for forging a relationship and it was a persuasive one. By joining forces, the two men would be emulating Abraham Lincoln's famous political partnership with black statesman Frederick Douglass. Lincoln and Douglass, two of the greatest men of their day, had put their heads together on numerous occasions to solve the country's "race problem," and their pairing and obvious mutual respect sent an important message to the country. Perhaps now was the time for a new team of forward-thinking leaders to tackle contemporary racial issues, and both Booker T. and Roosevelt had come to the conclusion that it would be practical, effective, and mutually beneficial to create a union of their own. By the time they finished their conversation, they knew that their first meeting would not be their last.

TR was also visited by Senator Thomas Platt, the most powerful figure in the New York Republican Party. Platt decided, albeit reluctantly, that he had to offer the phenomenally popular war hero the state's gubernatorial nomination in the upcoming 1898 election. He didn't like TR; his stint as police commissioner had proved that he was a renegade who would be difficult to control. But then again, it would be political suicide not to capitalize on Roosevelt's triumphant moment. When Platt made the offer, TR's response was an enthusiastic "I would be delighted!"

And delighted he was when he won the November 8 election by a margin of 17,786 votes. "I am more than contented to be Governor of New York, and shall not care if I never hold another office," he wrote to a friend. The Roosevelts—with their ever-expanding family (including their sixth child, Quentin, who was born in 1897)—moved into the Governor's Mansion in Albany. Inauguration Day on January 2, 1899, was so bitterly cold that the military band's bugles froze and couldn't squeeze out a sound. However, the harsh weather did not deter spectators from attending the ceremony. Thousands of people came to shake TR's hand and offer their good wishes. Edith, who was not always comfortable with crowds, cleverly held a bouquet with both her hands to avoid pressing flesh with all those eager strangers. TR was proud to be a political leader in his home state, and Edith, who ran her household as if it were a corporation, was thrilled to have TR's ten-thousand-dollar-a-year salary, a state-subsidized domestic staff, and a sizable (if somewhat institutional) house at her disposal.

Despite a pre-election promise to consult Platt on all appointments and policies, the independent-minded new governor predictably had his own ideas about everything from public works to tax reform, and his thinking was rarely in synch with the GOP machine. Furthermore, TR had difficulty narrowing his vision. Instead of focusing on New York state, he had a tendency to behave as if he were running the entire country (if not the world). With his characteristic energy, TR devoured issues large and small, domestic and international, including the nationwide problem of race relations.

TR's views on race were complicated and could be traced back to his youth. He "grew up in an atmosphere of Victorian privilege, was bombarded from early childhood with ideas that stressed the superiority of the white race and the inferiority of non-whites," suggests historian Thomas G. Dyer. Even the adventure sagas he enjoyed reading as a boy—his beloved *King Olaf*, for example, or the *Ring of the Nibelung*—taught him that he belonged to a superior race. On a more personal note, his mother's sentimental memories about her plantation upbringing promoted the myth that slaves were dependent and childlike. TR absorbed all of these attitudes and sometimes showed a bewildering combination of prejudice and enlightenment. As he matured, he became a proponent of "equipotentiality," the theory that individuals could succeed regardless of race, and he challenged conventional thinking by arguing that blacks had been held back by a lack of education. He believed they could grow with opportunity and stressed that men should be judged on the basis of merit, not color.

From his lofty perch in the liberal North, TR said he saw signs of progress for African Americans. "[T]he Race is doing well right now," he wrote optimistically in a letter. "Their friends are doing all they can for them and we cannot afford to stir up antagonism just now and I feel Washington will agree with me on this." The "Washington" in question was Booker T., who was, in fact, America's most conspicuous example of the race "doing well," as were his friends Paul Laurence Dunbar and William Edward Burghardt Du Bois. When these three black superstars appeared onstage together at a Tuskegee fund-raiser in Boston on March 21, 1899, they were hailed as "the foremost representatives of what education has done for the American negro during the past 30 years."

Paul Laurence Dunbar was a young poet who was popular with both white and black readers. The *Boston Daily Globe* described him as the "Elevator Boy Who Became a Poet," and the colorful headline wasn't far from the truth. Dunbar's parents were former slaves who moved from Kentucky to Dayton,

Ohio, after the Civil War. He was the only black student in his class, yet he excelled. Writing was young Dunbar's passion, and he was so good at it that his classmates elected him editor of the school newspaper and president of the literary society.

He aspired to be a poet, but that was not a viable ambition for a poor boy who had to support his mother. After graduating from high school, Dunbar went to work as an elevator operator in an office building for a weekly salary of four dollars, somehow managing to write in his spare time.

In 1892, Dunbar scraped together enough money to self-publish a collection of his poetry he titled *Oak and Ivy*. He was an enterprising young man who sold his booklet for a dollar. Even the passengers in his elevator were prospective customers, and Dunbar was so persuasive that, when the door opened on the ground floor, they often stepped out carrying a freshly purchased copy of his work.

Word of the boy genius spread gradually throughout the country, and he attracted the attention of critic William Dean Howells. Dunbar often re-created the sounds of the South in his poetry—the "dats" and the "de's" that characterized the speech of rural blacks of the time—and readers clamored for more of these quaint "colored" pieces about the "little brown baby wif spa'klin' eyes," the "easy-goin' feller," and the singing "Malindy." (A line from "Malindy" inspired the famous "Who Dat" chant recited by fans of the New Orleans Saints football team.) Howells praised Dunbar's artful use of African American dialect and predicted, "If he should do nothing more than he has done, I should feel that he had made the strongest claim for the negro in English literature."

Dialect was what made Dunbar popular, but he used standard or "literary" English to express his deeper feelings about

race. "I know why the caged bird sings," he wrote in "Sympathy," a poem that inspired the title for Maya Angelou's groundbreaking autobiography seventy years later. "It is not a carol of
joy or glee."

The other prominent African American to appear with
Booker T. on the Boston stage that afternoon was W. E. B. Du
Bois, a man famous for being an intellectual at a time when
many people believed that blacks were intellectually inferior.
Even as a child, Du Bois made it his mission to prove that he
was *superior*, not equal, to the whites around him. He grew
up in Great Barrington, Massachusetts, and while his western
New England community was small, his ambitions were large:
he would settle for no less than a first-class education at the
best possible schools. Du Bois distinguished himself in high
school and continued his studies at Fisk College, Harvard University, and the University of Berlin. Like Booker T., he was a
Harvard "first"—the first black person to achieve a doctorate in
history, which he received in 1895, the same year that Booker T.
accepted his honorary degree.

Unlike Booker T., however, Du Bois never cast himself in the
role of humble man of the people. He was always described
as "brainy" and "cultivated," and he dressed the part, outfitting himself in elegant gloves, a walking stick, and gold spectacles to emphasize his elevated status. "A man who thought
so much of himself that he couldn't stoop," was the way one
not-so-admiring person summed him up.

Yet Du Bois was not a snob. He was committed to using his
great intellect to help his race. His Harvard dissertation, "The
Suppression of the African Slave Trade to the United States
of America 1638–1870," offered the first comprehensive study
of the subject. After he received his degree, Du Bois wrote

The Philadelphia Negro, the first sociological study of urban blacks in America. He exchanged letters with Booker T. about the possibility of teaching at Tuskegee, but ultimately took a position as professor of sociology at the University of Atlanta.

Booker T. had invited Dunbar and Du Bois to join him at Boston's Hollis Street Theater, and the dynamic trio proved to be quite a draw. Nearly every seat in the hall was taken, and there were impressive Bostonians in attendance, including abolitionist Julia Ward Howe.

The program began with a spirited performance of "Good News" by the popular Hampton Institute quartet. Du Bois was the first speaker, and his subject was the life of Alexander Crummell, a black Episcopal priest and a proponent of Pan-Africanism, whose many good works in New York and Africa were not appreciated during his lifetime.

The audience listened politely, but Booker T. was the main attraction and, when it was his turn to speak, he was welcomed with thunderous applause. There was a moment of levity when twelve-year-old Portia Washington rushed up onto the stage and kissed her father. This was a happy reunion because Portia was attending boarding school in Framingham, Massachusetts (Olivia Washington had been educated in the North and Booker T. thought Portia would benefit from following in her footsteps), and father and daughter had not seen each other for quite some time. Margaret Washington, who was sitting in the theater, disapproved of her stepdaughter's public display of affection—but, then again, she usually disapproved of Portia.

Booker T. made his usual appeal for Tuskegee, urging the audience to remember that "so long as the rank and file of my own people are in ignorance and poverty, so long will this ignorance and poverty prove a millstone about the neck of your brothers and sisters in the South." "He held the big audience almost breathless," a journalist from the *Boston Journal* reported. Paul Dunbar offered comic relief by reading some of his lively dialect poems, and the trio wrapped up the presentation with a toe-tapping and hand-clapping finale of popular spirituals.

A distinguished woman named Elizabeth Baker Lewis was in the audience that afternoon. She was a graduate of Wellesley College and the wife of Harvard football coach William Henry Lewis. He was a recent graduate of Harvard Law School, the author of *A Primer of College Football,* one of the first (and the most authoritative) books on the sport, and the genius behind the Harvard football team's astounding, undefeated season in 1898. After hearing of his remarkable achievements, people meeting Lewis for the first time were surprised to discover that he was black.

Like Booker T. and Paul Dunbar, Lewis was the poor but ambitious son of Virginia slaves. His high grades in schools impressed his teachers and won him a scholarship to Amherst College, where he was elected captain of the football team and class valedictorian. Du Bois was so intrigued by Lewis's reputation that he attended Amherst graduation that year to see the boy wonder with his own eyes, and ended up introducing him to his future wife. Lewis was accepted by Harvard Law School, where he distinguished himself in the classroom and on the football field. His phenomenal performance as the Crimson's center lineman, and the fact that he was appointed captain by his teammates, proved that there was no color line on the Harvard gridiron. Lewis was the first black player to be voted all-American in 1892, and he won the honor again in 1893.

Lewis planned on practicing law after graduation, but setting up an office and attracting clients would take time and, now that he was a married man, he had a family to support. When Harvard offered him a coaching job, he accepted. Lewis helped Harvard pummel Princeton and Yale, and the team's stunning victory (thanks to an innovative play Lewis modeled after a Napoleonic military maneuver) transformed him into a local celebrity. He was the man of the hour at a banquet celebrating the big win and he received a deafening ovation when he entered the room. Lewis's biggest fan that night was his fellow alumnus, Governor Theodore Roosevelt. TR came to his alma mater to praise the team, and especially Lewis, who struck him as being the very best combination of brains and brawn.

The energetic young lawyer managed to find time to work with his team, write and publish his football manual, start his practice, *and* cofound the Massachusetts Racial Protection League, a watchdog group dedicated to defending black civil rights. Lewis and the other members, many of whom had grown up in the liberal North and had Ivy League degrees, did not share Booker T.'s enthusiasm for industrial education, and they made no secret of the fact that they disapproved of his leadership.

In 1898 they invited the famous educator to attend one of their meetings. During a seemingly convivial moment over coffee and cigars, Booker T. encouraged the Bostonians to voice their thoughts on race. They seized the opportunity to condemn him and his policies, and William Henry Lewis emerged as his most vocal critic. He told Booker T. to go back south and "attend to his work of educating the Negro" and "leave to us the matters political affecting the race," implying that the Tuskegee principal did not measure up to the high intellectual standards of the Northern black elite.

Instead of becoming defensive and firing back in kind, Booker T. calmly and diplomatically addressed the group. He had faced tougher audiences than this condescending bunch and he usually prevailed. "Gentlemen, I want to tell you about what we are doing at Tuskegee Institute in the Black Belt of Alabama," he said with great dignity. Instead of defending himself against Lewis's complaints, he matter-of-factly described his school and its accomplishments and ambitions. His words were so quietly persuasive that even Lewis had to think twice about his objections. Gradually Lewis began to warm to Booker T. and his ideas, and he eventually became one of his biggest fans.

The packed theater suggested that accomplished members of the race such as Booker T. could draw a sizable, right-minded audience in sophisticated cities such as Boston. But there were African Americans whose influence reached well beyond intellectual and philanthropic circles. For the first time, the works of black musicians and composers—most notably those of Scott Joplin—were crossing color lines throughout America, and their songs were popular in homes where they themselves would not have been welcome.

Earlier in the century, around 1834, a new musical genre called the "coon song" had emerged when a white minstrel performer named George Washington Dixon blackened his face and sang about the comic misadventures of "Zip Coon," a buffoonish "darkie" who was always getting into trouble. A century later, the song's refrain, "o zip a duden duden duden zip a duden day," would evolve into "Zippity Doo Dah," the Academy Award–winning song from Walt Disney's 1946 animated film, *Song of the South.*

Thanks to Zip's popularity, "coon songs" sold millions of

copies over the years, prompting white and black composers alike to write feverishly and cash in on the craze. In 1896, the catchy melody "All Coons Look Alike to Me" became a huge hit, earning twenty-six thousand dollars for tunesmith Ernest Hogan, who happened to be black. The great success of Hogan's song left him open to criticism, especially from African Americans who wondered why he promoted racial stereotypes in his work. However, several black composers and lyricists, including Paul Dunbar (coauthor of a song called "The Hottest Coon in Dixie"), eagerly jumped on the coon song bandwagon and made money doing so. Like today's rap musicians, they believed it was acceptable if they used racial epithets to describe themselves.

In 1899, the most exciting new talent on the musical scene was an African American pianist named Scott Joplin. He was born in Texas in 1867. His parents had six children to support, so there was never enough money, but music was always a part of Joplin's life. His father, a former slave, was a talented violinist and his mother sang and played the banjo. Home became a less harmonious place after his father walked out on the family and his mother had to work long hours as a domestic. But Joplin's love of music endured. He taught himself to play the bugle, the guitar, and any other instrument he could find, and he even accompanied his mother to the houses she cleaned, hoping he might find a piano to play.

Julius Weiss, a German Jewish music professor who lived near the Joplins, heard about the boy's passion and dedication and gave him free music lessons. Eventually Joplin became the proud owner of his very own secondhand piano and his talent blossomed. The gifted teenager started playing his own compositions—"He just got his music out of the air," a fan marveled—and he performed professionally in saloons, dance halls, and social clubs throughout the Midwest.

In 1894, Joplin settled in Sedalia, Missouri, a rough-and-tumble frontier crossroads overrun with bars and brothels. During the day, he studied music at W. G. Smith College, a black school, and at night he entertained at various honky-tonk venues. The popular music of the 1890s was dreary. Slow, lugubrious waltzes such as "After the Ball" (the first song to sell over a million copies of sheet music) were the last sighs of a century on its way out. But in Sedalia, there was a new sound that was fresh and exciting, and Joplin was eager to make it his own.

When asked where the term *ragtime* came from, Joplin always answered, "Because it has such a ragged movement." "Rags" were compositions generally played on a piano, with the left hand responsible for the chords, or octaves, while the right hand countered with "incessant syncopation." The player's fingers moved so energetically that they seemed to be in the throes of a musical race-to-the-finish, although Joplin cautioned, "It is never right to play Ragtime fast," and performed his music at a deliberate pace. Ragtime had its origins in gospel and plantation songs, the music of slavery, and there were also elements of it in many contemporary songs, such as the rousing marching tune "Hot Time in the Old Town Tonight." Though Joplin did not "invent" ragtime, he was the composer who made it popular. His buoyant syncopations caught the ear of local music publishers and began to sell. Consumers bought sheet music when they wanted to hear a particular song, and composers and publishers made money on each sale (the way record royalties would be calculated in years to come). The idea was to promote songs that were easy to play at home so that customers were more likely to buy them.

In the summer of 1899, Joplin presented "Maple Leaf Rag," his latest composition, to John Stark, Sedalia's premier music dealer and publisher. Stark was dubious about accepting the piece because it was unusually complex, even for a rag, and he feared that Joplin was the only one who could play it properly. Some (possibly apocryphal) anecdotes suggest the composer tricked Stark into taking a chance on his song. In one version of the story, Joplin bet Stark that a random stranger would be able to play the rag at first sight, and brought in a young black boy from the street who proceeded to do just that. Unbeknownst to Stark, the boy was a plant who had been practicing the complicated piece for months. In another version, Joplin walked into Stark's store with an adorable little black boy in tow. The child danced enthusiastically while Joplin played his piece, and Stark was enchanted. The truth of such stories notwithstanding, Stark snapped up "Maple Leaf Rag" because he recognized it was the sound of the future.

Booker T. Washington, W. E. B. Du Bois, Paul Dunbar, Henry Lewis, and Scott Joplin (who boasted to a friend that "Maple Leaf Rag" would make him the "King of Ragtime composers") were at the center of a new generation of black achievers. However, despite their many successes, these men knew that their position in white society was still tenuous. In a poem titled "We Wear the Mask," Dunbar wrote, "We wear the mask that grins and lies,/it hides our cheeks and shades our eyes," conveying just how carefully African Americans, no matter how distinguished, had to present themselves to the world.

JUMP JIM CROW

---◆◆◆---

Despite the triumph of a handful of talented African Americans, the typical black person was *not* doing well in 1899. Terrified of the power that seven hundred thousand registered black voters could wield in local elections, Southern states introduced literacy tests and poll taxes to disenfranchise these citizens. Lynchings were common. Historians at Tuskegee kept track of the number of lynchings in the country each year. They recorded 101 in 1898 and 85 in 1899, including the incredibly vicious execution of Sam Hose. On April 12, Hose, a black farmworker in Georgia, was accused of murdering his employer, raping the man's wife, and battering their infant child. Even though Hose may have killed in self defense, and the other charges of rape and assault were most likely fabricated to incite the mob, outraged Georgians did not wait for "due process." They administered their own form of justice, which consisted of tying Hose to a tree, cutting off his ears, fingers, and genitals, and setting him on fire. For those who were unable to join the two thousand vigilantes, "souvenirs" of the event, including the victim's knuckles, were on sale at local stores.

Many of these vigilante executions were popular public events, attended by men, women, and children, and photographed for posterity. After these high-profile executions, professional photographers printed gruesome postcards memorializing the "occasion," and they were mailed off to friends with bizarre "wish you were here" sentiments. Incredibly, Palmetto, Georgia, the town where the Hose lynching took place, was only ninety miles away from Tuskegee.

Black people's daily lives were complicated and restricted by "Jim Crow," the state laws that mandated separate, and supposedly equal, treatment of African Americans in public facilities. Jim Crow was originally a popular character created in the 1820s by a white minstrel performer named Thomas Dartmouth "Daddy" Rice. One day, when Rice was walking the streets of Cincinnati, he watched a young black boy—or an old black man, depending on who was recounting the story—sing a spirited version of the song "Jump Jim Crow."

> *Come listen all you galls and boys I's jist from Tuckyhoe,*
> *I'm going to sing a little song, my name's Jim Crow,*
> *Weel about and turn about and do jis so,*
> *Eb'ry time I weel about and jump Jim Crow.*

Rice was inspired to darken his face with charred cork, dress in tattered clothing, and sing and dance an exaggerated version of that number. The act was so popular that it became a mainstay in minstrel shows, especially when Rice added risqué verses. Audiences begged for "Jim Crow" and, at some point in time, the name became synonymous with the larger black community. Hence, the codes regulating what blacks could and could not do were called Jim Crow laws.

Whatever Jim Crow laws professed to accomplish, separate was *separate*, but never equal. As Booker T. frequently pointed out in newspaper editorials and letters of protest to railroad officials, when it came to travel, black passengers paid more and got less. In some states, finicky Southerners demanded segregated seating, complaining that colored people weren't clean. Booker T. countered with the question, How could black travelers maintain proper hygiene when they were denied access to washrooms? And even if there were "facilities," men and women had to share them—an outrageous violation of decorum at the time. As for the cars set aside for blacks, Booker T. complained that they were "poorly ventilated, poorly lighted, and, above all, rarely clean." Worse still, they attracted disreputable whites who wanted to drink, smoke, gamble, and indulge in other vices they wouldn't dare practice in "polite" society. With his rigorous travel schedule, Booker T. was constantly confronted by these iniquitous rules and joined W. E. B. Du Bois in organizing protests against them.

The weight of so many crusades was taking its toll on Booker T. Friends noticed that he looked exhausted and they decided a vacation from his grueling schedule, and a dramatic change of scenery, would be good for him. They proposed an all-expenses-paid trip to Europe. Booker T. thanked his benefactors but pointed out that he was largely responsible for the fund-raising at Tuskegee, and that the school could not operate without the donations he generated. His friends came up with a solution for that problem, too: they would pay for his trip *and* provide enough money for Tuskegee to stay afloat during his absence.

A grateful Booker T. set out on his first vacation in eighteen years. "I had always regarded Europe, and London, and Paris, much as I regard heaven," he said, in trying to describe his excitement. Francis Jackson Garrison, one of the trip's benefactors, sent Booker T. a check for a hundred dollars to cover the cost of any special clothing or luggage the Washingtons might need for their European tour, and he also provided letters of introduction to important and interesting Americans who lived abroad.

Booker T. planned a vigorous itinerary of destinations and activities. But his biggest and potentially most perilous adventure was crossing the Atlantic. Booker T. was apprehensive because he had heard that other African Americans had been shunned or treated rudely during ocean voyages. His patrons searched long and hard for a shipping line that promised to respect the Washingtons. The Atlantic Transport Line, for example, suddenly had no openings when it was established that the passengers in question were black. Francis Garrison, who was making the arrangements, was outraged. "I am bound that no indignity shall be put upon Booker Washington and his wife. It will be an honor to any line to have them as passengers," he fumed. The Red Star Line's *Friesland* was the right choice. The captain, the crew, and even the Southerners on board treated Booker T. with the "greatest kindness." Once he allowed himself to relax—and it didn't come naturally to him—Booker T. fell into a long, restorative sleep for hours each day.

After ten days at sea, the *Friesland* deposited its passengers in Belgium, and from there the Washingtons traveled to Holland. Booker T. was impressed by the industry and self-sufficiency of the Dutch. They seemed to accomplish so much on small plots of land, and without incurring any debt. But he was less than complimentary about Holland's women. "I do not think I exaggerate when I say that I have not seen in all Holland a single beautiful woman," he wrote.

Presumably the women in Paris, the Washingtons' next stop, were more impressive, but Booker T. reserved his praise for Henry O. Tanner, an African American painter who was making a name for himself in the highest artistic circles. Tanner was the eldest child of the Right Reverend Benjamin T. Tanner of Philadelphia. He moved to Paris, the capital of the art world in the late nineteenth century, and won critical acclaim for paintings such as *Daniel in the Lion's Den, Flight into Egypt,* and *The Still Hunt.* When Booker T. mentioned to some of his American friends that he was going to the Paris Salon to view the work of "a young colored man," they were astonished. Even white liberals doubted that a black artist could rise so high. But Tanner's latest effort, *The Raising of Lazarus,* was displayed prominently and received rave reviews. *La Findel Journal* called it "one of the best renderings in the Salon."

Booker T. was often criticized for promoting industrial education over intellectual and artistic pursuits. In this case, however, he couldn't say enough about Tanner's talent, and he urged his fellow African Americans to reach into their pockets to give the young artist the support he deserved. "Few of the race are able individually to purchase Mr. Tanner's original paintings," he acknowledged in an article he wrote for an American newspaper. "But hundreds are able to secure the photographs of these productions. . . . these photographs can be had for a small sum, and they should adorn the homes of thousands of our people in America." He even listed Tanner's address to make it easier for his readers to contact the artist and place their orders. He wanted Tanner's accomplishments to inspire other blacks to pursue their own artistic dreams.

In early July, the Washingtons traveled to England, where they were received by statesmen, diplomats, aristocrats, and royals, who invited them to parties and weekends at their country estates. Joseph Choate, the American ambassador, hosted a reception where Booker T. met the writer and humorist Samuel Clemens, better known as Mark Twain, for the first time. No doors—or gates—were closed to him, including at Windsor Palace, where Booker T. was invited to take tea with Queen Victoria herself.

After three eventful months it was time to sail home on the *St. Louis*. In the ship's library, Booker T. found *My Bondage and My Freedom*, a memoir by Frederick Douglass that described his 1845 voyage to Europe and offered a sobering account of racism at sea. Douglass wrote that he was not permitted to stay in a cabin because of his color, and that he suffered other indignities: several hotheaded passengers from Georgia were so insulted to find a black man on their ship that they threatened to throw him overboard. Booker T. was happy to report that he and Margaret were treated with the greatest respect during their crossing. In fact, the entire trip had been revelatory because they were never in a situation when they were made to feel that being black was a disadvantage. They had experienced a vacation from discrimination, but the race war still awaited them at home. Booker T. felt rested and was ready to fight. He also had a new strategy in place.

PRIDE AND PREJUDICE

———•◆•———

"If your head is in the lion's mouth, use your hand to pet him," was Booker T.'s very practical strategy for dealing with hostile Southern whites. In public he was reasonable, conciliatory, and by some standards, accommodationist. But if he didn't always speak his mind, it was because absolute candor would have been imprudent, if not suicidal. "A black man who overplayed his hand lost his life at the table, instantly, violently, with table upturned, cards and chips scattering, and a body crashing on the floor," was the dramatic way one historian summed up the situation. In private, behind a screen—or as Paul Dunbar might have said, behind a mask—Booker T. used his considerable power and resources to mount a war of "secret activism."

An ugly new mechanism of disfranchisement, the Hardwick Bill, was coming before the Georgia legislature. It would empower a board of regulators (white, of course) to evaluate voting applicants to determine if they "understood" the state constitution. There was every reason to believe that most "regulators" would dismiss a black man, no matter how educated, and approve any illiterate white. "The world is watching the South as it has never done before," Booker T. told the *Atlanta Constitution*, hoping to shame Georgians into doing the right thing. Then he appealed to the legislators' higher natures. "There is one, and but one, way out of our present difficulties and that is the right way. All else but right will fail." His pleas worked, and the bill was defeated by an overwhelming majority.

Next, Booker T. turned his attention to matters in Louisiana, where a watchdog group called the Afro American Council was in the process of challenging the constitutionality of a grandfather clause that allowed whites to bypass the literacy tests and poll taxes instituted to disqualify blacks from voting. This kind of court battle required a great deal of money. Booker T. agreed to oversee the campaign and to pay for the legal fees himself, if necessary, but he was careful to participate anonymously so he wouldn't offend anyone who might disapprove of overt political activism on his part.

In addition to blocking bills and fighting Jim Crow laws, Booker T. set out to change the very thinking that caused prejudice. Bigots such as Mississippi politician James K. Vardaman complained that the black man was "a lazy, lying, lustful animal which no conceivable amount of training can transform into a tolerable citizen." The way to obliterate that ugly stereotype was to give the race a brand-new image that reflected thirty years of progress.

Booker T. tried to do just that when he moved into a new house on the Tuskegee campus. The Oaks was a large and impressive Queen Anne home with a parlor, library, dining room, den, several bedrooms, and—a first for the area—indoor plumbing. Every brick and every bit of woodwork was crafted by Tuskegee students. Like Sagamore Hill, TR's manse, The Oaks was fashioned to look comfortably old and seasoned when it was actually new.

The house was controversial while it was being built because some people considered it too extravagant for its occupants. William Bancroft, a Quaker philantropist, happened to be on campus during construction and was distressed by what he saw. "I noticed a *very large* house," he wrote to Booker T. disapprovingly. "If it is for thy use, and if thy private means are not very different from what I suppose them to be, this seems very hard to reconcile with thy position and the needs of the school." In other words, what business did Booker T. have building a mansion for himself when Tuskegee was desperately in need of money?

Tuskegee trustee William Henry Baldwin Jr., who was president of the Long Island Rail Road and a conscientious New England philanthropist, as well as a great friend to Booker T., fired back a defense. He explained that the students who built The Oaks were paid for their work and that the house would be used for entertaining important friends of the institution. Finally, he pointed out, "It is imperative that if we expect Booker Washington to live and to do good work, for him to have comfortable surroundings." Booker T. stayed in The Oaks and it became his castle. But it was also a symbol of accomplishment and uplift. "The actual sight of a first class house that a Negro has built is ten times more potent than pages of discussion about a house that he ought to build, or perhaps could build," he said. If an African American lived in a nice house, it signified he was an important member of the community, and eventually he would be treated like one.

Booker T.'s efforts to promote the "new Negro" included a sophisticated publicity and public relations campaign. He charged Emmett Jay Scott, the bright young African American journalist from Texas who served as his personal secretary, with the job of creating press releases that featured positive stories about Booker T. and other noteworthy blacks. The idea was that if people read good news about African Americans for a change, they were more likely to discount the damaging stereotypes. Whenever Booker T. received an award or addressed a distinguished group, Scott sent the news to the press.

"Need Tub and Toothbrush: Booker T. Washington Recommends Both to Negroes, for Daily Use," was one *New York Times* headline. Even the jokes Booker T. told during his speeches were picked up by newspapers, especially the comic tale of a slave who learned the power of self-help. "I remember an old negro who wanted a Christmas dinner," Booker T. recalled. "He prayed night after night, 'Lord, please send a turkey to this darky.' But none came to him. Finally he prayed: 'O Lord: please send this darky to a turkey.' And he got one that same night." That anecdote was printed everywhere; Booker T. got so much coverage that Tuskegee had to subscribe to a clipping service to keep up with it.

Booker T. also made a point of giving lengthy interviews to journalists because newspaper articles were solid forums for his ideas. "Do you think the time might ever come, that any circumstance might ever arise, by which a black man might become president of the United States?" the *Memphis Commercial Appeal* asked him point-blank in a conversation about the future of the black man in America. "I should hope so," was Booker T.'s reply.

The most effective weapon in Booker T.'s "new Negro"

campaign was his own story. He decided to write a book that would be part autobiography and part promotional calling card for Tuskegee. Nineteenth-century readers had an appetite for "slave narratives"—autobiographies by African Americans who offered firsthand accounts of their experiences as slaves and the struggle for emancipation—and some had become bestsellers. *Narrative of the Life of Frederick Douglass, an American Slave*, published in 1845, was so popular that Douglass updated it three times to keep readers abreast of all the new developments in his ongoing saga.

In the 1870s and 1880s, fewer slave narratives were published because the subject was no longer topical. But Booker T. hoped that his autobiography, which he planned to call *The Story of My Life and Work*, would be an inspirational book that transcended time, place, and genre. He selected J. L. Nichols, a thriving subscription house, to publish it. Subscription houses, unlike conventional publishers, bypassed bookstores and sold their books through trained agents who went door to door.

Armed with sample pages of text and pictures, the agent visited likely prospects and delivered a snappy sales pitch emphasizing the book's strong points. "From Slave Babe to Leading Educator, Author, and Industrial Advocate," read the tagline for *The Story of My Life and Work*. His story "tells what all the world is seeking to learn," another brochure boasted. Nichols planned on marketing the book to admiring African Americans. Many authors, including Mark Twain, sold their works in this targeted way and were happy with the resulting royalties.

Booker T. hired writer Edgar Webber to help him with the project when it was in its formative stages. Webber attempted to shape the material into a winning personal history, but he wasn't particularly good at the job, and *The Story of My Life and*

Work was vague, badly organized, and a little dull. Meanwhile, Booker T. contracted Boston journalist Max Bennett Thrasher (who had accompanied him on tour the previous year) to write image-enhancing articles about Tuskegee and its principal for magazines and newspapers. Unlike Webber, Thrasher was a skilled writer who was able to mimic Booker T.'s folksy tone. When the occasion demanded, Thrasher even became the voice of Margaret Washington, for whom he penned a feature on sewing and hygiene for *The Women's Home Companion.*

The Story of My Life and Work sold well despite its flaws, but Booker T. was sure he could do better. He invited Max Thrasher to help him pen a *second* autobiography, one designed to appeal to more discriminating readers. They started working on a new version, called *Up from Slavery,* and this time Booker T. had the benefit of a real writer and real editors. The *Outlook,* a popular magazine with a broad readership, planned to serialize the book before it was published in book form, and its expert staff offered Booker T. valuable advice. "Talk about yourself more," its editors urged, because they believed "the personal element in such a life" was "tremendously interesting and valuable."

Booker T. made up his mind that this time he was going to write more of the book himself. He dictated detailed notes to Thrasher, then reviewed them and wrote a rough first draft. "My general plan is to give the first place to facts and incidents and to hang the generalizations on to those facts," he told his editor. Story first, then philosophy, was his new plan. And that story was shaping up to be a classic—an Algeresque, triumph-over-adversity saga, with the novelty of having a black protagonist at its center.

Not only was Booker T. the subject of two versions of his life story, but he also turned up as a pivotal character in a popular novel. In 1900, a successful African American journalist named Pauline Hopkins had a daring idea. She acknowledged that there were black "historians, ministers, poets, judges and lawyers" who were doing a fine job of speaking out against racism. But she wanted to reach a larger audience and suspected that a classic romance novel, "a simple, homely tale, unassumingly told," would be the way to do it. Hopkins wrote *Contending Forces,* a lively melodrama complete with heroes, villains, star-crossed lovers, concealed identities, last-minute revelations, and thrilling reconciliations. But the real purpose of Hopkins's potboiler was to expose the evils of racial discrimination.

Contending Forces tells the story of Sappho Clark, a beautiful young mulatto who fights to preserve her dignity and virtue in a world that is hostile to people of color. She is subject to a brutal assortment of travails, including rape, blackmail, and betrayal. But even as Sappho and her fellow protagonists navigate the torturous plot, they "faithfully portray the inmost thoughts and feelings of the Negro with all the fire and romance which lies dormant in our history," Hopkins wrote in the introduction to her book.

When modeling her leading men in *Contending Forces,* Hopkins turned to two real-life black heroes, Booker T. Washington and W. E. B. Du Bois. Du Bois's fictional counterpart was Will Smith, Sappho's brilliant and adoring young lover, while Booker T. turned up as Dr. Arthur Lewis, an important educator who was in love with Will's sister, Dora. Hopkins used her roman-à-clef to illustrate an important philosophical debate that was playing out between the two leaders. Like Du Bois, Will believed that blacks had the right to a classical education, and that there were times when they had to stand up and fight for their rights. Dr. Lewis, on the other hand, subscribed to Booker T.'s industrial education vision of racial uplift. "If you want honey you must have money," was his philosophy, and he advocated patience and industry over activism. Hopkins gave equal weight to both men and their arguments: in her able literary hands they were smart and sympathetic characters who, despite their differences, could coexist. (And they each got the girl in the end.)

There was one funny side note to Booker T.'s fame and success. Even though he received more respect than most African Americans, some people were nonetheless confused as to how to treat an accomplished black man. One Southern gentleman swore that he considered Booker T. a great man, yet could never break the unwritten rule of the South and address a "colored" man, however distinguished, as "Mr. Washington." He admitted that he was greatly relieved when Harvard awarded Booker T. his honorary doctorate because he could call him "Dr. Washington," and the "Mr." problem was solved.

THAT DAMNED COWBOY

———————◆———————

In 1899, while Booker T. worked on his two autobiographies, TR published his latest book, a memoir with overtones of a boy's adventure story. *The Rough Riders* was a rousing eyewitness account of TR's experiences during the Spanish-American War, the kind of derring-do tale he read voraciously as a child. TR enthusiastically chronicled every aspect of the campaign, from raising the regiment and whipping it into shape, to the battle at Las Guasimas and the arduous voyage home. TR was an experienced author with eighteen titles to his credit, but *The Rough Riders*, serialized in *Scribner's* magazine and published in book form, proved to be his most successful and most controversial work.

TR quite often spoke without thinking, and his impulsiveness got him into trouble. This seemed to be the case with *The Rough Riders* because he offhandedly suggested that the black soldiers who fought in Cuba were less heroic than their white counterparts. "They are peculiarly dependent on their white officers," he wrote. "None of the white regulars or Rough Riders showed the slightest sign of weakening; but under the strain the colored infantrymen began to get a little uneasy and to drift to the rear, either helping wounded men, or saying that they wished to find their own regiments." TR told them that he would shoot the first man who went to the rear, and when they understood that he meant business, "the 'Smoked Yankees,' as the Spanish called the colored soldiers, flashed their white teeth at one another as they broke into broad grins, and I had no more trouble with them," he wrote. TR didn't blame them for being cowardly. "I attributed the trouble to the superstition and fear of the darkey, natural in those but one generation removed from slavery and but a few generations removed from the wildest savagery."

Not only was TR's accusation shockingly ignorant, but it was also inaccurate. Black soldiers had fought bravely in the war, and TR had said as much to Booker T. during their very first meeting, according to journalist Max Bennett Thrasher, who was traveling with the Washingtons at the time. Eyewitnesses from the Cuban front instantly came forward to defend their maligned comrades. Sergeant Presley Holliday, an African American cavalryman, wrote an impassioned defense in the *New York Age,* claiming that the soldiers in question had been ordered to the rear to help the wounded and to retrieve supplies. TR subsequently softened his account of the incident by suggesting that the soldiers were following orders, but it would take more than backpedaling to repair his relationship with offended blacks.

It was a shame that TR's rash comments overshadowed his more enlightened attitudes about race, because his actions should have spoken louder than his words. The new governor signed a bill banning "local option" segregation in New York's public schools because he believed that the classroom was no place for a color line. "My children sit in the same school with colored children," he said in defense of his position. And in January 1900, TR invited Harry Burleigh, an important black composer and soloist, to perform at the Governor's Mansion. The Roosevelts' guests were charmed by the baritone's soulful rendition of "The Absent-Minded Beggar" and the evening was a great success . . . until Burleigh tried to check into a hotel and discovered that all doors were closed to him. No decent hotel in Albany would allow a black man—even a distinguished one—to occupy a room. When the Roosevelts were informed of Burleigh's predicament, they immediately invited him to spend the night at their house.

The other problem that arose after the publication of the hugely popular *Rough Riders* was that TR's memoir made it sound as if he fought the war single-handedly. It was *his* book, but there was something inescapably narcissistic about the way he placed himself at the center of the action. "Mr. Dooley," a humorous character created by journalist Finley Peter Dunne, reviewed *The Rough Riders* in his popular newspaper column and, after recounting TR's self-described heroics, he suggested, "if I was him I'd call th' book 'Alone in Cuba.' " The title stuck. A starstruck young woman who was introduced to TR at a reception gushed that, of all his works, *Alone in Cuba* was her favorite.

The new governor was more of an egoist than a team player. One year into his two-year term, he boasted, "I think I have been the best Governor within my time, better than either Cleveland or Tilden." He was hostile to the interests of big business, he ignored GOP head Thomas Platt's cronies when it was time to make appointments, and, whenever possible, he ignored *Platt* himself—which convinced the outraged boss to kick him upstairs before he destroyed the party machine. Washington was the perfect place to park the troublemaker, Platt decided, and if he had his way, TR would be President McKinley's running mate in the 1900 election.

Senator Mark Hanna, McKinley's campaign manager and the Republican Party's national chairman, had a visceral, negative reaction to the idea and the two Republican heavyweights tossed TR back and forth like a hot potato. While Platt tried to push him out of New York, Hanna did his best to keep him away from the presidential election. TR knew what was going on and was not happy about it. He claimed he wasn't interested in the vice presidency—in his opinion a decorative, do-nothing position. The job paid only $8,000 per year, $2,000 less than what TR earned as governor, the vice president had to pay for his own housing in Washington, and the Roosevelts were already having money troubles as it was.

Practical Edith always had to think about money. Though the Roosevelts were blessed with an illustrious name and pedigree, the previous generation's fortune had dwindled to a mere memory. TR had lost massive amounts of money on his cattle investments. Now he lived on his earnings, and with six children to support and educate, the family would struggle on a reduced income, although "struggling" meant maintaining servants and a country estate. Edith kept a tight rein on expenses and dressed simply, wearing the same gowns and hats for several seasons. The Governor's Mansion in Albany made life a little easier because it was free. But the vice presidency came with unavoidable expenses that would force Edith to strain to make ends meet, so she was against the idea.

Despite his and Edith's objections, TR showed up at the Republican convention on June 16 looking like the perfect candidate. He was the heroic Rough Rider, right down to his wide-brimmed, Western-style hat. One wise delegate looked at TR's headgear and promptly informed his friends, "Gentleman, that's an acceptance hat." The crowd chanted, "We want Teddy! We want Teddy!" and marching bands serenaded his hotel room. In the end, TR could not resist their collective adoration, and agreed to be McKinley's running mate, proving that he was a team player after all. Hanna wasn't fooled for a minute and frantically argued, "Don't any of you realize that there's only one life between this madman and the White House?" but no one was listening. The ticket was set with the awkwardly phrased slogan, "William McKinley, a western man with eastern ideas, and Theodore Roosevelt, an eastern man with western characteristics." An overjoyed Platt regained control of Albany and the New York Republican Party, while a disgruntled Mark Hanna snapped at his friend McKinley, "Now it is up to you to live."

It was considered undignified for an incumbent president to actually go out and campaign for reelection, so McKinley stayed home in Ohio for the summer and politely greeted voters from his front porch, while an enthusiastic TR went out on the road and did all of the work. Making the best of the situation, Hanna sent the self-styled cowboy to the Western states to stump for votes among his fans. He was usually accompanied by a cortege of Rough Riders, who turned every event into a Wild West show. TR was so visible and so vocal that he, not McKinley, became the face of the election. Voters showed their overwhelming support at the polls on November 6, 1900, when the Republicans defeated Democrat William Jennings Bryan by a landslide.

Booker T., who was blessed with impeccable manners and keen political instincts, immediately sent a congratulatory telegram to the vice president elect. TR's response was swift and cordial. On November 10 he replied, "My dear President Washington. Your telegram gave me peculiar pleasure." As nice as it was for Booker T. to receive a polite thank-you, what followed was even more rewarding. "Now, when you come up North next, I particularly want to see you," TR continued. "I have had some long talks recently with my friend Lewis of Harvard. There are points where I do not entirely agree with him and I want to consult you about them." TR had told Henry Lewis that Booker T. was "a man for whom I have the highest regard and in whose judgment I have much faith."

"Consult" was a strong word and it suggested that TR was turning to Booker T. for guidance, a smart move in light of his recent insult of the African American soldiers. But a potential partnership was a timely and strategic development for Booker T. as well, for it signified that he had the ear of the most popular politician in America.

Emmett Scott, Booker T.'s secretary, was so excited about the letter that he scribbled an emphatic comment in the margin before passing it along to his boss. "You have him sure!"

BEST BEHAVIOR

———•◆•———

Booker T.'s ongoing image-enhancing efforts included his students at Tuskegee, and he was always looking for ways to improve them. When he returned from Europe in 1899, he hired an exciting new lady principal to supervise the girls on campus. Margaret Washington was the acting lady principal, or dean of women, but when her responsibilities on campus expanded, Booker T. invited Josephine Bruce, once the most famous black socialite in America, to take her place. Bruce's husband, Senator Blanche Bruce, then registrar of the U.S. Treasury, had passed away earlier in the year, so the recent widow was looking for a new role to engage her energy and talents. After some haggling over salary, she agreed to come to Tuskegee to oversee "all that pertains to the life of girls at the school."

Like Olivia Davidson Washington and Margaret Washington before her, Josephine Bruce shared Booker T.'s belief that proper conduct opened the door to opportunity and success. When she arrived on campus, however, she discovered that the job was going to be more difficult than she imagined. Many of her students were poor and unsophisticated, and came from homes absent of "refining influences." Tuskegee offered some advantages, such as classes in dressmaking and hygiene that led to better grooming, and a strict honor code that promoted morality, but the school's rural Alabama community provided few opportunities to observe, let alone practice, social niceties. Bruce saw to it that even if her girls couldn't experience society firsthand, they could read about it. Her efforts to cultivate manners at Tuskegee matched a larger etiquette movement that was sweeping across the country.

After the Civil War, the financial boom in the North and the corresponding economic collapse in the South turned society upside down. The new rich had the money to buy the breeding they lacked, so there was a proliferation of etiquette manuals, forty new ones published in the 1880s alone, to show them the way. Mrs. John Sherwood, the "arbiter elegantiarum" who wrote the popular book *Manners and Social Usages*, applauded her countrymen's newfound obsession with good manners: "There is no country where there are so many genuinely anxious to do the proper thing as in the vast conglomerate which we call the United States of America."

Readers devoured guides such as *The Habits of Good Society, A Handbook for Ladies and Gentlemen, The Young Lady at Home and in Society*, and *The Bazar Book of Decorum*, which offered rules that ranged from practical to absurd. The advice "Change your clothes when they are dirty," as one manual took pains to point out, was basic common sense. Less obvious rules included the caveat that the number of guests at a dinner party should never be "more than the Muses [nine], or less than the Graces [three]." If these regulations seemed overly precise and even dictatorial, they did offer a handy blueprint for good behavior. But, given the fact that their authors sneered at Democrats because they considered them "common, rude, and dirty," they certainly had no advice to offer former slaves who might be interested in self-improvement.

Eventually blacks saw the need to create their own etiquette books, and, for the first time, teachers such as Josephine Bruce could use them in the classroom. *On Habits and Manners*, published by the Hampton Institute, was actually written by a white woman named M. F. Armstrong (a relative of General Samuel Armstrong, who supervised the project). It was billed as a textbook for "recently freed slaves or other students who had had no exposure to middle-class life" and included chapters on "Care of the Person," "Table Etiquette," "Social Behavior," and other fundamental topics—the same "tub and toothbrush" lessons Booker T. Washington learned when he was a student there.

On Habits and Manners urged blacks to be especially careful about their conduct while traveling, although the book acknowledged that "manners on the road may involve at times peculiarly difficult and trying positions, and cases where the courtesy will seem very one-sided." "One-sided courtesy" was an excessively polite way of describing segregation and discrimination, yet Armstrong suggested that "propriety of deportment on your own part will do more than anything else towards securing for you fair and proper treatment from others."

In 1891, a black lawyer, journalist, and activist named R. C. O. Benjamin took time from his busy professional life to pen an etiquette manual titled *Don't: A Book for Girls.* Its delicately etched green cover showed a well-dressed young lady sitting demurely in a walled garden, a cat sleeping in her lap and birds flying sweetly in the foreground. The only unusual element in the classic, pastoral scene was the "young lady" herself. She was African American.

Benjamin was well qualified to give advice about good manners because he had an unusually distinguished background. He was born on the island of St. Kitts, where he attracted the attention of wealthy patrons who sent him to Oxford, England, for a college education. He moved to America in 1869 and became an attorney, but journalism, not law, was his passion. In time he acquired several newspapers, including Alabama's popular *Negro American.* His motto was "Life is what you make it," and the words were apt because he was constantly reinventing himself.

Benjamin decided to become an arbiter of etiquette because he wanted to help black women overcome what he called "a state of hereditary darkness and rudeness." Former slaves were "slowly but surely emerging from the night of barbarism into the light of civilization." He wanted to speed them along the road to refinement, and most of his rules began with the word *don't.* Don't be idle; don't slight work; don't be selfish; don't gossip; and don't be slattern. He was especially concerned about the proper use of language, and presented a long list of don'ts that would immediately betray humble origins and illiteracy. "Well-bred persons usually speak slowly, with proper emphasis and without abbreviations," he cautioned. "Don't say gents for gentlemen, or hist'ry for history."

Benjamin took the trouble to create his handsome little book because he believed that "our girls are the pioneers of a race," and *Don't: A Book for Girls* was light and optimistic because its author was confident that blacks had the power to improve their lives. His attitude darkened as the decade progressed and he was deeply discouraged by the resurgence of racism. One day he saw a white man harassing black voters in Lexington, Kentucky, and when Benjamin came to their defense, the bully pulled out a gun and cold-bloodedly shot him in the back. Benjamin died, and his murderer got away with the crime by claiming he acted in "self-defense."

In 1899, E. M. Woods, author of *The Negro in Etiquette: A Novelty,* asked his readers to face up to some unpleasant realities regarding race. Woods, an African American, was the principal of a school in St. Louis when he wrote a pamphlet called *The Gospel of Civility.* It became so popular that he expanded it into a full-length book with illustrations depicting black men and women in real-life social situations. As his captions indicated, Woods's figures had *attitude.* "Sidewalk is as free for me as it is for you," boasted a proud black gentleman carrying a walking stick and dressed in white tie and tails (in the daytime). "Come in, if you can get in for the dirt," said a bandana-clad house-keeper to the surprised caller at her door. Woods was sassy and unashamed to tell it like it was. His book advised members of his race to stop "shambling," "shuffling," and saying "thank you Boss." Since suspicion of rape was the leading cause of lynchings, Woods warned African American men about the dangers of paying undue attention to white ladies: "Colored men, don't you know that white men don't like too much gallantry from negro men around their women."

In his own way, Woods was promoting an early form of black pride. Why, he wondered, did so many blacks behave as if they wanted to be white? "People who are constantly trying to get into another race remind me of a poodle dog trying to catch its tail," he scoffed. In a chapter on "The Black Husband and

White Wife" he even argued against intermarriage, explaining, "No Negro lugging a white wife on his arm has ever risen to eminence in the United States or gained the popular respect of the two races." Without naming names, he was using Frederick Douglass's much-criticized marriage to Helen Pitts as an example.

Woods also pointed out that, as blacks moved about in the world, they had to learn the difference between business and social courtesy. "Too many so-called intelligent people fail to comprehend this fine distinction," he warned. "The gulf between business equality and social equality is as wide as that between mere acquaintance and near relatives."

LAZY DAYS

———•◆•———

The excitement of winning the election passed quickly, and TR came face-to-face with his worst nightmare. The new vice president, the foremost advocate of the "strenuous life," had nothing to do. "We're all off to Washington to watch Teddy take the veil," Thomas Platt chortled on the eve of the March 4 inauguration. Once TR was sworn in, he would be out of sight and, eventually, Platt hoped, out of mind. That's what usually happened to vice presidents: they performed figurehead duties such as presiding over the Senate, then faded into oblivion. It seemed as if TR would be no exception. He worked a grand total of four days—from March 4 to March 8, at which point the Senate adjourned until the following October, and TR was free to go home to Oyster Bay to settle into the life of "enforced idleness" that came with the job.

After a few weeks, Edith noticed that her normally high-spirited husband was desperate for activity and battling depression. His pent-up energy had to go somewhere, so he decided to resume the law studies he had abandoned as a young man. Practicing law could be his fallback profession if, as he suspected, his days in politics were numbered. But even as TR purported to be a realist about his gloomy prospects, he fantasized about being the Republican candidate for president in 1904. The deck was stacked against him because party bosses Hanna and Platt were determined to keep him on the shelf. At the moment, TR was thinking about mining untapped resources in the South, namely the black vote.

One of the reasons Southern blacks were on his mind was that TR had just finished reading an advance copy of Booker T.'s *Up from Slavery.* He liked it so much that he shared it with Edith, and then dashed off an enthusiastic thank-you letter to its author. "My dear Mr. Washington," TR wrote on March 21, 1901. "Mrs. Roosevelt is as much pleased as I am with your book. I shall not try to tell you what I think about it, my dear sir, for I do not want to seem to flatter you too much. . . . I do not know who could take your place in the work you are doing."

TR also indicated that he wished he could sit down with Booker T. to discuss future plans. The two men met at TR's Madison Avenue office on April 1. One of the topics that came up during their conversation was the possibility of TR coming to Tuskegee later in the year. President McKinley had visited the campus in 1898 and his appearance occasioned a huge celebration, including a parade of proud students and a day of inspirational speeches. "Integrity and industry are the best possessions which any man can have, and every man can have them," McKinley had told his enraptured audience. "Nobody can give them to him or take them away from him." He also had the highest praise for his host, Booker T., whom he called "one of the great leaders of his race." The presidential visit, which was good for morale, was also great for PR and put Tuskegee on the map.

Two years later there was even more of a reason to show off Tuskegee. The school that started out with one teacher, thirty students, and a leaky roof now boasted 86 faculty members (including the agricultural genius George Washington Carver), 1,100 undergraduates, a 2,300-acre campus, and buildings bearing names such as Huntington and Rockefeller, in honor of the financial titans who donated them. Amazingly, the entire property was free from mortgage, but the school's annual operating expenses were as high as $80,000, and Booker T. still raised most of that money by going from door to door.

Thanks to the persuasive powers of *Up from Slavery*, which was a bestselling serialization and book, a new mogul with deep pockets stepped forward to offer support. Booker T. had been courting philanthropist Andrew Carnegie for ten years, but the self-made millionaire seemed indifferent to Tuskegee's needs. Then he read Booker T.'s new autobiography. "Give that man a library!" was his enthusiastic response, and he did just that by pledging $20,000 to build a new home for the school's collection of 12,000 books.

Booker T. hoped to attract more attention, and more donors, by hosting the extremely popular Theodore Roosevelt. He proposed that the vice president come to Tuskegee and make side trips to Montgomery and Atlanta, where Booker T. would arrange for warm receptions from the Chambers of Commerce. TR was enthusiastic about the plan because he believed that establishing a political toehold in the South would help build a constituency. He also had personal reasons for going south. Roswell, the plantation where his mother was born, was right outside Montgomery. TR held very romantic notions of his

Southern roots and was eager to see the idyllic Bulloch family seat. Booker T. and TR traded letters and telegrams over the next few months, finalizing arrangements for an official vice presidential visit the following fall.

While TR waited for his duties to resume in Washington, he leapt at the chance to attend the Pan-American Exposition in Buffalo in May 1901. President McKinley was scheduled to open the exposition, but Mrs. McKinley became ill at the last minute and was unable to travel. Roosevelt happily agreed to take his place and the McKinleys rescheduled their trip for early September.

Like the World's Columbian Exposition in Chicago in 1883 and Atlanta's Cotton States and International Exposition in 1885, the "Pan" in Buffalo was conceived to be a "beautiful spectacle" worth traveling across the continent to see. The first World's Fair of the twentieth century intended to celebrate Progress by commemorating the country's exciting new age of electricity and machinery. Everything was suddenly faster, brighter, and more efficient. Some of the wonders slated to debut at the fair included a machine that addressed (and "licked") envelopes, climate-controlled incubators occupied by real babies (who needed to have their diapers changed every two hours), and a futuristic X-ray machine that could see deep inside the human body.

The fair opened on May 21. TR was on hand to officiate, and he brought along Edith and the children. It was a perfect outing for the fun-loving Roosevelts. The festivities, filmed by technicians using Thomas Edison's revolutionary movie camera, included a rousing military parade and the show-stopping release of three thousand carrier pigeons. The children enjoyed the Indian Pow-Wow and the risqué hootchie-kootchie show, but Edith was impressed by the fair's fine display of art, including works by Augustus Saint-Gaudens and Cecilia Beaux. As for TR, he thought the Electric Tower, the exposition's 375-foot, eye-catching symbol of progress and power, was "bully."

The fair's most impressive technological achievement was its use of electric lighting. Powered by nearby Niagara Falls, the Pan boasted an unprecedented display of illumination. Buildings of all sizes were outlined by "tiny dots of fire" that turned the landscape into the "most important and artistic nocturnal scene that was ever made." Some observers exclaimed that it looked just like fairyland, while others wept at the sight of such magnificence.

In addition to being beautiful and impressive, the exposition was also great fun. The Midway, the heart and soul of every world's fair, featured a broad range of entertainment, from a "Trip to the Moon" to a Hawaiian Volcano and a Mirror Maze. Ordinary Americans who would never travel abroad had the opportunity to see turbaned Moors, bowing geishas, and natives from "darkest Africa." Pongos, Zulus, Ashanti, and other tribe members could be found in the African Village, where they danced and simulated their customs for crowds of fascinated spectators. They may have looked wild and threatening, but some of these "natives" were seasoned professionals who had performed similar routines at the Chicago World's Fair.

"Darkest Africa" wasn't the only place at the Pan where blacks were on display. Two other attractions—the Old Plantation and the Negro Exhibit—portrayed the African American experience. The contradictory nature of the two exhibits reflected the country's general schism on race. The Old Plantation paid homage to the South before the Civil War. In this fanciful re-creation of the past, the slaves were happy uncles and aunties who sang as they picked cotton, and joked and strummed the old banjo in daily minstrel shows. Playful "pickaninnies" greeted tourists at the door of the stately colonial mansion—the classic "big house"—that fronted the exhibition. The Old Plantation offered such a colorful, idyllic, and utterly unrealistic portrait of antebellum life that visitors probably wondered why Southern slaves chose emancipation over servitude.

If the Old Plantation celebrated the past, albeit one that never really existed, the fair's official Negro Exhibit was all about progress and the future. Buffalo marked the second showing of the exhibit, which first appeared in the Paris Exposition of 1900. When the French expressed interest in paying tribute to the advancement of the "American Negro," the black community came up with inspired ways to illustrate progress. In fact, W. E. B. Du Bois was one of the chief curators of the exhibit, which featured dioramas depicting the journey from the cotton field to the schoolhouse, as well as charts graphing the rise of literacy, population, prosperity, and other indications of progress for African Americans. Booker T., who also helped to shape the exhibit, met with President McKinley himself to discuss Tuskegee's role. Ultimately, four black educational institutions—Tuskegee, Howard University, Atlanta University, and Fisk University—were represented.

But the most interesting component of the Negro Exhibit was a display devoted to "Negroes as Authors." In 1899, President McKinley suggested including a library of works by African American writers in the materials going to the exposition in Paris. Daniel Murray, the son of a freed slave and an assistant librarian at the Library of Congress, was charged with assembling the collection. Murray had great resources at his disposal, but he was determined to find lesser-known books and pamphlets that were not available in the library. He scoured the country for material, inviting fellow librarians to recommend additions to his "Colored Authors' Collection."

Murray quickly put together a list of 1,100 titles and selected an impressive five hundred to send to Paris. Booker T., Du Bois, Dunbar, and Douglass were on the list, as were R. C. O. Benjamin (the author of *Don't*); John E. Paynter, a black cadet whose memoir, *Joining the Navy*, was included in the library of all government vessels; and Phillis Wheatley, the first documented African American poet. Every author had an interesting backstory, but Wheatley's was truly remarkable. She was a young slave in Boston in 1772 when she wrote *Poems on Various Subjects*. There was such an outcry of disbelief that an *African* could have authored the eloquent work that Wheatley was interrogated by a committee of eighteen Boston dignitaries, including two of America's founding fathers, John Hancock and Thomas Hutchinson, the governor of Massachusetts.

The group was so impressed by the young woman's intelligence and dignified demeanor that it published a public notice of "Attestation" confirming her authorship. "We . . . do assure the World, that the Poems specified in the following Page, were (as we verily believe) written by Phillis, a young Negro Girl, who was but a few Years since, brought an uncultivated Barbarian from Africa. . . ." Wheatley's book of poetry was published in England in 1773, but over a hundred years later, people were still amazed to discover that men and women of color could write. In an article describing the Negro Exhibit, the *Washington Post* suggested that "the number of authors of African descent will assuredly astonish the millions who visit the gay French city this year." The collection was housed in a little library outfitted with wooden bookcases, shadow boxes, and photographs of notable African Americans, such as Booker T. The display wasn't much to look at, but its content was so impressive that the French awarded it seventeen medals.

When the exhibit debuted in Buffalo, however, it was tucked away in the Manufacturers and Liberal Arts building, a less enticing (and less trafficked) place than the Midway, where the crowd-pleasing Old Plantation was located.

As promised, the McKinleys made their appearance in Buffalo the following September. Attendance had not been as high as the fair's organizers predicted, so they came up with the idea of "President's Day" to boost ticket sales. The First Couple arrived via a special train on the afternoon of the fourth and went to the fairgrounds the next morning. President McKinley delivered an eloquent speech to the one hundred thousand spectators who had gathered for the occasion. "Expositions are the timekeepers of progress," he told the crowd, invoking the theme of the fair. "They record the world's advancements. They stimulate the energy, enterprise, and intellect of the people, and quicken human genius." After the ceremony, he spent the rest of the day—and night—touring the Pan and enjoying its attractions. It was a hot Indian summer in Buffalo, so fairgoers found themselves sporting what came to be called the "Exposition Tan," a saffron hue that tinted the flesh on hands, faces, and necks that had been exposed to the sun.

The McKinleys took a break from the heat on September 6, when they visited Niagara Falls. The President returned to the fairgrounds later that afternoon, in time for a well-publicized appearance at the Temple of Music. James B. Parker, an African American waiter working for the Bailey Catering Company, was determined to see the President in person, so he took his place in the long line snaking around the building. The heat didn't bother him—he was a Southerner who was used to standing under a blazing sun. Parker was born a slave in Atlanta in 1857, and grew up to be a large man—over six feet five and about 250 pounds. Despite his intimidating size, he was described as being "gentlemanly" and a "man of few words." He had been working in the North for a few years and his current job at the exposition was a temporary position until something better came along.

When the ceremony began at 4:00 PM, the line moved very slowly (although McKinley was famous for having such an efficient handshake that he could greet as many as 125 persons per minute). As he waited, Parker had plenty of time to contemplate the other people in the crowd. He saw a nondescript young man ahead of him. He was dressed in somber black, with a white handkerchief wrapped around his right hand. It looked as if he had been injured. Parker noticed that the young man stared intently at the President, as if he couldn't wait a moment longer to shake his hand. Finally it was his turn, and the young man stepped forward. Parker watched as McKinley bowed graciously in his direction, and suddenly the man's handkerchief improbably exploded into flames.

A WILD RIDE

————•◆•————

The sound of a gunshot startled the crowd in the Temple of Music. The man in black was concealing a gun beneath his handkerchief, and his target was William McKinley. He took a second shot at the President and was taking aim for a third when a stunned James Parker lunged forward and knocked him to the ground with all his might. "It seemed to me that my own heart was in my mouth," Parker later recalled, "but with a jump I threw my left arm around the man and knocked his hand down."

McKinley's Secret Service agents joined in the fight, overpowering the would-be assassin and dragging him from the room. He was Leon Czolgosz, a self-proclaimed anarchist who had come to the Temple of Music with the express purpose of murdering the President. His bullets pierced McKinley's breast and abdomen, and the President instantly lost all color and, on the brink of collapse, managed to gasp two sentences. "Be easy with him, boys," he told his guards when he saw them descend upon Czolgosz. His other thought was for his wife. "Don't let her know of this—and if she does don't let it be exaggerated," he said, mindful of her frail constitution.

McKinley was rushed to the Pan's on-site infirmary, a rudimentary facility that usually treated fairgoers suffering from heat prostration, food poisoning, bee stings, and the like. A dazed but proud James Parker made his way through the crowd. The newly minted hero was happy to have helped. "Just think," he told a reporter from the *Atlanta Constitution*, "old father Abe freed me, and now I saved his successor from death, provided that bullet that he fired into the President don't kill him."

Provided . . . actually, the doctors who raced to the scene of the shooting were guardedly optimistic about McKinley's prognosis. He was a large, strong man who seemed to be withstanding the assault. Dr. Matthew Mann, a local gynecologist, was pressed into service because Buffalo's leading surgeon was out of town. He and his associates firmly believed that speed was the key to saving the President's life. Instead of taking the time to move him to a real hospital, they operated on the spot. That may have been a terrible mistake.

The Pan American Exposition celebrated Progress but its infirmary was a relic from the past. Though it stood in the midst of a monumental light show powered by thunderous Niagara, the primitive medical facility had no electricity. As the sun set, one of the doctors frantically wiggled a hand mirror to reflect its final rays, hoping to brighten the dimming room. Lack of illumination wasn't the only problem. Dr. Mann did not have the proper instruments at his disposal for abdominal surgery. McKinley was a portly man and the bullets had traveled deep into his body, but there were no retractors on hand to hold his abdominal cavity open.

The surgery commenced. Mann found one of the two bullets, but the other eluded him. He could have used Thomas Edison's famous X-ray machine, which was on display at the fair, but he was a little suspicious of the newfangled device and feared it would do more harm than good. To simplify the search, Mann convinced himself and his team that the other bullet had lodged itself in a benign place. Furthermore, he decreed that there was no need to drain the wound to prevent infection, and ordered the incision closed. The operation was pronounced a success and McKinley was transported to the home of John Milburn, the head of the exposition.

When the shocking news of the assassination attempt reached TR, he was at a fish-and-game resort in Isle La Motte, Vermont. An eyewitness reported that "a look of unmistakable anguish came to his face, and tears immediately filled his eyes." TR raced to Buffalo to be on hand for the tense vigil. He once said of the vice presidency, "The man who occupies it may at any moment be everything, but meanwhile he is practically nothing." At this very moment, he was in the uncomfortable position of being McKinley's understudy, on his way to becoming "everything." The *New York Times* waxed poetic when it described him as "standing to-night in the shadow of a Nation's grief, and at the same time confronting the tremendous responsibility of having to step into the place of the Chief executive." But TR refused to acknowledge the fact that he might be poised to become president. He was brusque with the cheering crowds who greeted him in Buffalo and curtly silenced one overeager fan who suggested that he might be getting a promotion. "Do not speak of that contingency," he commanded. "Our one thought and prayer now is for the President."

TR was genuinely happy when the doctors announced that McKinley was responding to treatment. On September 7, he sent a letter to Booker T. regarding their plans for his visit to Tuskegee, and he included a cheery postscript. "Before you receive this, the President I am sure will be out of danger," he wrote optimistically. Satisfied that McKinley was on the mend, a relieved TR left Buffalo on September 11 to join his family for a vacation in the Adirondacks.

While the President recovered, bulletins describing everything from his temperature to his bowel movements were issued multiple times a day. The doctors had every reason to believe things were going well. In a matter of days, the President was sitting up and asking his doctors for a cigar and newspapers (which they promptly denied). Mark Hanna, the patient's closest friend, saw a rainbow in the sky and considered it a good omen: he called it the "McKinley star."

An assassination averted, the country breathed a collective sigh of relief. And no one was happier than James Parker. Thousands of fairgoers wanted to see "that man Parker," the "Herculean Negro" who had come to McKinley's defense. Souvenir hunters bought the buttons off his jacket for a dollar apiece, and when the buttons were gone, they competed for the jacket. Tributes honoring him were in the works in Savannah and in Washington, DC. In Charleston, South Carolina, a proud Booker T. Washington stood before an assembly of five thousand African Americans and told them they should rejoice because a Southern black man "had saved President McKinley from death."

Eyewitnesses recounted stories of Parker's bravery in newspaper articles. On the day of the shooting, two ladies from Syracuse—Miss Millie A. Jacquin and her friend, Miss Elizabeth Mahley—assured the *Buffalo Times* that Parker was the first man to take hold of the assassin and force him to the ground. In another article, Czolgosz himself complained that "it was the stunning blow delivered upon him by Parker that prevented him from firing another shot." But when Captain Wisser of the U.S. Artillery Corps filed his official report about the assassination attempt, there was not a single mention of Parker. It was as if he never existed. One newspaper editor asked point-blank if the African American hero was being "denied his moment of glory because he was a Negro."

The question of who was responsible for saving the President's life became moot when, on September 13, McKinley took a sudden turn for the worse. He had trouble breathing and suffered from extreme prostration. The doctors who had been so optimistic about his recovery reversed their position and predicted the worst. "The end is only a question of time," presidential secretary George R. Cortelyou announced in a bulletin to the press. Cabinet members tried desperately to reach TR, who by this time was on a remote mountaintop in New York state. As luck would have it, the vice president and his companions had picked that day to explore Mount Marcy, the highest peak in the Adirondack region. Using megaphones and rifles, guides tried to communicate with the expedition, but they did not establish contact until after 5 PM. "The President appears to be dying, and members of the Cabinet in Buffalo think you should lose no time in coming," telegraphed Elihu Root, the secretary of war.

TR was shocked to hear of McKinley's decline and, later that same evening, made up his mind to proceed to Buffalo immediately, even though it was foolhardy to traverse thirty-five miles of treacherous mountain roads in total darkness. Relays of horses raced through the night, navigating one hairpin turn after another. "Push along! Hurry up!" "Go faster!" he shouted to his drivers during the descent, more concerned with speed than danger.

Not a minute was wasted, but when TR pulled up to the special train waiting to rush him to Buffalo, he was too late. President McKinley had expired at 2:15 AM, while Roosevelt was still in transit. A stunned TR jumped aboard and arrived in Buffalo in the early afternoon on September 14. He borrowed inaugural finery because he had not taken the time to pack, and, at 3:35 PM, took the oath of office before a small gathering of statesmen, friends, and reporters at the home of Ansley Wilcox, TR's host. It was a solemn moment, the room as "silent as the house of death itself," reported one of the journalists. TR pledged to "continue absolutely unbroken the policy of President McKinley for the peace, prosperity and honor of our beloved country." When the ceremony was over, he met privately with McKinley's cabinet members to invite them to stay on. America had lost three presidents to assassins in the past thirty-six years—first Abraham Lincoln, then James Garfield, and now McKinley. In the midst of great upheaval, TR wanted his countrymen to believe that he represented stability and continuity.

Feeling the need to clear his head after the ceremony, TR took a brisk walk up the street. He emphatically declined protection from the Secret Service. "I do not want to establish the precedent of going about guarded," he told the men who tried to follow him. The new President, the youngest chief executive in the history of the United States, did not contemplate mortality and imagine assassins behind every bush. And if one did materialize . . . he was more than ready to fight back.

When TR returned to the Wilcox house, he met with his private secretary, William Loeb, to take care of some pressing matters, including appointments that had to be canceled because of the sudden turn of events. Loeb handled most of the letters on his own. "I am directed by President Roosevelt to express deep regret that he cannot come," he wrote over and over again, working his way through a mounting pile of mail and telegrams. But TR took it upon himself to communicate with select correspondents, and one of them was Booker T. Washington.

On stationery bearing the letterhead "Executive Mansion," he wrote, "My dear Mr. Washington, I write you at once to say that to my deep regret my visit south must be given up." The trip to Tuskegee would have to wait. But in this instance, TR had more on his mind than rearranging his social calendar. "When are you coming north? I must see you as soon as possible," he added with some urgency. "I want to talk over the question of possible future appointments in the south exactly on the lines of our last conversation together. I hope that my visit to Tuskegee is merely deferred for a short season." He signed it, "Faithfully yours, Theodore Roosevelt." Thanks to TR's sudden promotion, Booker T. had come up in the world, too. He now had the distinction of being advisor to the new President of the United States.

THE PEOPLE'S PRESIDENT

———•◆•———

Americans were shocked and saddened by McKinley's death and they demonstrated their patriotism in a uniquely American way: they went shopping. "Never before in the history of the world has there been a greater demand for black goods, bunting, and their accessories," the *New York Times* reported the day after the President's passing. Suppliers from coast to coast were swamped with orders from businesses, private citizens, the rich, the poor, and even Hebrews, the *Times* took pains to point out. The country was on a grieving spree, and mourners spared no expense when they draped their offices, homes, and bodies in black. For those who wanted instant gratification (and showy souvenirs), buttons juxtaposing McKinley's photograph alongside an American flag were manufactured speedily and rushed to stores.

Even as Americans were publicly in mourning, they were excited by the prospect of a lively new president to go with the lively new twentieth century. McKinley had been a solid and dependable chief executive who embodied virtues that were highly valued in Victorian times. However, 1901 marked the start of a new age, and TR represented the future. He was young, brilliant, energetic, daring, and quick to laugh. "It was not only that he was a great man, but, oh, there was such fun in being led by him," an admirer observed. And, unlike McKinley and his perpetually ailing Ida, TR was blessed with a healthy wife and a houseful of hale and hearty children. The Roosevelts were a celebrity version of the go-getting, up-and-coming family next door. They were famous but relatable, and everyone wanted to know all the colorful details of their new life in Washington.

On September 17, TR and Edith, now the President and his First Lady, traveled to the capitol to attend McKinley's funeral. Despite the solemnity of the occasion, certain social obligations had to be fulfilled. Edith paid a formal sympathy call to Mrs. McKinley, even though she knew the widow was too grief-stricken to receive her. That evening, Edith returned to Oyster Bay to pack up her children and household, while TR accompanied the funeral cortege to the McKinley homestead in Canton, Ohio. He returned to Washington on September 20, but the President's House was being cleaned inside and out for its new occupants, so he moved in with his sister Bamie and her husband, William Cowles, who maintained a residence in Washington.

On September 21, he reported to the White House for his first day of work. The presidential offices were located on the second floor of the mansion, adjacent to the First Family's not-so-private living quarters. Once the Roosevelts moved in, TR's commute would consist of exiting his bedroom and walking down the hall. Until then, he entered the building through its famous mahogany front doors, turned left in the marble and mosaic vestibule, and walked, or rather, sprinted, up the stairs. If he wanted to avoid the crowds awaiting his appearance, he turned right after entering and rode up on the elevator.

On the second floor, TR passed through a reception room flanked by guards, an anteroom, and an executive room, before reaching his private office, which overlooked the Potomac River. There were additional rooms for TR's staff of secretaries and telegraph operators, and a separate office for the members of the cabinet.

TR had treaties to negotiate, canals to build, politicians to appease, federal appointments to make, pardons to grant, and dozens of other urgent matters vying for his attention. However, one pressing issue shot to the top of his list of things to do. It was his duty to select the official name for the President's House, and the stationer was standing by impatiently, waiting for his decision.

When the mansion was first built, in 1792, people referred to it as the "President's Palace," and even the "President's Castle." But those fancy names, with their royal connotations, seemed terribly inappropriate in a democracy. The building was dutifully renamed the "Executive Mansion," a term so utilitarian that it bordered on dreary.

Luckily, the residence had a popular nickname that suited its quiet majesty. After the invading British set fire to the mansion during the War of 1812, it was rebuilt and repainted a brilliant shade of white. Its stunning new appearance inspired admirers to call the place the "White House."

The more TR deliberated, the more he believed it was time for a change. Every state in the Union had an executive mansion. The President's house needed an identity all its own.

From now on, he decreed, the official name of the most famous home in America would be "the White House."

TR was besieged by callers during his first week in office. Lines of supplicants presented themselves to the White House's all-powerful gatekeepers, hoping to schedule a meeting with the President. Cabinet members and senators were guaranteed an audience Mondays, Wednesdays, and Thursdays between the hours of 10 and 12 AM, but ordinary folk were at the mercy of the staff. Despite the recent assassination, TR was incredibly accessible. The stairs leading to the executive offices were busy at all times. Anyone could present a card and ask to be seen, and there was always a chance a petitioner might make the list. After all, the President worked for the people, so they had a legitimate claim to his time. TR came out of his office several times a day to greet his visitors and, if he wanted to continue a conversation that began in the office, he often invited the lucky guest to join him for breakfast or lunch.

Politicians from the South were particularly eager to meet with the Yankee chief because they were suspicious of his policies and wanted to get to know the "enemy." Democrats from Mississippi, Georgia, and North Carolina were among the first to visit, and they expressed hope that TR's administration would be a "success," which was their way of asking if the Republican president intended to be fair to the South. "I am going to be President of the United States and not any section," TR assured them. "I don't care for sections or sectional lines." Not only was he half-Southern, he pointed out, but he had lived in the West. "I feel that I can represent the whole country," he announced with characteristic confidence.

Reassurances aside, Southern Democrats were concerned about how TR planned to fill federal appointments in their states. One of the President's most tedious duties was to appoint new judges, post office heads, portmasters, and the like, in locations throughout the country, and it was his prerogative to fill the positions as he saw fit. He could uphold the age-old system of patronage by giving the jobs to loyal Republicans, including ones who were black (which would be viewed as a doubly hostile act in the South). Or he could ignore partisan politics and award appointments on the basis of merit, selecting the best person for the job. Either way, it was a taxing and time-consuming process that left many presidents exasperated and worn out. Abraham Lincoln found the business of making appointments far more challenging than waging war. "You look anxious, Mr. President; is there a problem from the front?" he was asked one day by a concerned friend. "No," Lincoln replied with a sigh. "It isn't the war. It's that postmastership at Mudtown, Ohio."

TR was a sworn enemy of the patronage system when he served as civil service commissioner, and he was even more opposed to it now that he was President. He wanted to make fair and informed appointments, but he wasn't entirely familiar with the best candidates, especially in the South. Local senators and congressmen were happy to tell him what to do—the problem was that they *liked* patronage, and were apt to supply lists of family members, friends, and cronies to fill the positions. TR needed an advisor he could trust—someone who knew the landscape and who could help him to identify appropriate appointees. The more he thought about it, the more convinced he was that Booker T. was the man to show him the way. It was time for the two men to have a serious conversation.

Booker T. happened to be in Washington that week, staying at the home of his friend Thomas Calloway, the organizer of the

Negro Exhibits in Paris and Buffalo. TR's secretary informed him that a slot had been cleared for him to meet with the President at 9 PM on Sunday, September 29. It was an unusual time to conduct business, but TR's rigorous, around-the-clock schedule, which was the talk of Washington, was the explanation. Also, it had probably crossed the President's mind that the lateness of the hour might allow for a little privacy, something that was in short supply these days for him.

Reporters watched TR obsessively because their editors insisted that there was no detail too insignificant to print. The fact that "President Roosevelt rose early to-day, walked to the White House" was considered news. As was: "At 1:30 PM the President left the White House for luncheon," or, "At 4 o'clock he went out for a horseback ride." Most of the stories described day-to-day politics and the never-ending procession of visitors.

Most presidents merely tolerated reporters because they considered them a necessary evil, but TR understood their significance and actually welcomed them into his inner circle. "In our country, I am inclined to think that almost, if not quite, the most important profession is that of newspaperman," he said. During his first week in office, he sat down with representatives from Washington's three major wire services and laid out the ground rules of his administration. He promised to be accessible to all journalists who played fair. They should know that if he indicated information was "background" and didn't want to be quoted, he meant what he said, and the foolish writer who betrayed his confidence would be punished, even ostracized.

TR was true to his word. He beckoned the press "boys" in for candid chats at least once a day, usually while he was with his barber. If a topic excited him, TR jumped up from the chair, lather and all, while he expounded on the subject, then sat down again. And the reporters weren't the only ones asking the questions. TR was just as likely to turn to *them* for information. One day he spotted a familiar face among the reporters lingering in his outer office. "Come in here," he said. "I want to shake hands with you." He led the man over to a corner and, within seconds, they were engrossed in a lively conversation about political matters in a distant state. Every journalist hoped for that moment of recognition: "You go into Roosevelt's presence, you feel his eyes upon you, you listen to him, and you go home and wring the personality out of your clothes."

Eventually TR gave the press a gift they appreciated more than his time, his candor, or a great scoop. One day he saw a bedraggled group of reporters waiting outside in the rain. He felt so sorry for them that he was inspired to set aside a small room for reporters inside the building, the first home of the White House press corps.

TR respected journalists, but he had less patience for cameras, especially the ones that were turning up everywhere in the hands of amateurs. One widely reported presidential tantrum took place on Sunday, September 22, TR's first day off. He was spied strolling through downtown Washington with his brother-in-law, Douglas Robinson. They entered the German Reformed Chapel and were seated in the President's pew. The congregation was excited by TR's presence, but out of consideration, his fellow churchgoers kept their distance and allowed him to worship in peace. After the services, when the chief executive exited the chapel, he came face-to-face with the dark side of celebrity. A fifteen-year-old boy was waiting on the sidewalk, proudly poised to "snap" TR's picture with his brandnew Brownie camera.

The boy was one of the 250,000 early adopters who paid a dollar for the handy device that revolutionized photography. The Eastman Kodak Company's popular new product was a black cardboard box outfitted with a simple lens, and its chief virtue was that anyone could operate it. Gone were the days of tedious studio sessions with professional photographers who stood rigidly behind oversized apparatuses. The Brownie was portable and could "easily be operated by any school boy or girl," the company's advertisement boasted—all they had to do was aim and turn a switch. The camera's foolproof functionality and low price made it appealing when it went on sale in 1900. Its unique marketing campaign turned it into a bestseller.

The Brownie was invented by Frank Brownell, so there appeared to be a connection between the camera's name and that of its creator. However, George Eastman of Eastman Kodak had something else in mind when he christened his product. He wanted the camera to appeal to children so he named it after a popular group of cartoon characters created by the legendary illustrator Palmer Cox. "The Brownies," the stars of Cox's bestselling books and stories, were elflike figures with chubby midsections and pointed ears. Children loved the funny little creatures and followed their comic misadventures in *The Brownies at Home*, *The Brownies around the World*, and *The Brownies in Fairyland*. By reproducing their fanciful images on his camera box (essentially a turn-of-the-century version of a merchandising "tie-in"), Eastman was connecting his product to an established brand *and* packaging it as a toy. His ingenious marketing plan even included regional "Brownie Camera Clubs" for boys and girls under the age of sixteen. Members were encouraged to take lots of photographs (film cartridges cost fifteen cents for six exposures) and send them to Kodak. The best shots were eligible for a prize.

The lad poised to snap TR's picture had his eye on one of those prizes. "Kodaker after Roosevelt," reported the *Atlanta Constitution* when the story broke. President Roosevelt emphatically ordered the pint-sized paparazzi to "Stop that!" and motioned to a nearby police officer to help. Shaking his finger at the boy, TR told him he should be ashamed for "trying to take a man's picture as he leaves a house of worship." Generally speaking, TR was all for progress, and publicity, but not when they got in the way of propriety. The new president complained that he was suffering from the "shots of camera operators," and that he feared them more than "any possible bullets of Anarchists." To keep pesky professionals and this new breed of amateur photographers at bay, the police announced that they would arrest "anyone attempting to take a picture of the President at short range or in such a way as to annoy him."

THE FAMILY CIRCUS

———•◆•———

America's unbridled curiosity about everything Roosevelt was amplified when Edith, Kermit, and Ethel arrived in Washington on the evening of September 25 (Archie, Quentin, Alice, and Ted would follow later). TR greeted his family at the door of their new home and whisked them inside for a quiet reunion. The Roosevelts' first evening together was probably the last moment of privacy they would enjoy for a very long time.

With six children and a large household to manage, Edith often felt like the ringmaster of a perpetual circus, and the past months had been particularly difficult. The children had their usual assortment of maladies—Ted's bronchitis, Archie's chicken pox, Quentin's mothball up the nose. However, late in August, Alice and Quentin developed serious illnesses—she had a painful abscess in her jaw, while he suffered from a severe ear infection—that required them to be hospitalized at the same time. TR and Edith were so concerned that they arranged to sleep at the hospital while their children recovered. After that brush with disaster, the family weathered a seismic shift in their lives as TR went from being a restless vice president with too much time on his hands to a head of state with too much to do. Immediately after the McKinley funeral, the backstage family dramas began when Kermit was in a horse-and-carriage accident in New York City, and Alice petulantly refused to move to Washington until she was good and ready.

Now Edith had to add "First Lady" to her long list of responsibilities. She was happy about TR's new salary of fifty thousand dollars per year. "I shall not have to count the pennies!" she wrote gleefully to her sister soon after TR became president. Even though Edith was frugal by nature, she had found managing the family funds a difficult job because there always seemed to be more expenses than money. She kept clothing costs at a minimum and cut corners in a way that prompted one catty socialite to gossip that Mrs. Roosevelt spent only four hundred dollars a year on her wardrobe . . . and looked it. Edith didn't pay attention to remarks like that, but she did long for financial freedom. Now at last, they could afford fine living.

Not that Edith was going to be extravagant. In fact, she decided to break with tradition and run the White House herself, as carefully as she administered her other homes. She would select the menus, supervise the servants, and keep a tight rein on expenses. She would even continue her practice of doling out a small cash allowance to TR each day, although he was hard put to remember how he spent it.

Her customary support staff was in place: Mame, the crotchety nanny who took care of the younger boys (and who had attended to Edith when she was a child); Miss Young, the governess; Henry Pinckney, TR's manservant; Annie O'Rourke,

Above: Booker T. preparing for graduation from the Hampton Normal and Agricultural Institute, as depicted in *The Story of My Life and Work*, Booker T.'s first autobiography.

Above, left: Eight-year-old Theodore Roosevelt, looking every inch the privileged young gentleman. (Courtesy of Brown Brothers)

Left: In this illustration from *The Story of My Life and Work*, "Little Booker" and his mother are shown praying for freedom on the Burroughs plantation.

In this 1885 publicity shot for his book *Hunting Trips of a Ranchman,* TR is at his frontiersman best wearing a custom-made buckskin suit and brandishing a rifle. (Courtesy of the Library of Congress)

TR at Harvard, the consummate scholar and clubman. (Courtesy of Brown Brothers)

TR in 1900, the year before he unexpectedly became America's twenty-sixth president. (Courtesy of the Library of Congress)

Booker T. starting out as the principal of Tuskegee. He was determined to turn a makeshift classroom with a leaky roof into a proper school. (Courtesy of the New York Public Library)

Booker T. in 1901, at the time of his dinner with the Roosevelts. (Courtesy of the New York Public Library)

A dapper W. E. B. Du Bois at the Paris Exposition in 1900. (Courtesy of the University of Massachusetts)

Paul Dunbar, the gifted African American poet who came to Tuskegee at Booker T.'s invitation. (Courtesy of the Ohio Historical Society)

Booker T.'s second wife, soul mate, and Tuskegee's first lady principal, Olivia Davidson. (Courtesy of the New York Public Library)

Alice Hathaway Lee, the lovely young woman who won TR's heart and became his adored first wife. (Courtesy of the Library of Congress)

Edith Carow Roosevelt, TR's beloved childhood friend who grew up to be his second wife. (Courtesy of the Library of Congress)

The Washington family in 1899: (*from left*) Ernest Davidson, Booker T. Jr., Margaret, Booker T., and Portia. (Courtesy of the Library of Congress)

The Roosevelts, America's exciting new first family: (*from left*) Quentin, TR, Ted, Archie, Alice, Kermit, Edith, and Ethel. (Courtesy of the Library of Congress)

This anti-Roosevelt cartoon was considered tasteless and shocking because it showed the First Lady sitting at the same table with Booker T. Washington.

A cartoon designed to remind voters of the ongoing connection between Booker T. and TR.

Another political cartoon intended to create resentment among white Americans. The caption reads: "The cullud folks am bon-ton sense Bookah Wash'n'ton dined at de White House."

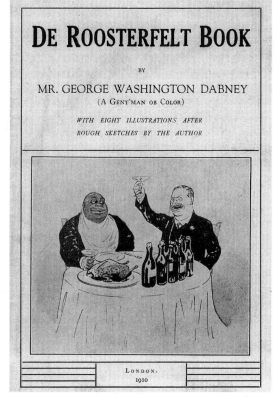

An image from *De Roosterfelt Book*, a vicious lampoon of the Washington/Roosevelt dinner penned pseudonymously by one "George Washington Dabney."

TR visited Tuskegee in 1905 and stood side by side with Booker T.

the family cook; and three other domestics brought down from the Roosevelt homes in Oyster Bay and Albany.

There were no official dinners on the President's calendar during his first weeks in office, but the unofficial meals were a daily challenge. Fortunately, Mrs. O'Rourke had been with the Roosevelts for many years and was used to their ways. She was assisted by two Irish sisters, Rose and Mary Sweeney, who had also moved with the family from New York, and the staff of kitchen workers who had served the McKinleys.

TR and Edith had a straightforward approach to eating. They believed in "plain food and high thinking," or as daughter Alice said sarcastically, "coarse food and plenty of it." Breakfast, served promptly at 8:15, consisted of hard-boiled eggs, fresh baked rolls, and fruit, which on a lucky day meant ripe cantaloupe or fresh peaches and cream. Lunch at 1:30 was a spartan affair of cold meat (usually leftovers), bread, and fruit. Dinner was simple but plentiful, with generous servings of lamb chops, new peas, potatoes, and edible leaves, followed by favorite family desserts such as pecan sandies or Bavarian creme.

TR had such an aversion to fancy food that he was indignant when a magazine made the mistake of calling him a gourmet. He preferred what we now call comfort food to elaborate delicacies and was happiest when dining on a large bowl of milk and bread. He also loved fresh food—wild asparagus from his garden at Sagamore Hill, and Potomac bass, caught by Major Richard Sylvester, who was a fine angler as well as Washington's Chief of Police.

At first light, the White House steward headed to the market to buy provisions for the day's menu. The grocery bills, which the President paid personally, were high because TR had a habit of extending last-minute invitations to friends, acquaintances, and the capital's countless politicians. Three times a day—and at a moment's notice—Mrs. O'Rourke had to be prepared to add an extra plate, so she tried to keep more food on hand than she needed. Roosevelt brought "joy to the Grocer, the Butcher, and the Baker," a newspaper quipped about the President's mealtime largesse.

But, on at least one occasion, Mrs. O'Rourke was not up to the challenge. Two hungry guests who had lunched on under-sized portions of leftover liver and bacon were overheard making plans to have a more substantial meal as they left the White House. "Let's go to the hotel and get something to eat," they whispered.

Culinary issues notwithstanding, Edith was comfortable with the domestic side of her new life. What she really wanted and needed was a secretary to assist her with the "business" of White House entertaining—a social secretary, as they were called in upper-class circles. The idea came to her during William McKinley's funeral. Edith had sent several notes to Ida McKinley expressing her condolences, but they were never acknowledged. Of course, there were extenuating circumstances: Mrs. McKinley was a recent widow and was in poor health. However, Edith refused to leave propriety to chance during her watch. She decided that the First Lady needed a system for communicating with the outside world as well as a trusted amanuensis to implement it. On September 26, her first morning in the White House, she summoned a young woman named Isabella Hagner to interview for the position.

"Belle" Hagner was a plucky young lady with a poignant riches-to-rags story. She was the daughter of a prosperous

Washington physician and a popular socialite who, along with her younger brothers, had enjoyed a happy and privileged childhood. Then a series of tragedies swept it all away. Her parents died suddenly, leaving their offspring penniless. Like a heroine in a dime novel, sixteen-year-old Belle rose to the occasion. She wasn't beautiful, but she was smart and a well-liked member of Washington society. Her most marketable asset, she discovered, was her elegant penmanship, and it was this talent that led her to a career. The best hostesses in town hired Belle to write their invitations and oversee their guest lists, and she dazzled them with her command of ballroom diplomacy. Between assignments, she worked as a lowly clerk in the War Department, until the new First Lady summoned her to the White House.

Edith explained that she wanted Belle to handle her correspondence and her calendar—to answer every letter, schedule every appointment, and compile every list, although it was impossible to anticipate all of her responsibilities in advance. She assumed that Belle was interested and asked if she could start right away—at that very moment, in fact. Belle followed Edith to the desk in her study, and in doing so, became the White House's first social secretary. A colorful announcement in the *Boston Daily Globe* called Belle "the social premier of the Roosevelt administration" and listed one of her duties as being "the task of smoothing out those ruffles that result from petty jealousies and animosities among the women of Washington society in the official circle."

In sorting out which of the women—and men—who aspired to come to the White House would be welcome, Belle was Edith's first line of defense. Previous administrations had drifted into an open-door policy for guests attending public receptions. Politicians were bad enough (after gatherings, Edith liked to say that the windows had to be opened "to let out the politicians"), but sometimes low characters—even prostitutes—had the nerve to show up at the gates. Edith had higher standards. "Morality, restraint, and good manners were to her thinking prerequisites to receiving White House invitations," points out historian William Seale in his book *The President's House.* It was Belle's responsibility to let the *right* people in and, more important, to keep the *wrong* people out.

Edith's campaign to rehabilitate Washington society was ambitious. She scheduled weekly meetings with the wives of TR's cabinet members and relied on them to be her eyes and ears—"a sort of genteel secret police"—in the outside world. The ladies reported on good and bad behavior, and the First Lady adjusted her guest lists accordingly, eliminating anyone who was suspect.

Social concerns aside, Edith's most pressing challenge at the moment was finding a way to squeeze her family, their pets, and a retinue of servants, including her social secretary, into the relatively small living space assigned to the President. The Roosevelts were used to larger domiciles; the Governor's Mansion in Albany was a palace compared to their White House apartment. Here most of the first floor was considered public space. For several hours a day, generally from ten to two, the palatial East Room, with its chandelier and mirrors, was open to visitors. On the south side of the house, the Red, Blue, and Green rooms and the State Dining Room were reserved for special guests and dignitaries. These rooms were separated from the public vestibule by a large, multicolored glass screen designed and built by Louis Comfort Tiffany in 1882. Upon seeing the colorful, almost gaudy, glass mosaic wall for the first time, one elderly White House visitor thought it had been assembled from old broken bottles. She actually complimented the President for being so thrifty.

One of the problems with allowing a stream of strangers into the President's House was that tourists were ruthless in their quest for souvenirs. Whenever the guards looked the other way, they clipped the curtains, cut holes in the upholstery, scratched their initials in the furniture, ate picnic lunches on the stairs, and walked off with anything that wasn't bolted. Consequently, the public rooms always looked a little shabby and in need of refurbishment.

Upstairs, the private living area presented a different set of problems. When Edith looked around, she saw rooms that needed painting and redecorating, insufficient sleeping quarters, an empty, low-ceilinged attic that somehow had to house bedrooms for the incoming servants, and, the most head-scratching problem of all, two antiquated bathrooms to accommodate eight family members, including the President. What she *couldn't* see was worse. The mansion's floors were so decayed and precarious that they had to be propped up with giant timbers during receptions to prevent them from caving in.

Edith was not enthusiastic about spending the next four and possibly eight years in an historic wreck, so she instantly took matters into her own hands. Her main objective was to turn the residential area into a true home for her family, and that meant redecorating. Soon fleets of painters, carpet layers, curtain hangers, electricians, plumbers, and other laborers crowded into the mansion to make it habitable.

Edith selected the children's bedrooms carefully. Alice and Ethel had their own rooms. Ted, who was away at boarding school most of the time, would bunk with Kermit. And Archie and Quentin—two little boys who were always looking for trouble—were placed right next door to their watchful parents.

There was a library on the second floor that doubled as the family's living room, and for intimate meals with family and friends, there was a private dining room on the first floor. The attic was cleaned for the four white maids who came from Oyster Bay, while, as in the past, the colored help was quartered in the basement.

Edith reviewed the house's tired old furnishings with a critical eye, banishing some pieces to storage and others to auction. She opened the windows, artfully arranged bouquets of flowers, and imported some simple furniture from Sagamore Hill. Suddenly the tired old rooms started to look airy, comfortable, and homey, and it took a lot of elbow grease to keep them that way.

The job of keeping the mansion clean fell to Possum Jerry, "the grey-haired, dignified colored person who keeps bright the furniture and fixtures at the White House," as the *New York Times* described him. There were over four hundred doorknobs in the White House and Jerry Smith had polished every one of them. "Anything dat suits de President, praise de Lawd, is good 'nuff fo' me," he told the interviewer as he began his daily chores, dusting the furniture, sweeping the stairs, buffing the doorknobs, shining the silver, and removing all traces of the swarms of visitors who passed through the mansion's famous doors. President Ulysses S. Grant hired him to be a stable boy in 1871, and one of his duties was to prepare Grant's favorite down-home dish of possum and potatoes, which is how he won his unusual nickname. Despite Smith's humble beginnings, he worked his way up the ladder to the position of house servant and now, eight presidents later, he was a senior member of the White House domestic staff.

"Tall and well-shaped with the complexion of an Othello . . . a knight of the white apron whose wand of office is his feather duster," was how a *Washington Post* reporter described him. Smith was such an established figure at the White House that no one thought it strange when, in 1895, he invited President and Mrs. Cleveland, along with the members of the cabinet and their wives, to a reception at his little house to celebrate his twenty-fifth wedding anniversary. The Clevelands declined but sent a set of silver spoons to commemorate the occasion. The secretary of state, the postmaster general, and several other statesmen accepted Smith's dinner invitation and reported that they enjoyed a "delightful evening." Smith always maintained that a person could be judged by how they treated black people. First Lady Ida McKinley, for example, was "just as nice to a colored person as she is to a White. It don't make no difference what your color is," he said.

Smith also said that dead presidents were often as friendly as live ones. He frequently saw Lincoln's ghost floating up the stairs and always saluted him with his duster. The late President Grant liked to chat when he appeared, but the recently assassinated William McKinley had difficulty communicating and could make only buzzing sounds whenever he tried to speak.

Edith whipped the place into shape in record time, but there was one domestic problem even she couldn't solve. She was dismayed to discover that the Roosevelts shared their tight quarters with some unwanted squatters—the mansion's perpetual population of rats. Presidents and their families came and went, but the White House rodents were always in residence. For years discreet employees had denied their existence, but by the fall of 1889 the vermin infestation became headline news. "The Executive Mansion is overrun by an affliction other than office-seekers," quipped the *Washington Post.* President Benjamin Harrison and his wife were fed up with the "tedious rascals" and summoned state-of-the-art "ratologists" to get rid of them. A special poison was laid throughout the house, but it was like "pie" to the rats, who grew fat and multiplied on their tasty new diet.

They also became bold. Their loud gnawing made it impossible to sleep, and, when they were hungry, they were fearless. If the cook turned her back on a chicken or a roast she was preparing for the President's dinner, a wily team of rats raced out and dragged it away. W. H. Hasmer, a famous rat hunter, was contracted (at a daily rate of ten dollars) to mount a massive assault on the cunning enemy.

Hasmer came armed with an arsenal of ferrets and terriers. The hungry ferrets chased the rats through the mansion's underground network of pipes and tunnels, while the terriers moved in for the kill when the culprits came up for air. The bloodbath lasted for two weeks, and one ferret disappeared, never to be seen again. Hasmer pronounced the operation a success. The rats were gone. The problem was that they always came back.

Now, whenever Edith heard a bang and a crash followed by a scuffle, it meant that someone, probably one of her children, was trying to catch a furry interloper. Her new home, cramped and infested, was falling down around her, and she discovered that making the best of it was a full-time job. She and TR downplayed the building's inadequacies by insisting that they were content. The President stated emphatically that he would not move to a larger residence. The White House suited him just fine.

Ethel and Kermit were finding it easier to adjust. They were the star attractions at the White House, and spectators gathered every day to watch them frolicking on the lawn, showing off their new bicycles. Accompanied by Henry Pinckney, TR's African American manservant from Sagamore Hill, the children rode all around the capital, speeding by the Washington Monument and other historic sites, enjoying freedoms that would not be experienced by presidential children in the future. Pinckney peddled as fast as he could to keep up with his young charges, but they delighted in playing hide-and-seek to elude him. On one of these jaunts, he was half a block behind them and "scared blue" about losing them in the crowded streets. A policeman called out, "Them the President's kids?" When Pinckney nodded in assent, the policeman said it was a great thing to have kids in the White House. "Kinder gets hold of the people," he observed.

In short order, Kermit and Ethel took over the White House and were thrilled with the mansion's haunted house features, especially the ramshackle attic and the elusive rats. They negotiated with the head gardener to allow their colony of white rabbits to enjoy free rein over the grounds (although he drew the line at turning the hothouse conservatory into a rabbit buffet). They located the mansion's best hiding places, including a large decorative planter in the reception area of the executive offices, where they waited patiently for the perfect moment to pop out and say "Boo!" to unsuspecting visitors. Punishment was normally out of the question because TR, whom Edith often described as her seventh child, was more likely to get down on the floor and play "bear" with his high-spirited youngsters than scold them, although he was furious when he caught them tossing spitballs at a portrait of Andrew Jackson.

Kermit and Ethel enjoyed each other—and sometimes the company of children whose parents worked at the White House—because they liked to have a rough-and-tumble good time. However, Ethel despised arranged visits with overdressed little socialites who came expecting high tea and dolls. She told them to go home and change their clothes so they could play in the stables. Boys, on the other hand, knew how to have fun.

While it was thrilling to rule the White House for a few weeks, Kermit and Ethel were counting the hours until their younger siblings arrived. With Archie and Quentin to complete their gang, the real adventure would begin. There were so many newspaper articles about the escapades of the Roosevelt kids that the *New York Tribune* chided the First Lady with the headline "Mrs. Roosevelt So Busy She Has Hardly Time Enough To Watch Her Children."

Edith, who considered her personal life to be just that, was shocked by the outpouring of interest from across the nation. For example, speculating about where the Roosevelts would go to school had become a national obsession. "You can't think how much anxiety pervades the country about the children's education," she marveled. "I receive letters from schools and tutors every day."

Which school? There were as many answers as there were Roosevelts. Three of the children were enrolled in proper private schools. Ted was at Groton in Massachusetts, where he tried to get his peers to stop talking about his father's new job. Kermit was starting at the University School in Washington, which was only a ten-minute walk from the White House. Ethel was enrolled at Cathedral, and, for Archie, it was the no-frills public school—the nearby Force Academy, where all of his books and supplies would be free. TR was a firm believer that "boys should at sometime in their life, get the give and take of a public school." As for Quentin, the child Edith called her "fine little bad boy" (and possibly her favorite), she was keeping him home, where she would oversee his lessons personally. She secretly hoped that she would become pregnant and there would be another Roosevelt baby to keep him company.

Seventeen-year-old Alice was the only rebel in the family. She announced to her shocked parents that she was finished with finishing school, and histrionics followed. She cried and darkly alluded to ways she might disgrace the family if they forced her to attend. TR and Edith reluctantly gave in. They also agreed to let her stay in Oyster Bay for the moment. There was more than enough drama in the White House without Alice.

She was scheduled to have her coming-out party in January and the anxious debutante had high expectations for the evening. What Alice wanted was a dazzling dress with a bit of décolletage, a beautiful ballroom, plenty of champagne, and lavish party favors for her guests. However, she was going to have to settle for what she considered a stodgy, second-rate evening in the State Room at the White House. As far as she was concerned, its décor was no better than a train station waiting room, a nasty combination of late General Grant and early Pullman, with too much gilt, plush, and heavy furniture to be a fitting backdrop for a thoroughly modern young woman. There wasn't even a proper dance floor, so the existing one would have to be topped with "crash," an ugly linen covering that screamed of frugality.

Alice was so desperate to have her own way that she offered to pay for all the "extras" from the generous allowance she received from her maternal grandparents. But Edith said absolutely not: she would have to resign herself to what her parents could afford, and that did not include a couture gown, sparkling wine, expensive trinkets, or a customized dance floor.

Her father and stepmother were living in the past, Alice felt. Their old-fashioned rules were "a hangover from the brownstone-front existence of my stepmother when they had little parties with a modicum of decorous dancing and an amusing fruit punch," she later observed. In Alice's opinion, her parents simply did not know how to entertain at the White House.

BEHIND CLOSED DOORS

————•◆•————

When Booker T. arrived at the White House on Sunday, September 29, for his scheduled 9:00 PM meeting with TR, the building was quiet. The Roosevelt children were sleeping (bedtime was usually eight o'clock), and reporters were unlikely to be around at this late hour because most assumed there would be no important news on TR's day of rest.

Booker T. was escorted to TR's library by two black servants in traditional livery. African Americans had played an important part in White House history from the very beginning. It was a rare president (notably James Buchanan, who preferred white, traditionally trained British servants) who didn't employ a sizable African American staff—an army of porters, valets, messengers, waiters, maids, cooks, footmen, laundresses, and laborers—to keep the mansion running. "The tone of the house was distinctly southern," according to White House historian William Seale, and, in fact, most of the president's servants were Southern blacks. Though they "performed a thousand duties," they were generally invisible because they worked backstairs and behind the scenes. Within the black community, however, some of them had become legends.

One of the first was Benjamin Banneker. Although he never worked at the White House, he was thought to have been a key member of the team that planned the capital. Born in 1731, the grandson of an English dairy maid and a slave who had been a gifted scientist and engineer in his native Africa, Banneker was a curious little boy who followed in his grandfather's footsteps and grew up to be a skilled surveyor and astronomer. He was so skilled, in fact, that in 1791 he was recruited to work with urban planner Pierre-Charles L'Enfant in designing America's new capital city.

Described by the *Georgetown Weekly Ledger* as "a large man of noble appearance" who "resembled Benjamin Franklin," Banneker was praised as an "Ethiopian, whose abilities . . . already prove that Mr. Jefferson's concluding that that race of men were void of mental endowment, was without foundation." Banneker was an author, scientist, mathematician, farmer, astronomer, urban planner and, like Franklin, the publisher of his very own almanac.

Some overly enthusiastic admirers credited Banneker with single-handedly re-creating L'Enfant's plan for Washington after the Frenchman was fired from the project and left town in a huff. In fact, Banneker played somewhat of a lesser role— Congress had a copy of the original plan on file—but he was a remarkable surveyor and scientist nonetheless.

When construction commenced on the President's House in 1792, many of the carpenters, bricklayers, stone masons, and general laborers were black. Not that most of them had any say about where they worked. They were slaves whose owners hired them out as day laborers. "Jim," Len," "Jess," and "Bill," to name a few of the men listed in the financial ledgers, did the work while their masters pocketed their "wages." Even the White House's architect James Hoban collected sixty dollars a month for the services of the slave carpenters he owned and leased to the project.

The day was long, usually twelve hours. While some blacks, like Hoban's builders, were trained artisans, many were un-skilled laborers who toiled on backbreaking jobs such as lifting, digging, and hauling. The swampy site was hot and buggy, and one observer noted that it looked just like a bustling plantation, with an army of blacks as far as the eye could see. Interestingly, these slaves were not chained: there was no point in running away because there was no place to go.

John Adams, the first president to actually live in the White House, was not a slave owner. But many of his successors, in-cluding Thomas Jefferson, staffed the mansion with slaves. The President was responsible for paying for his own servants, so it was more cost-efficient to import already owned workers from home. Most of the African Americans who cleaned, cooked, served, sewed, maintained the gardens, and performed innu-merable other domestic chores were nameless, but occasionally a staffer stood out. This was the case with Paul Jennings, a for-mer slave who led an unusually public life.

Jennings was born on James Madison's Virginia plantation in 1799, and was never far from his master's side. In 1809, when still a young boy, he accompanied the family to the White House, where he worked as Madison's bodyservant. After Madison died in 1836, Jennings stayed with the impoverished Dolley Madison, until she was forced to sell him to Senator Daniel Webster. The President's widow was so poor that, in a dramatic reversal of circumstances, Jennings used his meager personal funds to support *her.*

Jennings made an arrangement with his liberal-minded new master to buy his freedom. But in 1848, he set aside that plan to help a desperate group of slaves organize a dramatic escape from Washington on a ship called the *Pearl.* Jennings was going to join the fugitives and even wrote a note of farewell and thanks to Webster. At the last minute he had second thoughts about the dangerous undertaking and backed out, retrieving his note before Webster saw it. The fleeing slaves were not as lucky. The *Pearl* was captured and its seventy-six passengers severely punished. They were sold downriver to the infamously harsh slave traders in Georgia and Louisiana.

Eventually Jennings purchased his freedom and became a civil servant in the Government Pension Office. He lived quietly until 1863, when he teamed up with a coworker named John Brooks Russell to publish a memoir, *A Colored Man's Reminiscences of James Madison.* Jennings's recollections of Washington in the early part of the century were revelatory.

When the British invaded Washington in 1812, the Madisons evacuated with the help of their faithful colored servants, Jennings, Sukey, James Smith, and others. Jennings wrote that, contrary to popular folklore, Dolley Madison did *not* save the famous portrait of George Washington from the invaders—it was the mansion's gardener and doorkeeper who carried it to safety in their cart. According to Jennings, early Americans were not very respectful of the First Family during their hour of need. After fleeing the White House, Dolley and her retinue sought shelter in a private home, but the mistress of the house took one look at her prospective guests and cried, "Miss Madison, if that's you . . . go out! Your husband has got mine out fighting, and d— you, you shan't stay in my home; so get out!" Dolley beat a hasty retreat and, presumably, found a more welcoming citizen to take her in.

Jennings's memoir was brief, only twenty-four pages, but he painted a vivid and sympathetic portrait of the Madisons. Readers enjoyed being privy to a servant's-eye-view of the presidential household and a popular new genre, the benign White House tell-all, was born.

Three years later, in 1868, a slave-turned-dressmaker named Elizabeth Keckley penned *Behind the Scenes,* a more sensational White House confidential. Like Jennings, Keckley was born on a plantation in Virginia. She grew up to be an accomplished seamstress and was able to use her skills to support her white owners when they fell on hard times. Eventually Keckley bought her freedom and moved to Washington, where she designed dresses for Mrs. Jefferson Davis and other important political wives. Her dream was to work at the White House, and her growing reputation as a first-class modiste enabled her to do just that.

Keckley had the honor of meeting Mary Todd Lincoln in 1861, after the new First Lady dropped a cup of coffee on the ball gown she was planning to wear to an inaugural event. Keckley saved the day by whipping up a flouncy mauve concoction of her own design. The President pronounced it "charming" and Keckley's fate was sealed. She became Mary Todd Lincoln's personal dressmaker . . . and confidante. Keckley discovered that her temperamental employer had a taste for pretty things (she ordered sixteen dresses in one season) and secrets. Mrs. Lincoln confessed to Keckley that she owed twenty-seven thousand dollars to Stewart's department store in New York City, and what's more, she was determined to keep her increasingly troubled finances from her unsuspecting husband.

President Lincoln liked "Madame Elizabeth," or "Lizzy," as he called her, and asked her to comb his hair before he went out in public, including the very night he was assassinated. That evening, Keckley was the only person a devastated Mary Todd Lincoln wanted to see. She also turned to her faithful dressmaker when she needed to raise money to pay her debts. The two women met secretly in a New York City hotel and arranged to consign Mrs. Lincoln's collection of dresses and jewelry to an auction house. Keckley was flattered to be treated like a trusted friend—in fact, Mrs. Lincoln called her "my best living friend" in one of the many letters they exchanged. Unfortunately, the sale generated negative publicity for the President's widow, who was accused of undignified behavior. In the public's eye, Keckley was guilty by association.

Penniless, depressed, and down on her luck, Keckley chose this moment to write her memoirs. She envisioned the book as part slave narrative and part apologia. It would be her opportunity to tell her life story *and* to defend herself and the former First Lady. With the help of a professional writer named James Redpath, she completed a manuscript and sold it to a publisher. Keckley's intentions may have been noble, but Carleton & Company had something else in mind. An early advertisement called *Behind the Scenes* "A Literary Thunderbolt" and promoted Keckley as someone who "has much to say of an interesting, not to say startling nature, in regard to men and things in the White House, Washington, and New York." As an added enticement, the publisher printed twenty-four of Mary Todd Lincoln's letters to Keckley, private correspondence in which the former First Lady expressed her constant anxiety about money and her scorn for the "ungrateful country" that refused to support the widow of its greatest president. There was unflattering information about Mrs. Lincoln throughout the book, especially Keckley's revelations about her employer's moodiness, hypochondria, and shopaholic tendencies. And what wasn't unflattering was too personal for public consumption. Mrs. Lincoln blamed Keckley for betraying her confidence, even though the distraught dressmaker insisted her publisher printed the letters without her knowledge, and their unlikely friendship soured.

There was some controversy among critics as to whether Keckley, a former slave, could have written the book, but the question of authorship did not trouble readers nearly as much as the idea that Lizzy and servants like her were listening at the keyhole and repeating what they heard. The *New York Citizen* dismissed the memoir as "the backstairs gossip of negro servant girls." And the *New York Times* called Keckley's disclosures "gross violations of confidence" and suggested she should have "stuck to her needle." There was a backlash against *Behind the Scenes* and the book and its author were vilified by critics, and lampooned in a poisonous parody titled *Behind the Seams; by a Nigger Who Took in Work from Mrs. Lincoln and Mrs. Davis.*

Booker T. would have been familiar with the memoirs of Paul Jennings and Elizabeth Keckley—their books were part of the "Negro Authors" exhibition at the World Fairs in Paris and Buffalo. But, for his purposes, the best insider view of the White House had been written by Frederick Douglass. In his autobiography, *Narrative of the Life of Frederick Douglass,* the celebrated abolitionist offered accounts of his White House meetings with Abraham Lincoln during the Civil War, including his very first visit to the President's office. He called himself "The Black Man at the White House" and described how nervous he was to approach Lincoln about the plight of black soldiers fighting in the war. Considering that Douglass was, in his words, "an ex-slave identified with a despised race," he was given a warm welcome and found Lincoln to be a kind and patient listener, even when they disagreed.

During one of his subsequent meetings with Douglass, Lincoln made the governor of Connecticut cool his heels in the outer office while the abolitionist sat comfortably in the inner sanctum. "Tell Governor [William] Buckingham to wait," Lincoln ordered his secretary, "for I want to have a long talk with my friend Frederick Douglass." The ultimate compliment came in the form of an invitation to tea—not at the White House, but at a venue called the Soldier's Home, where the President often spent his evenings plotting the war with his advisors. Douglass had to decline because he had a speaking engagement that evening, but was mindful of the invitation's significance.

Emboldened by the President's attentions, Douglass decided to test the social waters at the White House by attending the annual New Year's Day reception. Heretofore, men and women of color had been barred from the event even though it was public and open to every American willing to wait in line. Since Lincoln had abolished slavery, Douglass hoped that the White House doors would swing open to members of his race. Instead, they slammed in his face. He was turned away by the doorkeepers, and when he made a fuss, they pretended to let him in, only to cleverly reroute him to another exit. Luckily, someone recognized Douglass and informed Lincoln about the gaffe. The guards relented, he was escorted into the East Room with the other visitors, and the President greeted him warmly with the words, "Here comes my friend Douglass. I am glad to see you."

Thirty-six years later, in the tradition of Douglass and Lincoln, Booker T. and TR were beginning their own White House entente. They settled into the library and TR spoke frankly to his guest. First of all, he told him that he had no intention of appointing a large number of colored people to positions in the South. Other presidents had tried that approach in the past and it just didn't work. However, if Booker T. would hear him out, he had a better plan, one that truly excited him and that didn't involve merely paying lip service to the black community. TR intended to pick the best man for the job, regardless of color or political affiliation. If that meant appointing a qualified white Democrat in the South, or a respected black Republican in the North, so be it. No quotas, no payback, no patronage.

Black appointments in the North? Now that was a novel approach. Booker T. paid close attention to TR's words and was encouraged by what he heard. The tactic, if properly executed, was a step toward true equality everywhere. And the chief executive seemed to be offering him the opportunity to suggest candidates and to weigh in on other people's recommendations. That would make Booker T. a presidential "czar" who could steer TR toward appointees who were fair-minded toward—and even friendly to—his race.

They chatted about nominees, and Booker T.'s first suggestion that night was, in fact, a white Democrat. Ex-governor T. G. Jones of Alabama supported fair election laws and championed education for both races. More important, he was vehemently opposed to lynching. Booker T. recommended him wholeheartedly for a judgeship in his state and TR promised to consider his advice.

That was easy, the two men may well have thought. They agreed to meet again in a few weeks to discuss more appointments. Booker T. was about to embark on a lecture tour of Mississippi but would perform due diligence on Jones and other recommendations, reporting back to TR before going on the road. Meanwhile, he promised to communicate with the President through his secretary, Emmett Scott, in order to dodge snooping reporters.

Despite their best efforts to be discreet, one journalist was already tracking the story. A sharp-eyed correspondent for the *Los Angeles Times* happened to be sniffing around the White House that night and filed an "Exclusive Dispatch" about Booker T.'s visit. He was correct about some of the details, writing that the "President wished to consult him in regard to his Southern policy." But the reporter went on to say that he found it curious that "the man who had been summoned to the national Capitol for a conference with the President of the United States thought it necessary to go to a cheap 'nigger' hotel in an unsavory part of the city" because the regular hotels wouldn't take him.

Actually, Booker T. was staying at the home of his old friend Thomas Calloway, an esteemed member of the black community who lived in a perfectly respectable part of the city. Accurate or not, the article proved that no matter how high Booker T. climbed, there would always be someone, in this case a snide journalist, to remind him that he was not welcome.

FATHERS AND DAUGHTERS

————— •◆• —————

As their meeting proved, TR and Booker T. were skilled statesmen who rarely encountered a problem they couldn't solve. However, at the moment, both men were confounded by a mounting crisis on the home front, and there was no solution in sight. They were up against an adversary like no other: their darling but incredibly difficult adolescent daughters. There was a war waging between the generations, and the fathers were definitely on the losing side.

Alice Lee Roosevelt was a handful. A family friend described the rebellious seventeen-year-old as "a young wild animal who had been put in good clothes." "Princess Alice," as she was called after her father became President, was blond and blue-eyed like her mother, and she had TR's indomitable spirit. But she had a mind and a temper all her own.

After her mother's untimely death, baby Alice was ignored by her grief-stricken father and spoiled by her aunts and maternal grandparents. Later, when TR married Edith, he felt guilty about betraying his first love. Unlike the children he shared with Edith, his daughter was a constant reminder of his "infidelity." According to Alice, he never, not even once, mentioned her mother—not to her, not to anyone. There were no anecdotes about their courtship, no fond recollections of their brief marriage, and no shared heartbreak about her tragic death.

Yet there were other times when Alice was immersed in her mother's world. She spent six weeks a year with her grandparents, the Lees, at their city and country homes in Massachusetts, and they happily indulged every whim of their beloved daughter's daughter. They gave her such a generous allowance that TR joked, "We'd better be nice to Alice. We might have to ask her for money." During her carefree visits to the Lees, she dominated the household, jumping on the furniture, stuffing herself with sweets, and spending money frivolously. But when she was back in the Roosevelt fold, she was expected to follow Edith's strict rules of decorum.

Edith wasn't a wicked stepmother by any means. She dutifully attended to Alice's needs as she was growing up, especially during any health crisis. Nonetheless, she *was* a stepmother. Edith always felt a little insecure about her pretty predecessor and her jealousy sometimes colored her actions. Edith told her son Ted that it was just as well that Alice Lee died young because TR "would have been bored to death staying married to her." Naturally, Ted wasted no time in taunting Alice with his mother's unkind words. Edith was the matriarch and, as far as she was concerned, there was no room in the Roosevelt family for another woman, not even the memory of one.

When Alice became an adolescent, she felt more and more like an outsider—"an interloper," she said—and she often behaved inappropriately to get attention. She confessed that when she first heard the news of the McKinley shooting, she feigned concern and then ran outside to dance a little victory jig. Unlike the rest of the family, she rejected religion and refused to be confirmed. And there was that matter of dropping out of school when it was time to go a girl's academy for proper "finishing."

Over time, Alice discovered that the best way to dodge strict supervision was to stay away from home. She ran with a privileged circle of Gilded Age progeny, including Vanderbilts and Harrimans, and decided that it was much more fun to spend time in their opulent Newport "cottages" than under Edith's penny-pinching thumb. Because most of her friends were ostentatiously rich, Alice constantly overspent her allowance to keep up with the Joneses (in fact, the Joneses who inspired the expression were one of Newport's oldest families), and, when she ran out of funds, she had to appeal to the Lees to bail her out of debt.

Alice thought that *she* was being tough and elusive when she refused to move to Washington with the rest of her family, until she realized that in truth her parents were avoiding *her.* Actually, Edith never asked her to join them at the White House (in fact, she encouraged Alice to stay away until they were "settled"). Somehow Alice convinced herself that it was vaguely embarrassing to have a working politician for a father and kept her distance. This enabled her to feel as if she were rejecting her parents, instead of the other way around. "It pleased me to pretend that I had ceased to take an interest," she wrote. An irate Alice stayed in Oyster Bay, stewing. If her father wanted her to come to Washington like her dutiful little siblings, he would just have to come and get her, she decided.

TR was bewildered by Alice and never knew what she might

do next—throw a head-splitting tantrum, smoke, drink spirits, keep company with inappropriate young men. It was one thing for a private citizen to have a difficult daughter, but it was unseemly for the President to have a child he couldn't control, and he didn't like it one bit.

Around the same time, Booker T. was also experiencing his own share of hand-wringing parental moments with *his* eighteen-year-old daughter, Portia. He was a strict father who raised his children in much the same way he raised his chickens. When it came time to feed the hens, he scattered their food all around the farmyard so they had to hunt and peck for it. He did it "to keep them from being lazy," he said. "They are just like human beings. If they get their living without having to work for it, they will not develop." The same rules applied to his children. Even though the Washingtons lived in a large, well-staffed house attended by students studying the domestic arts, Portia, young Booker, and Ernest were expected to be industrious at all times. They woke up early, performed chores, and labored long hours over their schoolwork.

Portia was busy but restless at Tuskegee. Until the age of sixteen, she had attended grammar school in comparatively cosmopolitan Framingham, Massachusetts, near Boston. Now, she was stuck on the rural Tuskegee campus under Margaret's watchful—and ever-critical—eye. Music was Portia's passion, but she was too advanced for the classes available at home, so instead had to study dressmaking, which she loathed. The girls spent hours each day making uniforms, a task that was repetitious and dull. Portia felt alienated and displaced, and longed to escape to a more stimulating environment.

In September 1901, a wonderful opportunity presented itself. Her father arranged for her to return to Massachusetts to study music at Wellesley College. Portia matriculated as a special student, meaning that she was not entitled to full student privileges. Instead of living on campus, she boarded with a teacher in a rooming house and spent most of her time with faculty members. There were rumors about protests from Southern families who did not want their daughters living in a dormitory with an African American. Whatever the reason, Portia was separated from the other girls and was once again a loner. She lived in two worlds, Tuskegee *and* Wellesley, and felt like an outsider in both.

Girls like Portia Washington and Alice Roosevelt would not be called "teenagers" until the 1940s, but they exhibited all the traits that would give adolescents a bad name in years to come. They were moody, insecure, and defiant. They had too much free time, they spent too much money, and they tried too hard to win the approval of their friends. Their behavior was unpredictable, even unacceptable. And to top things off, they were crazy about a new kind of music that expressed the turmoil young people felt inside. Ragtime was the music of rebelliousness; its pulsating rhythms were hypnotic and made its listeners feel euphoric—perhaps even a little wanton. At least, that's how they looked when galloping recklessly through a high-speed one-step or two-step on the dance floor.

Before ragtime, popular music was smooth and orderly, as was the ballroom dancing that went with it. Genteel young men and women gracefully waltzed, or executed the complicated steps of the quadrille with dignity and poise. But the new century's dances were fast and chaotic. Couples moved so quickly, and with such abandon, that they often seemed to be going forward and backward at the same time.

Though young people clamored for Joplin and his "Maple

Leaf Rag," conservatives protested that ragtime was an inferior form of music that was ruining dance. Worse still, they were certain it was destroying morals. In 1901, twenty thousand of the country's leading musicians denounced "rag time" as "rot" and announced they would no longer include "rags" in their programs. It is "musical hash, made of bad meat," one member of the Federation of Musicians complained. "The lowest standard in the musical world," seconded another. The American Society of Professors of Dancing was in complete agreement. At their annual meeting, they proclaimed "there can be no graceful dancing with rag-time" and voted to ban it from the ballroom.

Critics feared that ragtime would "stifle the nostrils of decency" once and for all and claimed that the music's "thumpity, thumpity, thumpity harmony" would have an unwholesome effect on young people. Of course, the real reason behind the mounting antipathy against this outrageous new sound lay in its African American origins. Young Americans were falling under the spell of "coon melodies" set to a different beat. The offending rags were composed by black musicians who played honky-tonk piano in cheap bars on the wrong side of the tracks. Ragtime's detractors accused it of being "symbolic of the primitive morality and perceptible moral limitations of the negro type." And they suspected its degeneracy was contagious. In some people's eyes, ragtime led directly to miscegenation. If a young white person—Alice Roosevelt, for example—accepted colored music today, the reasoning went, she might be willing to accept a colored husband tomorrow.

Both TR and Booker T. were distressed by the fact that their daughters' growing pains were subject to public scrutiny. TR was appalled by the frequent sight of Alice's name in the newspapers, and not in the usual biographical roundups about the Roosevelt children. In his experience, proper ladies avoided any kind of public exposure, their names appearing in newsprint only upon announcement of their birth, marriage, and death. In fact, it was rare to find a published photograph of the First Lady, and the few that circulated showed her with demure, downcast eyes, as if avoiding the camera's gaze. TR joked that Edie would divorce him if he forced *her* to be in the newspapers. On the other hand, news of Alice was everywhere. An article that circulated throughout America on September 24, 1901, reported that she had just received a windfall inheritance of one hundred thousand dollars from Nathaniel Hawthorne Cusack, an old bachelor who was a Roosevelt family friend. The story was particularly troubling because it linked the young, unmarried woman to money (which was considered vulgar) *and* suggested she'd had a relationship—however innocent or familial—with an unmarried man.

Portia, like Alice, also became the subject of unladylike and unflattering articles when newspapers picked up on the story of her situation at Wellesley. Booker T. came under fire for sending his daughter to a fancy Eastern college when he promoted industrial education for other blacks.

These fathers, so accomplished and capable in most aspects of their lives, simply did not have an inkling about what to do with their unpredictable eldest daughters. "I can run the country or I can attend to Alice, but I cannot possibly do both," TR said famously, and it is likely that Booker T. felt exactly the same way about his own challenging child.

BOLD MOVES

———•◆•———

After his meeting with TR, Booker T. raced home to Alabama as fast as the train could take him. He arrived at Tuskegee on Tuesday, October 1, and politely sent a thank-you note and a souvenir photograph of his home, The Oaks, to the Calloways, his hosts in Washington. Then he got down to the serious business of being TR's eyes and ears in the South, and scheduled a meeting with ex-governor T. G. Jones for that very night. He asked Jones if he was interested in the judgeship and, not surprisingly, Jones said he was. Their sit-down confirmed what Booker T. already suspected: Jones was the perfect choice to kick off TR's nonpartisan, best-man-for-the-job approach to federal appointments.

Booker T. dashed off a recommendation to the President, enumerating Jones's many virtues. He called him "a clean, pure man in every respect" and said that Jones "stood up in the constitutional convention and elsewhere for a fair election law, opposed lynching, and has been outspoken for education."

He gave the letter to his secretary, Emmett Scott, to deliver to the president personally, emphasizing the need for secrecy. It would be highly impolitic for there to be any more publicity about their new relationship.

Scott hopped on a train for the trip to Washington. Booker T. arranged for him to stay with the Calloways, which would make his visit a little less conspicuous. He also came up with a plausible excuse for his secretary's sudden presence at the White House. If any journalists asked, Scott should say something about being there to invite TR "to include Tuskegee on his itinerary when he goes South again." As anticipated, when Scott arrived at TR's office on the morning of October 4, the press grilled him about the nature of his business with the President. Predictably, when they heard his innocuous answer, they immediately became disinterested and did not probe for further information. "They bit!" Scott reported to a relieved Booker T.

It was a thrilling moment for Scott when he was escorted into TR's private office, especially since he passed other blacks in the waiting room (Paul Dunbar was one of them) who were *not* granted interviews that day. He found the President "full of cordiality" and "brimming over with good will." Scott handed over the letter from Tuskegee and made plans to return the next morning to hear TR's decision about the Jones appointment.

Things did not go as smoothly on October 5. Scott cooled his heels in the outer office for three long hours, a disappointment after his preferential treatment the previous day, and TR was in a challenging mood when he finally summoned him. He expressed surprise and dismay that Jones had voted for Bryan, McKinley's opponent, in the last election (although he knew that Jones was a Democrat). Despite a few misgivings, TR impulsively decided to take Booker T.'s advice. "Tell Mr. Washington without using my name that party will most likely be appointed," he informed Scott at the end of their interview. "In fact I will appoint him."

It was a big, bold move that was bound to please all factions, and Booker T. had made it happen. Southerners welcomed the choice of a white Democrat, while blacks and Northerners appreciated Jones's liberal, pro-equality sentiments. An "At the White House" column in one of the capital newspapers slyly noted that "Booker Washington, the negro leader, would be particularly pleased," suggesting that someone had spilled the beans about his new role as TR's political czar in the South. As for the journalists, they liked the angle that TR crossed the aisle for his appointee and quoted the President as saying, "I am going to make such appointments as will make every southerner respect the Republican party."

The Washington/Roosevelt partnership was off to a brilliant start. Letters and telegrams flew back and forth between the White House and Tuskegee, sometimes twice a day, with TR asking for advice about various appointments and Booker T. happily providing it. The individual candidates—Bingham, Roulhac, Blacock, and others—and their bureaucratic offices— a postmastership here, a judgeship there—were less significant than the fact that Booker T. was making decisions and building a power base with the President. He made a point of being color-blind, endorsing blacks who met his high standards, but condemning those who did not. He found Mr. H. C. Leftwich, a black man who held the position of receiver of public money in Montgomery, "in bad odor" and unworthy of his position because "he does not pay his debts and associates with immoral characters." On the other hand, he considered Mr. Nathan Alexander, an upright black druggist from the same city, to be "an active candidate for Mr. Leftwich's position."

Booker T. tried to be discreet about being a presidential power broker but eventually his influence became apparent, especially in the black community, and his friend Thomas Calloway warned that he would be "swarmed with influence hunters." Calloway, who was doing a little influence hunting of his own, offered to investigate the supplicants and secretly assess their value. However, Booker T. had spent his entire career building a network—"the Tuskegee machine," as some people called it. If he didn't have a personal opinion about a prospective appointee, he was never more than one or two discreet inquiries away from one.

On October 10, Booker T. departed for a whirlwind lecture tour of Mississippi that placed him in a different city—Natchez, Vicksburg, Greenville—each day. The main purpose of his trip was to speak out against lynching. Terrorist groups such as the Ku Klux Klan were resurgent in the South, and lynchings were increasing at an alarming rate. He knew the topic would be of interest to blacks, but he was surprised to find that whites were eager to hear his cautionary theory about the subject. Although blacks were the usual victims of lynchings, Booker T. insisted that it wasn't just a racial issue, but "lawlessness," plain and simple. He believed that lynching was another form of anarchy, the very kind of moral chaos that led to McKinley's assassination, and he pleaded for an end to mob rule.

Ever the diplomat, Booker T. tempered his strong message by saying that Mississippians had made great progress in racial matters. He even praised the state's railroads for providing colored passengers with better accommodations, although the truth, was in 1901, a railroad car could be a dangerous place for a black man, even a famous black man with a long list of accomplishments like Booker T. On public transportation, especially in the South, the light-skinned, well-spoken, and impeccably dressed educator was just another "darky," subject to the segregationist rules of the road. Booker T. had his share of war stories. There was one nerve-racking train trip when two ladies from Boston, philanthropists unfamiliar with the racial etiquette of the South, insisted he eat in their dining car. "I'm in for it now," he thought, keenly aware that black men had been lynched for less.

When Booker T. boarded the train carrying him to Washington for his second meeting with TR, a band of angry bigots who were offended by his speech followed him, hoping to teach this outspoken black man a lesson. Sometime during the night, they managed to sneak onto the train and hunted for Booker T. in all the public spaces, but they never thought to look for a black man in a pricey sleeping compartment. Whenever possible, Booker T. reserved a Pullman car so he could rest, read, and avoid contact with potential troublemakers. After three failed attempts to locate their would-be victim, the bumbling vigilantes gave up and went home.

Unaware of his close call with death, Booker T. passed the time reading. Catching up with all the recent newspapers and biographies was his customary activity while traveling, and his favorite subject was Abraham Lincoln. "In literature he is my patron saint," he said, boasting that he had read nearly every book and magazine article written about his lifelong idol. Booker T. was counting on his knowledge of Lincoln to help him navigate a tricky situation he currently faced.

Despite his seeming enthusiasm for working with the President, he was having second thoughts. Of course, Booker T. was extremely flattered by TR's attention, and it was an honor to be in his orbit. However, he feared that the agenda was too overtly political. The cautious educator usually tried to steer clear of partisanship because it was in Tuskegee's best interests that he *appear* neutral. Booker T. prided himself on getting along with everyone—Republicans and Democrats, Northerners and Southerners—and worried that aligning himself with a Republican president, and a Yankee to boot, might change all that.

The other problem he had to consider was a practical one. Booker T. had so many commitments, it would be difficult for him to find time to be a presidential advisor. As it was, he spent six months of the year on the road and was rarely home at his beloved Tuskegee, where he had a school to run. On top of everything else, this was a tense moment for his family. Margaret wasn't feeling well, which had caused her to skip the last few trips, and recently Portia had been the subject of several nasty newspaper articles about her supposed social ostracism at Wellesley. Booker T. was so angry about the way the press, especially in Chicago, was treating his daughter, that he asked Emmett Scott to set up individual meetings with the editors of all the Chicago "colored papers," presumably to mount a counterattack. There was no question that his agenda was full, but it was almost impossible to say no to the dynamic TR, whom he regarded as "the highest type of all-around man that I have ever met."

Booker T. had a lot of time to think during the forty-eight-hour train ride through Mississippi, Tennessee, Kentucky, Ohio, and Virginia. When his train pulled into Washington's Baltimore & Ohio station on the morning of October 16, he had convinced himself to be open-minded about a potential alliance with TR. "New responsibilities bring new opportunities for usefulness," he liked to say, and this opportunity felt particularly promising. Somehow, he would make it work.

He exited the train to the sound of the station's famous bell tower, which clanged incessantly to mark each arrival and departure. Despite the early hour, travelers vied for streetcars and the odd little glass-enclosed taxis known as "herdics." The nation's capital was a city of transients, always rushing in and out of town; in fact, most politicians didn't actually live in Washington. Their permanent residences were with their families in their home states, so they maintained temporary quarters in hotels, apartment buildings, and rooming houses. Far from the disapproving eyes of their wives back in Ohio, upstate New York, and other "hometowns" across the country, most of these men found life in the capital a never-ending bachelor party. Their arrival at the station, and the attendant ringing of the tower bell, was their signal to commence such fraternal activities as spitting, cussing, imbibing, womanizing, and, of course, politicking. Simply put, Washington was not a city famous for good behavior or good manners.

Booker T. was spared the trouble of jockeying for a hired car because he was being met by Whitfield McKinlay, a prosperous black real estate man who had agreed to be his host. Unlike the itinerant politicians who flitted in and out of town, McKinlay maintained a real home in the capital at 1918 Eleventh Street, NW, where he and his wife, Kate, were respected members of the black community. He was an ambitious man and a staunch Republican who, like Thomas Calloway, saw a place for himself in the Booker T./Roosevelt constellation. Emmett Scott had arranged for Booker T. to stay with the McKinlays, who were excited to meet their guest and promised to give him "the best room in the house."

The two men greeted each other outside of the station and set off in McKinlay's coach for Arlington National Cemetery, where they planned to visit the graves of black soldiers with Bishop Abraham Grant of the African Methodist Episcopal Church. As they passed the National Mall, Booker T. was reminded of the infamous slave markets and holding pens that had surrounded the landmark before the Civil War. In the "Yellow House," Robey's Tavern, and even in the basement of the exclusive St. Charles Hotel, "human cattle" were "herded" and sold within sight of the Capitol, and the Mall's lovely expanse of lawn was blighted by coffles of weary, manacled slaves awaiting transport to their new owners. Those days were gone, and Washington was more hospitable to African Americans, but there was still much progress to be made, in Washington and everywhere else in America.

October 16 was a happy day for TR because he was looking forward to the arrival of his two youngest (and most mischievous) sons, seven-year-old Archie and four-year-old Quentin, who were finally moving into the White House. Because it was a special occasion, the children would be permitted to join the adults for dinner. TR's old friend and hunting companion Philip Stewart was visiting from Colorado and he was a sociable sort who would fit right in with the group. Experienced guests knew to expect just about anything at the Roosevelt table, whether it was the odd sight of a kangaroo rat eating from a dish or a pet snake peeking from a pocket.

The only complication was that TR had also scheduled an after-hours meeting with Booker T. Washington. The two men had fallen into the habit of late-night conversations whenever Booker T. was in town. It occurred to TR that he didn't have to curtail the family festivities and that he could combine business with pleasure if he invited Booker T. to dinner. In fact, TR was the first President to conduct business during White House meals, a practice he started during his early days in politics. Edith always indulged his habit of bringing "strays" to the table, and she was a great admirer of the famous Dr. Washington.

TR acted on his impulse and dictated a note to one of his secretaries, inviting Booker T. to come at 7:30 that evening.

A second later, he uncharacteristically hesitated. As he wrote to a noted civil rights lawyer a short time later, "the very fact that I felt a moment's qualm on inviting him because of his color made me ashamed of myself." He hastened to send out the invitation before he could change his mind.

Booker T. was tired after his long journey and looked forward to spending a quiet afternoon with his hosts before setting off for his evening appointment with the President. When he arrived at the McKinlay house, he was handed an envelope that had excited everyone's curiosity. Its return address was the "Executive Mansion" (TR was still using the previous administration's stationery), and Booker T. assumed it contained details about his meeting with TR. He carefully opened the letter and read its contents. The forty-five-year-old man thought he had seen everything, but even he was surprised by what he held in his hand.

It was an invitation to dine with the President and his family that very evening.

In the entire history of the United States, no black man, woman, or child had ever been invited to have dinner with the President at the White House.

Booker T. contemplated the invitation and calculated the cost of an acceptance. He consulted the McKinlays and anyone else he could reach in a hurry, but there was no easy answer. Booker T. knew all too well that a working relationship was not the same as a social one. "You have no idea how many invitations I am constantly refusing because I want to avoid embarrassing situations," he once told a friend. Sometimes it was safer to decline social interaction with white folk than to cross the color line.

But Booker T. had just returned from Europe, where Queen Victoria had welcomed him to tea at Windsor Castle. Why should he hesitate to dine with his own president?

Though the invitation was addressed to Mr. Booker T. Washington, he couldn't help but see it as a bold recognition of all members of his race, and as he later noted in a letter, that's what made his mind up in the end. He realized that he had no right to refuse, or even hesitate, no matter what personal condemnation it brought upon his shoulders.

Booker T. picked up a pen and composed his reply carefully. "My Dear Mr. President," he wrote on Tuskegee stationery. "I shall be very glad to accept your invitation for dinner this evening at seven-thirty." He signed it, "Yours very truly, Booker T. Washington," in his neatest hand, and sent it off to TR, before he could change his mind.

DINNER IS SERVED

——————•◆•——————

The afternoon passed quickly as Booker T. conferred with friends, sent off telegrams, and considered his wardrobe. Would his daily uniform—a jacket, a tie, and a starched white shirt with a spanking clean collar—be appropriate for dinner at the White House? Or was he required to wear evening dress?

Booker T. posed the question to Mrs. McKinlay, but she had never been a guest of the President and did not know the answer. Whitfield stepped in with a quick solution. He jumped into his buggy and drove straight to the White House, where he consulted George Cortelyou, the administration's top expert on protocol. Cortelyou confirmed that the President would wear formal attire that evening and advised Booker T. to do the same.

Luckily, Booker T. had packed a black dress suit and he gave it to Mrs. McKinlay to send out for pressing. Meanwhile, there was nothing to do but wait. He wasn't sure how dinner with the President would play out, but at least he knew he would be properly attired for the occasion.

Mrs. McKinlay fussed over his suit until it was perfect, and her husband kindly offered to drive him to his destination so he could travel in style. Leaving enough time to be prompt for his 7:30 appointment, Booker T. climbed up into the McKinlay carriage. It moved purposefully through the district until it reached the White House, where it turned into the circular drive and halted under the mansion's impressive porte cochere. This was where bystanders gathered during the day to watch Kermit and Ethel perform daredevil tricks on their new bicycles, but tonight, the parklike area was deserted. Booker T. said good-bye and thanks to Whitfield, stepped out of the carriage, and slowly climbed the stairs—one, two, three, four, five—pausing in front of the two uniformed men who flanked the glass-paneled entrance.

Did he imagine a look of disapproval from one of the black doorkeepers—was it Possum Jerry?—as he crossed the threshold into the vestibule? Was the old servant thinking, Don't you know your place? No matter, Booker T. said to himself as he moved forward confidently. Tonight there was no such thing as a "place," and there were no limits to what a black man could or couldn't do . . . not if he were dining at the White House.

He was escorted across the entrance hall and around the multicolored Tiffany screen that separated the public area from the rest of the house. The mansion's private reception areas, including the Red, Green, and Blue Rooms, were on the other side. These days, the Roosevelts liked to meet and greet their guests in the Blue Room, which, despite Edith's efforts, still looked like an overstuffed parlor in a Victorian manse.

The period of mourning for President McKinley was in force,

and much had been written in the newspapers about the fact that the Roosevelts would not host any official events until the New Year, although it was perfectly proper for them to have small "family" dinners, such as the one tonight. This moratorium on large-scale entertaining was helpful in that it gave the new First Family time to determine their personal approach to White House hospitality.

Each president had a different style, and some administrations were more social than others. John and Abigail Adams had been the first presidential couple to occupy the White House, in 1800, but the building was still unfinished and barely habitable (Mrs. Adams used the drafty East Room to dry her laundry). With a mere four months remaining in his term, President Adams had time to host only one pleasant but hasty reception before moving out.

When Thomas Jefferson, the country's next chief executive, took office he championed a revolutionary approach to presidential social life: democracy. Some Americans envisioned their leader as a European-styled royal, with a palace and a high and mighty manner to go with it. But Jefferson wanted the new country to have a new etiquette. He preferred shaking hands to the courtly tradition of bowing, and he promoted egalitarianism at his dinner parties by seating his guests at a round table, so no individual ranked higher than another. He wasn't too proud to invite his butcher (and his butcher's son) to mingle with statesmen and members of Washington society.

Jefferson may have campaigned for a less imperial Washington, but the two presidents who followed him, James Monroe and John Quincy Adams, *liked* pomp, pageantry, and lots of rules. Monroe required foreign ministers to wear their full regalia when visiting the White House, and they were happy to comply because dressing up made them feel more important. Similarly, Adams, who had spent a great deal of time in Europe, maintained a strict dress code for his guests, insisting on silk stockings and satin shoes for evening receptions—and that was for the *men*.

Andrew Jackson, whose nickname was, after all, Old Hickory, was more down-to-earth. He liked common folk so much that he welcomed twenty thousand of them—"a rabble, a mob, of boys, negroes, women, children, scrabbling, fighting, romping"—to his inauguration in 1829. The masses swarmed over the food, broke the china, and soiled the furniture. The only way to get them to leave the White House was to lure them outside with promises of lemonade and ice cream.

Jackson hosted another such mob scene at the end of his term, and the guest of honor on this occasion was a giant cheese. The New York Dairymen's Association proudly presented the President with a 1,400-pound wedge of their finest cheddar. He sent it down to the basement to ripen, and when it reached pungent perfection, he invited the public to come and help themselves to a piece. Ten thousand cheese lovers showed up to sample the wonder of the dairy world, and they were not exactly a fastidious bunch. They dropped so much cheese—grinding it into the carpets and smearing it on the walls and furniture—that a foul odor permeated the mansion that took weeks, if not months, to dissipate.

When he became president, Martin Van Buren was so offended by the rank condition of the White House that he established a strict "Code of Etiquette" for receptions. First on the list of new rules—absolutely no food or drink would be served to guests, except at the table. And there would be no common folk at the upscale dinner parties he intended to host.

Van Buren believed in the three E's of entertaining: elegance, extravagance, and, above all, exclusivity.

Some presidents were unenthusiastic about entertaining. James Polk and his wife, Sarah, were staunch Calvinists who disapproved of alcohol, dancing, and any sort of frivolous behavior. They were not a social couple by nature, although they did help establish an important White House tradition. Polk was so short, thin, and physically unprepossessing that no one seemed to notice when he entered the room. Sarah wanted her husband to get the attention he deserved, so she came up with the clever idea of using a musical cue to signal his arrival. Whenever the Marine Band played a few bars from "Hail to the Chief," a march inspired by Sir Walter Scott's poem "The Lady of the Lake," the crowd knew President Polk was on the way. The strategy worked so well that the song has heralded the presence of every "chief" ever since.

The Franklin Pierces were gloomy, Abraham Lincoln was preoccupied, and Andrew Johnson was downright dull. After the Civil War, it took several years for the clouds to lift, but once they did, Washington was caught up in a veritable "orgy of entertaining," with the White House at its center. President Ulysses Grant and his wife, Julia, liked to have a good time and refused to be prisoners of his high office. Grant broke with tradition by dining outside the mansion, if he so desired, and he and his wife democratically returned social calls instead of requiring visitors to come to them. When it came to fine dining, the Grants set the bar very high. Their dinner guests were treated to twenty-nine courses of delicacies, accompanied by at least six different wines.

Those wines became a distant memory when Rutherford B. Hayes took the oath of office. The new president and his wife, nicknamed "Lemonade Lucy," refused to serve spirits, so the mansion was "dry" as a bone. Parties were on the tame side when rum flavoring had to stand in for the real thing, but rumor had it that certain White House stewards could be counted on to supply a quick shot of whiskey to desperate guests with an unquenchable "thirst."

Chester Arthur, jokingly referred to as "His Accidency" because he inherited the presidency when James Garfield was assassinated, revitalized White House entertaining with his silver palate. He loved fine foods and modeled his dinners after ones he enjoyed at the gilded tables of the fabulously wealthy robber barons of Newport, Rhode Island. "Never have epicures so enjoyed themselves at Washington," wrote one grateful recipient of his hospitality. He was also very concerned about the White House's shabby appearance and demanded appropriations for extensive remodeling. (If the government refused to pay for it he planned to reach into his own deep pockets to cover the cost.) Cartloads of the mansion's historical castoffs were sent to auction to make way for the spiffy new furnishings he selected. His term might have been short, but it was in the best of taste.

Like Arthur, William McKinley enjoyed hosting dinners featuring good food, wines, and colorful floral arrangements from the White House conservatory. But the most eye-catching display at many a McKinley affair was Mrs. McKinley herself. Ida was sickly, so her doting husband breeched table protocol at state dinners by sitting next to her instead of giving that honor to the ranking guest, as was the custom. It seems he had a very good reason for doing so. His "Mrs." suffered from epilepsy and often experienced paralyzing seizures at the dinner table. Whenever that happened, the President calmly tossed a large napkin over her head and left her covered until she gradually returned to her senses. Guests may have been uncomfortable during Ida's public "fits," but McKinley took them in stride and never missed a beat in conversation.

The question facing the newly installed Roosevelts was, how would they entertain in *their* White House? Would they be democratic and welcoming, like Jefferson? Formal and persnickety, like Van Buren? Or would they model themselves after the high-spirited Grants? One thing was certain: Edith was a skilled (and healthy) hostess who would never need a napkin tossed over *her* head. And, unlike most of the hosts who had passed through the mansion, the Roosevelts were American aristocrats, familiar with how things should be done, yet secure enough to break the rules. She and TR were in the process of devising their own brand of presidential hospitality, and their innovative approach was evidenced at this very moment by the unprecedented presence of a black dinner guest in their drawing room.

After waiting anxiously for the evening to begin, that guest, Booker T., was eventually joined by Philip Stewart (who was coming a short distance from the guest room on the second floor) and a parade of lively Roosevelts, consisting of TR, Edith, Kermit, Ethel, Archie, and Quentin. TR was in a good mood because he enjoyed having Stewart around. He considered the convivial Westerner his "playmate" and liked to take him out on "rides and scrambles."

The Roosevelts and their guests exchanged pleasantries and promptly (and rather unceremoniously) headed down the hall for the dinner table. Henry Adams, a friend and frequent visitor to the White House, would complain that, early on in their

White House days, the Roosevelts went into dinner "with as much chaff and informality as though Theodore were still a Civil Service Commissioner." He preferred a little more pomp and circumstance and a bar or two of "Hail to the Chief." But TR was such a charismatic figure that all eyes turned to him whether or not there was a musical cue. One dazzled White House guest from abroad compared him to a natural wonder. "I have seen two tremendous works of nature in America. One is Niagara Falls and the other is the President of the United States," he wrote admiringly.

The little procession would have entered one of the two White House dining rooms. The smaller one, though designated for family, was one possible destination, since as soon as the Roosevelts moved in they had ordered a bigger top for the table to accommodate TR's daily assortment of guests. But occasionally they used the State Dining Room for private dinners, depending on their mood and the size of their party. It was larger than the other space, but not so vast that they felt lost in it. In fact, the room was woefully undersized for large events, and there were times when the staff had to seat guests at spillover tables in the hallway. Yet with its twin chandeliers, giant mirror, and abundance of gilt, the State Dining Room was a more suitable backdrop for gentlemen wearing formal evening attire.

Both venues featured oval tables. On a typical evening *en famille*, TR and Edith generally liked to sit opposite each other in the middle instead of at the ends. On this night, Edith wisely placed herself between the fidgety younger boys, where she could keep an eye on them, and invited Booker T. and Philip Stewart to take the seats of honor on either side of the President. They were attended by white-gloved waiters, and the

President had his valet, Henry Pinckney, who had recently been promoted to the position of White House steward, at hand, anticipating his every need.

At these family meals, guests often sat down to a table of gay, miscellaneous china patterns—the bread and butter plates might sport colorful little flags, while the dinner plates bore a delicate Haviland design. When Edith became First Lady, she expressed an interest in the sets of presidential china that had accumulated in the mansion. She intended to organize the dishes for display and put a stop to the practice of selling off any broken or unusable pieces, because she found it undignified for the White House to deal in souvenirs. Instead the fragments were sent straight to the bottom of the Potomac River. Eventually, Edith ordered 120 place settings of gold and white Wedgwood (with the Great Seal of the United States prominently displayed at the top) to use at state dinners.

As for the food on those plates, TR loved to eat, and announced that he would serve "only the best" food, champagne, and cigars during his tenure, even though the President had to pay for most entertaining expenses out of his own pocket. The Roosevelts liked their "three squares" and they assumed their guests felt the same way. Americans were fascinated by the food that was served at the White House. No matter how many times TR protested that he, his wife, and their children ate like any average American family, people imagined them dining on exotic fare. The perennial interest in presidential cuisine sparked numerous cookbooks, including one titled *The White House Cookbook* by Mrs. F. L. Gillette and Hugo Ziemann, steward of the White House, first published in 1887.

The book offered a week's sampling of menus for each month of the year. For tonight, a Wednesday in October, for example,

Gillette and Ziemann recommended a savory, autumnal meal that included:

> *Mock Turtle Soup*
> *Boiled Fillet of Veal,*
> *Potatoes à la Delmonico*
> *Fried Egg Plant & Mashed Squash*
> *Olives*
> *Saucer Puddings*
> *Apple Snow*   *Crisp Cookies*

Recipes for the proposed dishes were included in the book.

Annie O'Rourke, the Roosevelts' cook, may or may not have followed the volume's culinary advice when she began her dinner preparations earlier in the day. She was more likely to select choices from a list of reliable family favorites since guests always seemed to like them. One such staple was the classic Southern combination of hominy with gravy, a dish so beloved by TR that it sometimes appeared on the table at breakfast, lunch, *and* dinner. He also pioneered the idea of serving vegetables harvested from the fields and gardens of Sagamore Hill, including sweet potatoes, fiddlehead ferns, dandelion greens, and wild lettuce.

No meal was complete without a basket of Mrs. O'Rourke's warm and buttery homemade biscuits with currants, affectionately called "Fat Rascals," or a plate of her sugar wafers, the recipe for which was handwritten on the inside jacket of one of Edith's personal cookbooks. The ever-critical Henry Adams was immune to the charms of the Irish cook's specialties, saying that he found the food in the Roosevelt White House to be "indifferent and very badly served." But he was a bit of a snob.

Unlike the Polks or the Hayeses, the Roosevelts served alcohol at their table—usually white wine and sherry. They didn't mind if other people indulged in spirits, although they seemed indifferent to them. Two decades of interminably long political and society dinners had taught TR a trick or two. Whenever possible, his valet filled his glass to the brim with crushed ice, and then topped it off with the smallest amount of wine. The President appeared to be keeping up with everyone else, but he was imbibing very little alcohol. Ironically, the large-glass-filled-with-ice ruse often made some observers think that Roosevelt was a tippler who drank too much. Henry Adams dismissed that rumor with yet another barb. "Theodore is never sober," he agreed, "only he is drunk with himself and not with rum."

Coffee was TR's real vice. He consumed vast amounts of it, literally gallons, all day long. His son Ted described his father's cup as being so enormous that it was "more in the nature of a bathtub." And there wasn't only coffee in it—TR's sweet tooth was so powerful that he required five, six, and even seven lumps of sugar at a time, creating a constant buzz that made him even more energetic and excitable.

The President's infatuation with coffee spawned a legend and a famous advertising campaign. According to Roosevelt lore, TR was dining at the Maxwell House in Nashville, Tennessee, when he was served a freshly brewed cup of the house blend. It was so hot and flavorful that he drank it down in a big gulp and said with a sigh of regret, "My, that was good to the last drop." Maxwell House took note of his words and, in 1917, when selling its coffee to the public, made his compliment the company's official slogan. TR was not mentioned by name until the 1930s, after he was dead and unable to comment upon whether he wanted to endorse the product.

Booker T. was doubtless a bit nervous at the outset of the dinner, but soon relaxed and felt perfectly at ease at the President's table. Edith was noted for her ability to make each guest feel as if he were the only person she wanted to see, and she conversed with princes, cowboys, and shopgirls with equal aplomb. Nothing could rattle her composure after three years of entertaining the rambunctious Rough Riders who regularly turned up for "grub." (One particularly "rough" rider was arrested for firing his gun at a woman and tried to reassure the horrified Roosevelts by explaining, "I wasn't shooting at the lady, I was shooting at my wife.") At least Booker T. was a man Edith admired.

TR was full of chatter and goodwill. The first thing that every guest noticed about the President was that he never stopped talking, and he did so with such emphasis that his words burst forth like "projectiles." Henry Adams complained that no one could get a word in edgewise. "Theodore absorbed the conversation," he wrote after one evening together, "and if he tried me ten years ago, he crushes me now. To say that I enjoyed it would be . . . a gratuitous piece of deceit." Another White House visitor said that when Roosevelt was at the table, "hardly an observation was made by anyone else . . . and in fact, it would only have been possible by the exercise of a sort of brutal force." Sometimes when TR was monopolizing the conversation, Edith sent him a not-so-subtle signal by quietly saying "Theodore! Theodore!" The President would sheepishly answer, "Why, Edie, I was only—" in mock defense, but he appreciated the fact that she helped to keep his ego in check.

As for Booker T., whether the topic was Southern politics, the "Negro problem," or the best way to raise chickens, he could hold his own at any gathering. He was smart and good-humored, but unlike his host, he took his time when it came to conversation. He chose his words carefully because he didn't always have the luxury of speaking his mind. But Booker T.'s folksy yet dignified style served him well at the tables of millionaires, statesmen, royals, and now, the President.

Philip Stewart also contributed to the lively atmosphere that night. He had plenty to say about Colorado (TR wanted to discuss the matter of federal appointments in that part of the country, as well as in the South). He and TR had gone hunting there in January and recounted tales for the children, who loved hearing about their father's adventures. Stewart was armed with his new Kodak camera on that trip and photographed the various animals they encountered, from a friendly jackrabbit to a vicious mountain lion. The lion had jumped down from its treetop hiding place to attack the hunting party's dogs. TR came to the rescue by boldly leaping into the fray of fighting animals and plunging a hunting knife into the big cat's heart.

Booker T. watched the wide-eyed children with interest. His dining room back home at The Oaks was an exceedingly proper place, where Portia and her brothers were seen and not heard. The young Roosevelts, on the other hand, brought pets to the table (snakes, mice, and other specimens, as their father had done before them), expressed opinions and reactions, and behaved, well, like *children*. Not bad children, but children nonetheless. It was getting late. Archie and Quentin were overexcited by their long and eventful first day in the White House, and their siblings had school the next day, so they were all sent to bed.

The gentlemen retired to the Red Room to discuss politics over coffee. One newspaper reported that "it is here, in the genial glow of the red hangings and the crimson shaded lights

that the President comes after dinner with . . . 'political au-
thorities' to discuss affairs of state." According to Booker T.,
they "talked at considerable length concerning plans about the
South." There were many more appointments to be made in
Mississippi, South Carolina, Texas, and other places. More important, it wasn't too early to start cultivating Republicans in
the South. TR needed votes for the 1904 election, and he envisioned Booker T., Stewart, and supporters like them acting as
grassroots emissaries who would use their influence to attract
new blood to the party. The reaction to the Jones appointment
in Alabama was encouraging. A group of prosperous white
businessmen (one was the postmaster of Tuskegee and a friend
of Booker T.'s) announced their intention to start a Republican
Club in Montgomery to jump-start TR's campaign.

All in all, the evening was pleasant and productive for all
concerned. But when Booker T. talked about the dinner in years
to come, it was the fact that TR's family was alongside him at
the table, not his new role as political advisor, that seemed to
mean the most to him. "I dined with the President and members of his family," he said on more than one occasion.

At about ten o'clock, Booker T. said good night. He and
TR would see each other in a week, on October 23, at the Yale
University Bicentennial in New Haven, Connecticut, where a
huge convocation was planned. He rushed off to catch the last
train to New York, where he had scheduled a full day of appointments. The Roosevelts and their houseguest retired, the
guards settled into their evening routine, and the White House
was quiet.

A BIG STINK

———•◆•———

A lowly *Washington Post* stringer finished his long, tiring shift by reviewing the routine, typewritten memorandum the President's secretary prepared and distributed to reporters every day. It summarized TR's daily agenda and included a list of his callers. "Congressman So-and-So met with the President to discuss thus-and-such an issue," was how the report generally ran. But, on this occasion, one name jumped off the page, and the reporter came to the extraordinary realization that a black man had been a dinner guest at the White House.

"Booker T. Washington, of Tuskegee, Ala., dined with the President last evening," he wrote in his column. That one line caused telegraphs to start clicking furiously in the capital, their shocking message reverberating across the nation like a thunderclap.

———•◆•———

WHILE TR SLEPT peacefully in Abraham Lincoln's canopied bed, Booker T. struggled to make himself comfortable in a Pullman compartment on a train bound for New York City. Both men were blissfully unaware of the powerful journalistic missile that had been launched during the night, and they woke up on Thursday, October 17, to what they thought would be an ordinary day.

In Washington, TR ate breakfast with his family, spent an hour receiving callers, and presided over a routine cabinet meeting that focused on the less-than-pressing issue of tea production in America. After a month in office, he seemed to be settling into a manageable routine. "It is no easy job to be President. But I am thoroughly enjoying it and I think so far I have done pretty well," he wrote in a letter to his son Ted, who was trying to adjust to his new role as the country's "First Son."

It was a more exciting day for the Roosevelt children because they learned their doting parents had ordered a Shetland pony to add to their ever-expanding White House menagerie. TR and Edith were trying to make their offspring feel at home in an environment that had a tendency to be a little stiff. Upon moving in, Archie listened to his father go over the house rules until he had to speak out. "I don't see what good it does you to be President," he grumbled. "There are so many things we can't do here." Interestingly, there were moments when TR felt exactly the same way.

In New York, Booker T. disembarked from the train and made his way to the Grand Union Hotel, which was located at Park Avenue and Forty-Second Street, directly across from Grand Central Terminal. His usual "home" when visiting the city, the hotel was large and respectable, with over seven hundred rooms, some of which could be booked for as little as a dollar a day. More important, the Grand Union maintained a fairly open-door policy and welcomed "almost every traveler," according to its advertisements, so Booker T. did not have to worry about being turned away because of his color.

Some hotels were famous for their service, others for their food, but the Grand Union was best known for its unique accommodations for drunks. Inebriated guests were escorted solicitously to "Drunkards Row," a corridor of ground-floor rooms where they could sleep off a bender in private, without risk of stumbling and falling from a window.

Booker T. checked into one of the hotel's "sober" rooms and glanced at the New York *Tribune,* where he saw a one-liner indicating that he had dined with the President. It was an innocuous announcement, so he didn't pay much attention to it, and spent the day meeting with prospective donors. At one point he dashed off a quick letter to TR recommending "a colored lawyer of intelligence" for an upcoming position in Mississippi.

In the early evening, Booker T. dined with his friend and Tuskegee trustee William H. Baldwin. After dinner, he visited John D. Rockefeller Jr. (another dedicated philanthropist) at the weekly Bible class he ran for young men at the Fifth Avenue Baptist Church, and he addressed the group with customary good humor. The day was long and tiring, and when he finally placed his head on his hotel pillow, he never imagined waking up to the media storm that followed.

The *Atlanta Constitution* was the first paper to break the story. It was filed out of Washington the night of the dinner and ran the very next morning. According to the five-inch headline, there were four important "facts" readers needed to know about the previous night's incident. "President Has Booker T. Washington at the White House for Dinner"; "All Roosevelt

Family Present at the Table"; "Washington was in Evening Dress"; and, finally, "Probably the First Negro Ever Entertained at the White House." The journalist implied that he was an eyewitness, commenting specifically on Booker T.'s arrival and departure as if he had been outside the mansion, watching his every move. Before dinner "he was at once admitted into the private apartments," the reporter wrote, and after the meal he left at about ten o'clock, "apparently very much pleased with his dinner and his chat with the president."

Booker T.'s secretary, Emmett Scott, was pleased about the dinner and the press coverage in the Atlanta paper. "It is splendid, magnificent! And you deserve it all," he enthused in a congratulatory note to his boss. He firmly believed that this "especial mark of the president's favor" was good news for the race, a sign that an important corner on the road to social equality had been turned. "The world is moving forward," he exclaimed, "and my heart bubbles over I am so glad!" Perhaps the *Constitution* was a touch provocative, emphasizing as it did the novelty of the President entertaining a black man at the White House, but Scott chose to see it as good publicity.

Then all hell broke loose.

Why? Because it had never before happened, and people were shocked by the notion that a Negro and a white man—the President of the United States, no less, and a former slave—sat together at a dining room table.

African Americans had visited the White House before, but had never been invited to dine there. Sojourner Truth, the noted abolitionist, met with Abraham Lincoln in his office, not in a dining room. Frederick Douglass *almost* had tea with Lincoln, but not at the White House. A famous black singer named "Blind Tom" performed at one of President James Buchanan's musicales without being offered refreshments. And when Blanche Bruce of Mississippi was in the Senate, he was invited to attend official executive mansion functions, but he was far too tactful to accept. Queen Liliuokalani of the Hawaiian Islands was the only White House dinner guest who might have been considered a touch "dark," but no one begrudged the tropical royal a place at the President's table. She was entertained by Grover Cleveland during an official visit to Washington.

Sitting down to eat with the "Negro Moses" was an entirely different matter. On the following day, October 18, the *Atlanta Constitution* revisited the story.

BOTH POLITICALLY AND SOCIALLY

PRESIDENT ROOSEVELT PROPOSES

TO CODDLE DESCENDANTS OF HAM

ACTION OF PRESIDENT IS ROUNDLY CENSORED

Indignant Southerners couldn't stop talking about TR's great affront to their sensibilities. The *Memphis Scimitar*, true to its name, viciously slashed the offending parties. "The most damnable outrage which has ever been perpetuated by any citizen of the United States was committed yesterday by the President when he invited a nigger to dine with him at the White House. . . . He has not inflamed the anger of the Southern people; he has excited their disgust." Memphis's *Commercial Appeal* insisted that "this is a white man's country. President Roosevelt has committed a blunder that is worse than a crime."

The *Kentucky Courier Journal* carried on about the high-wafting "Odor of that Dinner," with "Teddy and Booker hobnobbing over their possum and potatoes," while the *Raleigh*

Morning Post summed up the prevailing sentiment of the South in one word: "monstrous." The enraged reactions that appeared in bold-faced headlines from Maryland to Texas proved that Southerners didn't like it one bit. The consensus was that both men should have known better.

"And he calls himself half a Southerner!" Roosevelt's critics said in disbelief. They felt betrayed—even hoodwinked—by his apparently hollow promise his first week in office to "represent the whole country, not any one section." He was a damned Yankee after all, with no regard for decency or honor. The *Nashville Tennessee American* printed the most personal insult of all, saying that TR's beloved mother, who was raised on a plantation in Georgia, would have disapproved of her son's reprehensible behavior. "Had she been present when he seated Booker Washington at his table," the paper insisted, "she would doubtless have declined to sit."

From a Southerner's perspective, no proper lady, or gentleman, for that matter, would ever deign to dine with a black man. According to the *Geneva Reaper,* a newspaper from Booker T.'s home state of Alabama, TR was irredeemably tainted. "Poor Roosevelt!" a journalist wrote in mock lament. "He might now just as well sleep with Booker Washington, for the scent of that coon will follow him to the grave as far as the South is concerned."

Worse still were the comments reserved for Booker T. The *Memphis Scimitar* again aimed straight for the jugular when it called him "a nigger who happens to have cash enough to pay the tailor and the barber, and the perfume for scents enough to take away the nigger smell."

Coon songs were enjoying a burst of popularity in 1901, and one of the year's bestsellers was a number called "Coon, Coon,

Coon." Sung by Lew Dockstader, a corpulent white entertainer who performed in blackface, it was the comic lament of a black man who wants to be white.

Coon! Coon! Coon!
I wish my color would fade.
Coon! Coon! Coon!
I'd like a different shade.
Coon! Coon! Coon!
Morning, night and noon.
I wish I was a white man
'Stead of a Coon! Coon! Coon!

Immediately after the White House dinner, a satiric version replaced the popular standard. A barbed ditty called "Teddy's Mistake or Booker's Reception" set its timely lyrics to the melody of "Coon, Coon, Coon." "For he is a coon, coon, coon and Booker is his name" was the fashionable new way to sing the hit tune in the South. The parody suggested that, like the unhappy black man in the original song who went to great lengths to change his color, Booker T. was also a man ashamed of his own race. The respected educator had become the object of ridicule and derision. "That dinner," according to the *Argus*, "has undone the work of his life, and the best thing he can do is move North." It was such a shame, agreed the *Atlanta Constitution*. "Roosevelt has ruined the best negro in Alabama."

Clearly, the dinner wasn't just a dinner: it was a Pandora's box of racism that, once opened, was impossible to close. The dreaded specter of social equality had reared its head, and Southerners were so terrified they attacked from every angle. One objection was that the dining room in question belonged to the nation and not to TR. Roosevelt, therefore, had no right to express his personal attitudes about race in the White House, which "is intended to be the representative official home of the American people, not the private home of the person chosen to occupy it," as the *Raleigh Morning Post* argued. Though President of the United States, TR was no more than a high-class tenant who was required to represent public opinion and uphold tradition. It might have been acceptable for him to invite a distinguished African American to an official event, an invitation that any well-mannered black person would, of course, refuse. But an offer to dine with a man and his family signified *social* acceptance in the South, and that concept was unacceptable.

No matter who the guest, TR's practice of hosting "business" lunches and dinners to extend the workday was further grounds for objection. Mixing business with pleasure was an alien and distasteful concept to most Southerners. To them, any man who was welcome at the dinner table was, by definition, a friend. Needless to say, the notion of a black "friend" was a serious affront to the Dixie sensibility. "We people of the south have been born and raised so that we cannot accept the negro as our social equal and we cannot respect any man who does," announced a disapproving Confederate congressman in the *Atlanta Constitution.*

The only exception to tabletop segregation occurred behind closed doors in Southern kitchens. The colored "help" might sit down to eat with the children of the house because they were taking care of them. But this practice never suggested social equality: the children, no matter how young, were always considered superior to any black person in the room.

Southerners were as mystified by Booker T.'s defiant, cross-the-color-line behavior as they were by TR's. At the Cotton States Exposition back in 1895, he assured them that social equality was completely manageable—that the solution to the problem was so simple that he could, in fact, demonstrate it with one hand. The fingers and the palm work together, but go their separate ways, Booker T. had suggested, illustrating how blacks and whites could move forward on parallel, but decidedly distinct, paths.

Prior to the White House debacle, he had seemed determined to avoid all tricky social situations. White visitors to Tuskegee recalled that he never placed them in the awkward position of having to eat with him at his table. During meetings at The Oaks, when the scent of cooking wafted up to Booker T.'s office, signifying lunch or dinner, guests were tempted to suddenly recall an appointment they had scheduled, or complain of the onset of a sore throat . . . anything to avoid an invitation to join the Washingtons for a meal. But they needn't have worried. Invoking one pretext or another, Booker T. would considerately absent himself from the dining room, or arrange for his guest to be served privately. He observed the old customs, all the don'ts that were in force when he was a boy on the plantation.

That's what he did in the South, but in the North and everywhere else in the world, he moved freely. Southerners were unconcerned about Booker T.'s behavior in Yankee territory— places like Boston, New York, or even Europe. But the White House was sacred ground and it was almost in the South. Down home, a black man was supposed to know, and uphold, his boundaries.

Of course, interracial dining was not the only issue. When Southerners objected to "social" intercourse in the dining room, it was code for sexual intercourse in the bedroom. In

their minds, the inevitable result of social equality was miscegenation. If you eat with them, you may end up marrying
them, was the general thinking. "A dinner given by one man to
another in the home and privacy of his family means that the
guest may woo and win the host's daughter," the *Macon Telegraph* predicted ominously.

In this case, the host's daughter was the lovely and virginal
Alice Roosevelt, and several newspapers placed her at the table
to underscore the extent of TR's gaffe. However, Alice was not
sitting thigh to thigh with Booker T. at the infamous dinner on
October 16. She was still pouting (and waiting for an invitation to join her family) at her aunt's home in Farmington, Connecticut, over three hundred miles away. Nonetheless, it served
the rabble-rousers' purposes to promote the idea that TR had
subjected his innocent womenfolk to the terrible indignity of
breaking bread with a black man. No *real* gentleman would do
that. An incensed Georgian telegraphed his protest to the President. "You have made mistake. He who dines with negro, we
think no better. To compel his wife is worse."

Booker T.'s daughter, Portia, and TR's sons were fair game
for comments, too. Bill Arp, a Southern humorist who enjoyed
taking potshots at Republicans, suggested that the Roosevelts
and the Washingtons should become in-laws. Come Christmas,
he predicted, Portia could follow in her father's footsteps and
visit the White House. "Maybe Roosevelt's son will fall in love
with her and marry her without having to elope," he quipped.

The *Richmond Times* saw no humor in the situation and
blamed TR for undermining long-standing family values in
America. "It means the President is willing that negroes shall
mingle freely with whites in the social circle—that white
women may receive attentions from negro men: it means that

there is no racial reason in his opinion why whites and blacks may not marry and intermarry." The U.S. Census in 1890 revealed that there were roughly 1,132,060 mulattos in the country, 924,964 of them (including Booker T. and his wife) living in the South. It was therefore puzzling that so many Southerners expressed shock and revulsion at the thought of potential interracial couplings. How did all those Southern mulattos come into being? "The increase of mulatoes [sic] in the South tells a stronger and more convincing tale of social equality than any action of the President's ever could," pointed out the editor of the African American *Georgia Baptist.* In fact, the "lovely rainbow like population" the South "succeeded in making out of the coal black African," the *Topeka Plaindealer* suggested sarcastically, indicated that *white* men were the ones guilty of promoting miscegenation, not "the colored gentleman who might be honored by an invitation to dine with President Roosevelt or any other Southerner's family."

The fear of miscegenation may not have been foremost in the mind of every Southerner who objected to the dinner, but one prevailing concern was that of "Negro Aspiration." What if the honor accorded Booker T. inspired several million Negroes to believe that they were entitled to the same treatment? What if they demanded it? Suddenly there were signs of rebelliousness. On the Sunday immediately following the dinner, "two gaudily dressed negro women" entered a church in Louisville, Kentucky, marched to the front, and sat themselves down next to a mortified Confederate veteran and his wife. The reporter recounting the horrifying story of their behavior said it was thought to be the result of Booker T.'s dinner at the White House. The incident "fanned the flame of negro aspiration as it had never been fanned before," suggested the *Washington Post,* and that was very bad news for whites who were fighting to maintain their dominance over the black population.

Northerners responded differently. For the most part, they were supportive of the dinner, and they viewed Southern opposition with everything from bemusement to high-minded outrage. The *Boston Transcript* wrote sarcastically that the "hysterical and horror-stricken Southern shriekers" would realize eventually that "life is still worth living," even though a "gifted, interesting, and attractive olive-skinned Christian gentleman has broken bread and eaten salt at the President's table." The *New York Times* was predictably positive. "The South should be rejoiced," the paper chided, calling Booker T. and TR "two of the truest Americans born on our soil and two of the best and most intelligent and influential friends of the south now living."

Senator Joseph Foraker of Ohio, who was not always one of TR's fans, graciously allowed that Booker T. Washington was "highly qualified to sit at any man's table." Boston's William Henry Lewis, the black, Harvard-educated football coach who previously had differences with Booker T., stepped forward in staunch support. "I am sure that when our Southern brethren think it over they will be heartily ashamed of themselves, for no man living has done the South a greater service than Booker T. Washington," he told an interviewer.

The great humorist Finley Peter Dunne used his comic alter ego, "Mr. Dooley," to debate the issue. There was no question that "Tiddy" had insulted the "sunny Southland," and Dooley put his finger on the problem. "Fr'm time immermoryal," he said, "th' sacred rule at th' White House has been, whin it comes to dinner, please pass th' dark meat." It was all about "social supeeryority." Of course, he noted slyly, "a raaly supeeryor race nivir thinks iv that." Mr. Dooley believed that TR made a mistake by expressing his private values in a public space, although he saw humor in the condemnation coming from the South. "Thousan's iv men who wuden't have voted f'r him undher anny circumstances has declared that under no circumstances wud they now vote f'r him," he said.

For the most part, blacks were jubilant about the dinner. Government messengers could be heard shouting the news all over Washington. Yet some black newspapers averred that Booker T. had made a terrible mistake. In the South, the *Charleston Messenger* chastised him for accepting an invitation that "a self-respecting negro man, or any other gentleman" should have declined, "because of the strife acceptance of it would arouse." That same newspaper inaccurately argued that race relations had been better than ever in the South, until Booker T. spoiled everything. Now, the editor claimed, there would be hell to pay.

In the North, where Booker T. often locked horns with black intellectuals and budding militants who opposed his ideas about industrial education, the dinner aroused the ire of William Monroe Trotter, editor of the *Boston Guardian*. Like William Henry Lewis, Trotter was a smart and opinionated African American who had been educated at Harvard. But unlike Lewis, Trotter refused to see any merit in Booker T.'s bricks-and-mortar approach to racial uplift, and he used the dinner as an example of the Tuskegee wizard's selfish, me-first quest for power. In fact, he suggested that TR had invited the *wrong* Negro. Trotter considered Booker T. to be passive, subservient, and an impediment in the path of black progress, and he often used the words "Washington est delinda" in his articles, meaning "Washington must die." Condemnation from the black press hurt Booker T. more than hysterical jabs from Southern conservatives.

News of the scandal reached Europe, where the dinner was "the most universally discussed topic that has found its way across the Atlantic in many years," reported the Paris correspondent for the *London Express.* What the French found shocking was not that a black man had dined at the White House, but that it hadn't happened before. Typically, they were amused by the provincialism, even barbarism, of Americans. In their country, interracial dining would not raise an eyebrow, let alone spark a national furor. One of the most adored actors in Paris was a black clown named Chocolate. And, as the *New York Tribune* reminded readers, Booker T. Washington had been entertained by cabinet ministers and other notable Frenchmen during his visit to France in 1899. The *Journal des Débats* called the affair "a black incident in a White House," and asked, "Is the South going to secede anew to maintain the social slavery of the black race?"

Emmett Scott was devastated. He wrote to his boss while struggling valiantly to maintain a stiff upper lip. "My Dear Mr. Washington: I know just what you must be undergoing at this time! It all seems so pitiful and so pitiable," he consoled.

Then he switched tactics, using his skills as a public relations expert to spin a bleak situation into a better one. Acknowledging that it was terrible for Booker T. to be "misunderstood and traduced," Scott still believed the scandal had its "compensating features." Finally the President would have the opportunity to see the "inner, inner phase of Southern feeling."

Scott didn't say what he expected TR to do with these insights. Meanwhile, he was desperately trying to figure out a way to combat the tidal wave of bad publicity that threatened to engulf Booker T. and Tuskegee.

The press sniffed the enticing scent of scandal and doggedly chased the story and its principals, who were completely unprepared for the assault. Booker T., who was still in New York, was pursued by reporters who rivaled modern-day paparazzi in their determination to secure interviews. They followed him everywhere, begging for a comment. Those who were unable to badger him in person sent telegrams and letters demanding some statement or stand.

Although correspondents knew better than to pester the President, several of the country's more prominent newspapers, including the *Boston Globe* and the *New York Times,* seemed to have an extraordinarily vivid sense of what TR was thinking, suggesting they may have been beneficiaries of deliberate White House leaks. Roosevelt was "vastly amused," the *Globe* said in its headline, "while regretting that any one would find fault with his conduct, he feels that he has nothing to apologize for and nothing to be ashamed of." The *Times* claimed to have "overheard" the President telling a "friend" that he was "amazed that he could be so misunderstood by those who had criticized him." And the *Herald* bureau delivered the most provocative news of all: the word around the White House was that if the Southern papers kept up their abuse, "the President might answer them by inviting Mr. Washington to dinner a second time."

SITTING DUCKS

———— •◆• ————

Both Booker T. and TR decided that the best form of damage control was silence, hoping that a "no comment" approach would throw cold water on the flames of scandal.

That was wishful thinking.

As the South's shrill tirades against social equality, miscegenation, presidential impropriety, and uppity "coons" raged on, the scheduled trip to the Yale Bicentennial in the cloistered university town of New Haven proved to be perfectly timed. TR had been vice president when he was invited, but now his hosts had the honor of welcoming *President* Roosevelt to the festivities. And Booker T., representing Tuskegee, was one of many esteemed educators expected to attend. The school had a four-day celebration planned, including dinners, historical pageants, and official ceremonies.

The bicentennial was an important occasion for the Yale faculty and the "sons of Eli," as the students were called, but it was a big shock to all concerned when newspaper reporters descended on New Haven en masse to witness the reunion of TR and Booker T. Wednesday, October 23, marked the one-week anniversary of the now-infamous dinner, and journalists were determined to keep the story alive.

There was a rumor that Booker T. would sit beside TR when he received his honorary degree. And with so many banquets scheduled for the honored guests, it was more than likely that TR and Booker T. would find themselves dining in the same place at the same time—and maybe even at the same table. All eyes were on New Haven, hoping to see something shocking.

Some impatient reporters fabricated news instead of waiting for it to happen. Soon after his arrival in New Haven, Booker T. was compelled to break his silence because the *Brooklyn Eagle* ran a bogus interview attributed to him. He issued a terse statement to the Associated Press, reiterating that he had not made any statements about the dinner, nor would he do so while at Yale. "I want to state as emphatically as I can that I have given no interview and have refrained from any discussion of what occurred in Washington, although persistent efforts have been made to put words in my mouth." One of those persistent correspondents cornered him on campus, pretending to want his opinion of the bicentennial parade. But "How about that dinner with President Roosevelt?" was the inevitable next question, and for the hundredth time an exasperated Booker T. refused to answer.

TR's so-called escape from publicity hounds was faring no better. It was time to pick up the troublesome Alice from his sister's place in Connecticut and escort her home by way of New Haven, and his train was a magnet for reporters. TR was a little out of sorts about the trip because his security team informed him that he was not allowed to engage in any handshaking at

Yale. Given what happened the last time a president reached out to a stranger in a crowd, officials thought better of exposing TR to that kind of risk, but TR resented the implication that he wasn't capable of defending himself. Just in case, he carried a handgun at all times.

Booker T. was also being told what he should and should not do in New Haven. Edgar Gardner Murphy, a white proponent of racial equality in the South and a longtime champion of Tuskegee, sent him a telegraph strongly urging that he avoid contact with the Roosevelts during his trip. "Reported here that you are to meet Roosevelt and daughter at Banquet this evening. I earnestly hope you will not attend," he wrote. "The trouble is not superficial. I think your whole past influence in the south and the very existence of Tuskegee are involved."

News of where and with whom Booker T. dined had become such a national obsession that he was probably tempted to start fasting. These days it seemed that everyone had a story about a meal with Booker T., whose eating habits, one editor quipped, had become "the public property of the country." Major Henry Lee Higginson, a philanthropist who founded the Boston Symphony Orchestra, claimed that he was "sorry the President gave him a dinner without asking *me*. I have invited Booker T. Washington to my house . . . when he comes to Boston I shall do it again." Bishop Potter of Philadelphia also announced proudly that he had hosted Booker T. on a previous occasion. And Professor Charles Eliot Norton of Boston made a point of telling reporters that Booker T. graced his table the previous winter, and stressed, "Should he be here again this winter, I shall again hope for the honor." With so many racists speaking out against Booker T.'s right to dine, it became fashionable to claim him as a guest.

TR swept into New Haven on the morning of October 23, every inch the visiting dignitary. His entourage consisted of Alice, his sister Bamie and her family, and assorted staff members and guards. Even without the customary handshaking, TR was a sensation. Alice watched her father in action, noting that he was both dignified and relaxed (it was the first time she was seeing him perform his duties as president), and she decided that she liked the "ruckus" that came with being the "First Daughter," after all.

The reporters who expected to witness another installment in the ongoing racially fueled drama were sorely disappointed. Despite the fact that the two men attended the same events, they were never seen together, and that may have been by design. During the main convocation, TR was onstage, awaiting his honorary degree, while Booker T. was tucked away in the audience with the other academics. When Supreme Court justice David Brewer stepped up to the podium to give his opening address, he surprised the crowd by tackling the dinner head-on. Looking in TR's direction he said, "I am glad that there is one man in the United States who knows a true Washington, whether he is a George or a Booker."

The audience leapt to its feet in approval, applauding his bold words with an ovation that lasted for several minutes. TR bowed in acknowledgment and Booker T. looked pleased. This rousing affirmation seemed to validate their impulse to come together as equals at the dinner table—but this was the liberal North speaking. Other parts of the country continued to voice condemnation, and TR's confidence in his actions was starting to waver.

He sought advice from fellow Yale honoree Samuel Clemens.

Seizing a moment when they could speak privately, Roosevelt asked the popular writer point-blank what he thought about the situation. Was he right to invite a Negro to dine at the White House? Clemens thought about the question, then told TR that the President, because of his office, might have to curb his impulses and behave differently from ordinary citizens. Perhaps he had made a mistake. TR listened and seemed to take his answer seriously.

What Clemens didn't say, however, was that he thought Roosevelt was an irresponsible showoff who would do anything for attention. The writer was actually a big supporter of Booker T. Washington. He endorsed *Up from Slavery*, calling it "deeply interesting and impressive." But he actively disliked the President and wrote privately that he wasn't worthy to *untie* Booker T.'s shoelaces. In his opinion, TR was given to staging self-aggrandizing stunts, and that's how he saw the White House dinner. "The storm that burst on us must have enthused the circus soul of the little imitation cowboy," was Clemens's irreverent remark about Roosevelt and the dinner, and he went on to say that TR's "dime-novel heroics" backfired when he found that the public's reaction "wasn't all praise, but that the Southern half of it was furious censure."

When TR returned to Washington, he continued probing friends and associates for their reactions. He wondered what Philip Stewart was thinking—after all, he was there that night. "I suppose you have been amused at finding that our innocent dinner to Booker T. Washington has not only become a national but an international affair," he wrote. TR confessed to being perplexed by the uproar from the South because it never occurred to him that a courtesy extended to a man as deserving as Booker T. would provoke any kind of comment at all, let alone the fierce political and personal attacks he faced every day.

The "outburst of feeling in the South against us is to me literally inexplicable," he complained to Lucius Nathan Littauer, a Republican congressman from New York. TR was irritated and at times furious with the vociferous critics who spewed vitriol in his direction. But his deepest felt and most often expressed emotion was, as he put it, "melancholy." It saddened him, he said, to think "such feelings should exist."

To old friends like Curtis Guild, a fellow Harvard man and the inspector general of Havana during the Spanish-American War, and Henry Cabot Lodge, he let off steam in his letters, condemning the "idiot or vicious Bourbon element of the South." It was that "combination of Bourbon intellect and intolerant truculence of spirit," he wrote, "which brought on the Civil War." If the South wanted another confrontation, they should know that this Rough Rider never ran away from a fight. "If these creatures had any sense they would understand that they can't bluff me," he fumed. What's more, he would invite Booker T. to the White House "just as often as I please," he threatened.

That's what TR *said*, but Booker T. sensed a new coolness emanating from the President while they were in New Haven. Yes, he had been advised to avoid potentially compromising situations with the Roosevelts, but when their paths never crossed, it occurred to Booker T. that TR might be avoiding him. On his way home to Tuskegee, he sent a note to TR, hoping to get their partnership back on track. "My Dear Mr. President," he wrote. "I was unfortunate in my attempt to see you while you were in New Haven, but in any case I presume we could not have talked with any satisfaction there." He added that he hoped to see him the very next time he passed through Washington.

The reply from TR's secretary was polite and indicated that the President would be glad to see him at some unspecified time in the future. However, it wasn't the warm, personal response Booker T. had hoped to receive, and it gave him pause. If he may have been inclined to feel a little hurt or ignored, he quickly dismissed those passing insecurities. After having been home in Alabama for a few days, he realized that there was big trouble ahead, and the stakes were higher than a black man's right to sit at a white man's dinner table. Lives were on the line.

Democrats were using the dinner to discredit Roosevelt and the Republican Party, and their objective was to incite a deadly new wave of racial prejudice. Of course, some Southerners were genuinely offended by what happened in the White House. Others merely exaggerated their objections because they understood that they had been handed a powerful weapon to use against the current administration and the country's black population.

The prediction that TR's bipartisan appointment of T. G. Jones would initiate friendly relations between the North and the South did not sit well with all Southerners, especially Democrats who wanted to prevent Republicans from gaining ground in their territory. It served their purposes to make sure that TR remained unpopular, and the good news was that, these days, the President was doing their work for them. "Somehow, the look ahead does not seem so hopeless," rejoiced one Dixie Democrat when he heard about the dinner. He believed that TR could be counted on "to raise more of that stuff from the very hot place with that very short name than was ever raised before. There's a good time coming, boys," he promised his party.

Like-minded men throughout the South rallied to make the most of the controversy. In case anyone was taken in by the Jones appointment, they stressed that TR's naming of "all the Joneses, all the Smiths, and all the Browns ... to federal judgeships will not reconcile the white people of the South to the fact that the president of the United States ate at the same table with a nigger." In fact, many indignant Southerners believed that Jones should resign and "hurl the appointment back into the very teeth" of that Republican scoundrel.

In Maryland, where opposing candidates were engaged in a bitter battle for a Senate seat, the Democrats embraced the fight against social equality, or the "Negro Issue," as they called it, as their campaign platform. To illustrate the dangers of welcoming blacks to the dinner table, they commissioned a vulgar cartoon of Booker T.'s visit to the White House. IT HAS COME TO THIS! screeched the headline on a crudely rendered, nine-by-twelve-inch drawing. The upper corner of the picture showed President Roosevelt warmly shaking hands with a smug-looking Booker T. and greeting him with the words, "I wish you would dine with Mrs. Roosevelt and myself this evening." Below, a larger cartoon depicted the two friends happily ensconced at the table, with a smiling Edith Roosevelt sitting between them, contentedly pouring tea. The Democratic State Committee planned to distribute thousands of copies throughout Maryland on the eve of the election.

It was one thing to circulate a caricature of the President— politicians were fair game for any cartoonist. However, it was the first time in history that a president's *wife*, "a woman whom all Americans must honor and respect as belonging to the best type of American womanhood and American motherhood," was lampooned. This ungentlemanly act backfired on the

Democrats, who were blasted with criticism. "Those who have fathered this villainous picture have gone beyond all bounds," condemned one disapproving editor. Ultimately, the offending politicos were shamed into recalling the cartoon from metropolitan areas, although they quietly released it in rural communities, where it was less likely to spark a controversy. Ironically, the very existence of the disrespectful drawing proved that the men who claimed to be fighting social equality to "protect" Southern gentility had no gentility at all.

In South Carolina, Senator Ben Tillman, a staunch Democrat who was best known for being a proud white supremacist, sensed immediately that the dinner was a promising development for his party. "Use it for all its worth," he told his followers, urging them to act quickly and viciously, while the story was fresh in the public mind. "Pitchfork Ben," as he was called (he once threatened to poke President Grover Cleveland in the stomach with a pronged farm implement because he disagreed with his policies), delighted in making bombastic racist statements—the more offensive the better. His remarks about the dinner were choice, even for him. "The action of President Roosevelt in entertaining that nigger will necessitate our killing a thousand niggers in the South before they will learn their place again," he announced to his approving constituency.

"Ain't that a lovely sentiment to come out of the mouth of a United States Senator!" commented "Silas Larrabee," the *New York Times'* fictional, front-porch political analyst. The idea of killing Negroes to restore social equilibrium in the South was so outrageous that *Life* magazine suggested Tillman be sent to jail for "inciting murder." A year later, the joke was on Tillman when he received a sentence which, from his point of view, was worse than any jail. He started a brawl on the Senate floor, and his behavior was considered so grossly inappropriate that TR *uninvited* him from the most important White House dinner of the year.

Booker T. understood that Tillman and extremists like him were using the dinner to widen the existing divide between the races, and he feared their enthusiasm for exterminating blacks was becoming contagious. In Ball, Louisiana, for example, there was a high level of racial tension after a black man named Bill Morris was burned at the stake for assaulting a white woman. But it was a subsequent, and seemingly innocuous, incident that sparked an out-and-out race riot in the community.

A black caterer named Crea Lott was selling refreshments during a gathering at his church when a white police officer showed up and demanded to see his license. Lott had no license and allegedly became "impudent" when questioned. Instead of issuing a citation for the violation, the policeman left and returned with a large, armed posse. Why the overreaction? The vigilantes claimed that they were concerned that the "churchgoers" were plotting to avenge Morris's lynching, so they wanted to be prepared. But the real reason they were itching for a fight was that Lott dared to challenge their authority— the darkest side of "Negro Aspiration."

There was some controversy as to who started the gunfight that ensued between the factions, but the posse was out for blood, and Lott and his friends were armed and ready to defend themselves. By the time the shooting was over, nine blacks (including women and children) and two white men were dead. In reporting the story, the *New Orleans Picayune* observed that "negroes have been lately aroused to aggressiveness by the intemperate expressions in both the Northern and Southern press over the recent Booker Washington dinner with the President." TR's public endorsement of Booker T. had given his race a false sense of power, security, and entitlement. The posse's bellicosity could be attributed to the dinner as well, because when faced with defiant blacks, Southerners felt compelled to defend their so-called supremacy as never before.

If the ill will generated by the dinner had turned African Americans into sitting ducks, Booker T. was the most visible target. Emmett Scott's desk drawer overflowed with threats from people who believed that Booker T. deserved to die because he dared to dine at the wrong table. A group of angry racists (also natives of Louisiana) backed up their threats by pooling their funds to hire an assassin. The hit man, who was black, traveled to Alabama by train. His plan was to jump off before reaching the Tuskegee station so he could slip into town unnoticed, but it backfired when he was injured in the fall and needed medical help. Since the local hospital refused to admit blacks, he was rushed to the school infirmary. Booker T.'s doctors and nurses treated him so kindly that, in a change of heart right out of a redemption drama, the would-be murderer abandoned his mission, slipped out of the infirmary, and left town as soon as he was physically able.

Booker T. found the Democrats' subversive political agenda and the rampant violence it meant to provoke chilling. Here it was 1901, a new century. Yet African Americans were worse off than ever before. When he wrote to TR about the situation on October 23, he chose his words very carefully, knowing it was important to stay cool. If he made the problem seem too desperate, or too difficult, TR might retreat from it. "I have refrained from writing you regarding the now famous dinner which both of [sic] ate so innocently until I could get into the

South and study the situation at first hand." He went on to say that "a great deal is being made over the incident because of the elections which are now pending in several of the Southern states." As for the newspapers, they were using the story to sell copies.

Despite this, he didn't want TR to worry. "Pursue exactly the policy which you mapped out in the beginning," he urged, meaning please don't give up on your plan to promote equality in all parts of the country. Booker T. trusted that TR was "of such a nature that having once decided what is right nothing will turn you aside from pursuing that course." They had much to accomplish together, and the tempest would blow over eventually, Booker T. predicted. He sounded far more confident than he actually felt.

Because of the dinner, everything went horribly wrong, and quickly. When TR invited Booker T. to be his advisor, it was to fortify his power base in the South. Now Dixie despised him. As for Booker T., he was certain that a partnership with the President would enable him to help his race reach the highest level of government. Instead, he had lost valuable ground, his reputation was compromised, and, worse still, blacks everywhere were being held accountable for his "mistake." The situation was so contrary to their expectations, and so explosive, that neither man knew what to think or how to move forward.

There was *one* person who believed that the White House dinner was something to sing about, and that was Scott Joplin. Nineteen hundred and one had been a good year for the composer. He moved from Sedalia to St. Louis, where he was astonishingly productive. During this outburst of creativity, Joplin picked up the October 26 edition of the *Indianapolis Freeman*, a popular black newspaper, and a headline caught his eye.

PROF. WASHINGTON. DINES WITH PRESIDENT ROOSEVELT—AN
HONOR CONFERRED UPON THE LEADING NEGRO OF AMERICA.

The article covered all the whos, whats, and wheres of the story and observed that inside the White House that night "the usual order of affairs was not disturbed on account of the color of the guest of honor."

The words leapt off the page, and the seed of an idea took hold. Joplin had been thinking about writing an opera, a grand opera, rendered in his distinctive ragtime style. He admired President Roosevelt, and it occurred to him that Booker T. Washington's historic White House dinner was a worthy story to set to music.

He even had a title in mind. He would call it "A Guest of Honor."

UNDERCOVER

———•◆•———

Only two weeks had passed since the exciting moment when Booker T. proudly climbed the five stairs to the White House door, but what an exhausting and exasperating two weeks it had been. Thankfully, he was able to escape the limelight and clear his head at Tuskegee, where he was protected from the relentless assaults of reporters and racists. And at this point, he couldn't decide which of the two was worse. The dinner was a setback, to be sure, but Booker T. prided himself on his ability to find practical solutions to seemingly insolvable problems, and he was determined to fix this one as soon as possible. He had to think—and act—quickly.

Since his public affiliation with TR had ruffled so many feathers and set off such an astonishing display of fireworks, perhaps it was time to emulate freedom fighters of the past by taking the battle underground. If TR were willing, they could communicate through letters and emissaries (along with the occasional office meeting), and loud-mouthed Southern opportunists would not be the wiser. Let them rant about the evils of social equality, Booker T. resolved. While they hurled sticks and stones, he would work quietly, closely, and covertly with the President to appoint a nationwide network of qualified blacks and right-minded whites.

On October 31, Booker T. penned another letter to TR. His strategy was to be cool and rational at a time when the country was a cacophony of raised voices. "While I must confess that the outbreak over my dining with you was far beyond my expectations, I cannot help but feel that it was providential and that good is going to come out of it," he wrote. His upbeat tone inspired TR to respond in kind. "By the way, don't worry about *me*," the President answered reassuringly. "It will all come right in time, and if I have helped by ever so little 'the ascent of man' I am more than satisfied."

Both men were bluffing. They sounded calm and collected, but the letters they wrote to others betrayed their uncertainty. Nonetheless, there was work to be done and they had their own reasons for wanting to do it together. Booker T. hoped that by collaborating on TR's federal appointments he would gradually weed out the reactionary Republicans known as "lily whites," men who used politics to rob African Americans of their rights. He also wanted to replace black officeholders who were unqualified, or of "low character," with better choices. He knew that it was as important to keep the wrong man from getting a job as it was to appoint the right one. At the moment, Booker T.'s main objective was to eliminate politicians who supported lynching.

As for TR, he wanted the benefit of Booker T.'s advice and connections without the liability of an overt relationship. The lily whites were anathema to him, too, because of their racist policies, but they were also undesirable because they generally sat in the back pocket of Mark Hanna, TR's old nemesis and one of his potential rivals for the Republican nomination in the 1904 election. Replacing them would undermine Hanna's power *and* presumably win black supporters—two very good reasons to work in concert with Booker T.

Booker T. began by sending a steady flow of letters and telegrams to the White House. Some were general thoughts (he warned the President that "white men do not have an opportunity of knowing the real character and reputation of members of our race whom they recommend"), while others were practical assessments of individual candidates' virtues or vices. TR was cordial in the extreme. More important, he listened. "In Mississippi matters I am going to act exactly on the good advice you give me," he wrote appreciatively. Time and again, Booker T. got his way. Ironically, the foes of social equality were so busy protecting the sanctity of their dining rooms that they missed the more significant point that a black man was privately consulting with the President on important matters of state. Secrecy was always an advantage, so Booker T. cautioned Emmett Scott to keep these sub rosa summits with TR out of the newspapers.

TR, the foremost advocate of the strenuous life, also had a full and flashy public agenda during his first year in office. His first official "Message to Congress" in December called for regulation of commerce and industry, reform of immigration laws, and federal protection of the country's natural resources, to name a few of his progressive goals. A few months later, in February, TR took on a fire-breathing triumvirate of robber barons (J. P. Morgan, E. H. Harriman, and James Hill) who had formed a railroad monopoly called the Northern Securities Company, and his aggressive trust-busting stance sent a big "no toler-ance" message to big business. He was a fierce advocate for the building of the Panama Canal, and he personally convinced the warring factions in a momentous Pennsylvania coal strike to resolve their differences at the bargaining table. All of these ac-complishments were bold, crowd-pleasing antidotes to the bad press generated by the dinner.

One of TR's most ambitious projects that first year was the massive renovation of the White House itself. Some people were puzzled by the undertaking because, when the Roosevelts moved in, they announced that they were perfectly satisfied with their historic home. Now they were prepared to relocate for six long months while Charles McKim, one of the leading architects of the Gilded Age, would gut the building and ad-dress its many flaws.

There were several good reasons for renovating the White House. The mansion was in "a state bordering on architectural insanity," diagnosed Glenn Brown, the Washington architect who was advising McKim. There were serious structural is-sues, especially those rotting floors. Space was at a terrible pre-mium, with the family, their servants, a fleet of office workers, and all those persistent rats competing for territory.

After several months, the Roosevelts may have come to the conclusion that their new home was uninhabitable. On the other hand, they were a hardy bunch who had adapted to fre-quent moves in the past. Perhaps it was the ongoing tempest surrounding his dinner with Booker T. that inspired TR to view the building in a new light. Some said the "sanctity" of the White House had been violated by Booker T.'s egregious crossing of the color line; others believed that TR's nod to social equality was all the more meaningful because it took place in the historic dwelling. Whether or not Americans agreed with Booker T.'s right to dine with the President, they discussed the significance of the setting. *Where* the dinner occurred was as important as the meal itself.

If the White House was so beloved by Americans and held so much meaning for them, why was it falling apart, the President had to ask himself. Immediately after taking office, he polished the building's image by giving it a new name and a quick facelift. However, it would take nothing less than a substantial physical makeover to reclaim the White House's dignity and standing as a national icon. TR overheard a tour guide sarcastically call the building the "Booker Washington café." The President expressed his displeasure and put a stop to the man's derogatory comments, but words were not enough.

TR appealed to Congress for funds and won $540,000 for the renovation, which was scheduled to start that June. McKim and his crew commenced work, and the race was on to complete the job in time for the start of the social season the following December. McKim built the West Wing for the President's offices, remodeled the White House's second floor for the family, rerouted the visitor entrance to the basement, and enlarged the State Dining Room to accommodate more guests, which eliminated the need to set up unsightly spillover tables in the drafty hallway.

The result was a mansion fit for a president, and a splendid backdrop for elaborate entertainments. Post-renovation, the Roosevelts fervently embraced pomp and circumstance as their signature style of entertaining. Trumpets signaled their impending arrival in the Front Hall. While onlookers watched from below, the President and his First Lady majestically descended the Grand Staircase. "The President is distinctly tending—or trying—to make a 'court,' " the writer Henry James observed with surprise the first time he was invited to a diplomatic reception at the White House. James found the experience so imperial that he dubbed Roosevelt "Theodore Rex."

Everyone was talking about the *new* White House, which meant that maybe, finally, they might stop talking about what happened in the *old* one. All these changes notwithstanding, the infamous dinner would simply not go away. James K. Vardaman, the Mississippi Dixiecrat whose nickname was the "Great White Chief," was not fooled by the White House's spiffy new look. He accused the President's house of being "so saturated with the odor of the nigger that the rats have taken refuge in the stable."

His fellow Democrats decided that a provocative picture commemorating the event on a campaign button could be worth a thousand votes. The image guaranteed to raise the ire of conservative Southerners was the sight of TR and Booker T. sitting together at a table under a banner proclaiming "Equality," and that was the precise visual that Democrat Arthur Gorman used to promote his successful bid for a Maryland U.S. Senate seat in 1902. There was no end in sight to the postprandial mudslinging emanating from the South.

Regardless, TR and Booker T. forged ahead with their plan to work together. When a new collector of customs was needed in Charleston, South Carolina, Booker T. recommended Dr. William Crum, the worthiest of the candidates as well as a successful black physician, who was both a native of the city and a staunch member of the Republican Party. "He is as far different, in my mind, from the old irresponsible and purchasable Negro politician as day from night," Booker T. enthused to TR. Placing an African American in the collectorship of a major

Southern port would be an audacious move on the President's part, but TR was committed to proving that the door of opportunity was open to qualified men of any color. He submitted Dr. Crum's name to the Senate for confirmation, only to find himself at the center of another racial storm.

Charleston was the stomping ground of South Carolina senator Pitchfork Ben Tillman, who had been furious ever since TR barred him from the White House—the same White House where a black man had been an invited guest. Tillman and a large body of local white supremacists had no intention of allowing a Negro to assume a position of authority in their city. "That ain't the kind of place we believe in putting the black man in down in South Carolina, and we have been dealing with them long enough to know the best way to treat them," he argued none too eloquently. What followed was a long and arduous game of block and tackle. For three long years, starting in 1902, TR submitted Crum's name to the Senate, and for three long years, Southern politicians saw to it that the appointment was stalled. TR repeatedly used his presidential powers to give Dr. Crum the position on an interim basis, but, pending confirmation, the poor man was not allowed to collect a salary, and had to see patients on his day off to support himself.

Crum's confirmation was very important to Booker T. He assigned lobbyists to various senators to win them over to Crum's side, using his own money to fund their work, and he oversaw a pro-Crum publicity campaign. Crum himself wasn't convinced that winning the battle was worth such an immense investment of time, money, and effort—but Booker T. was. He wanted a black Republican in a significant post in the South, and he was willing to do anything to accomplish that goal.

But at what cost? Between the White House dinner and the

ongoing Crum debacle, TR was persona non grata in the South. An auditorium of angry Southerners hissed at the sight of his photograph, and officials in South Carolina warned that they could not guarantee his safety if he dared to attend a trade exposition in Charleston. With the upcoming presidential election at stake, TR's supporters decided to lay the groundwork for a renovation far more difficult than remodeling the White House: they set out to repair the President's tainted reputation. If they couldn't put an end to the damaging chatter about the dinner, perhaps they could tweak history *just* a little to make the incident more palatable. Their first thought was to look for evidence of an African American who was entertained at the White House while a *Democrat* was in office. That way, TR would not be the first to commit the breech. But their findings were not very convincing. The rumor that Grover Cleveland had invited Frederick Douglass to his wedding reception prompted the former president to flatly deny the accusation, and that was the end of that.

The next attempt at damage control was predicated on the notion that the meal in question wasn't a sit-down dinner at all, but rather an impromptu business lunch in TR's office! According to the new gospel proffered by revisionist Republicans, TR and Booker T. had been engrossed in a routine midday meeting when their conversation segued into a spartan, desktop lunch. Contrary to public opinion, there was no dining room, no wife (or daughter) in attendance, and, by the time TR's apologists finished their tall tale, there was barely any food. This account was wildly improbable, but the hope was that some gullible Southerners would swallow it and decide that TR wasn't so bad after all. Initially the story did not gain much traction (suspicious minds wondered why TR didn't clarify the nature of the meal earlier). But as time passed, and memories failed, the concept of a lunch, an unpremeditated, "hurried meal," took hold.

Booker T. had no illusions about spinning the dinner in his favor. Ever since that fateful meal, his name was invoked when a Negro crossed one of those imaginary color lines. TR's New Year's reception in 1903 was a perfect example. It was an annual event for federal officeholders, an opportunity for them to shake hands with the President and enjoy a glass of punch. This year jaws dropped at the sight of black faces in the crowd. African Americans who worked in low-visibility jobs such as registrar of deeds, or registrar of the Treasury, were always *invited* to these affairs, but normally they had the good sense to stay home. Tonight they showed up in force, and, shockingly, several had their wives in tow.

"Coons Lionized At White House," reported the *Atlanta Constitution* with its usual crude hysteria. "The Presence of Negro Women In Low Neck Gowns Created A Sensation," noted the salacious headline in the *Galveston Daily News*. Politicians who hailed from the South "left the mansion in high dudgeon" because they were so offended by the presence of the black guests, who kept to themselves and had a "lonesome time" in their corner of the East Room.

They may have been "lonesome," but they were there. The dinner set a precedent, and there was no going back. Blacks had the right to accept invitations from the President, and they were doing just that, despite the South's efforts to keep them in their place. When Senator Tillman and his ilk began reciting their litany of reasons to boycott the newly tainted White House— *again*—their protests sounded feeble, even stale. Booker T. was secretly pleased by such stories, even when they provoked a fresh round of accusations about the damage caused by that dinner. It meant that, against all odds, African Americans were making progress.

Some attempts to disgrace Booker T. were almost funny. Lulu Hadley, a white chambermaid at the English Hotel in Indianapolis, refused to make Booker T.'s bed when he was a guest, claiming that no respectable white woman would clean up after a "nigger." She was fired as a result, but the enterprising Lulu wasn't out of work a day. She immediately turned the situation to her advantage by becoming an advocate for white supremacy. The Negro was "a brute, ready to kill you when your back is turned," she asserted in a three-page editorial in the *Philadelphia North American*. She admired Booker T. Washington "in his place," she admitted grudgingly. Unfortunately, she complained, "he is out of it most of the time."

Lulu's writing was remarkably sophisticated, and the points she made about Roosevelt's mistake in inviting a black man to dine (he should be impeached!) and Booker T.'s crafty aspirations for social equality sounded suspiciously like propaganda from a higher source than a chambermaid in a second-rate hotel. The fact that she received large cash "donations" from benefactors in Louisiana, Texas, and other Southern states suggested that she may have been paid to play the part of the outraged gentlewoman.

An amusing incident occurred when Booker T. was on a speaking tour of Florida and he ran into an old white Southerner at a train station. The man greeted him with great respect, saying, "Suh, I am glad to meet you. Always wanted to shake your hand, suh. I think, suh, you're the greatest man in America."

"Oh no," demurred Booker T. He was surprised and flattered

by the compliment, but he immediately suggested that President Roosevelt was the better man. "No, suh!" was the rapid retort. "Not by a jugful; I used to think so, but since he invited you to dinner I think he's a . . . scoundrel!"

The *Baltimore Herald* found the anecdote hilarious and printed a version of the encounter. Booker T. sent it to TR with a note explaining, "This is a true story." TR howled when he read it and immediately wrote back to Booker T., saying, "I think that is one of the most delightful things I have ever read. It is almost *too good to believe. What a splendid confusion of ideas it does show!*"

On February 18, 1903, the ever-expanding body of Washington-Roosevelt folklore took a distinguished turn when Scott Joplin registered his ragtime opera, *A Guest of Honor*. According to Joplin biographer Ed Berlin, the finished work was an all-singing, all-dancing tribute to the White House dinner. Joplin had already dedicated an upbeat two-step rag called "The Strenuous Life" (after the title of one of Roosevelt's most popular books) to the President. But *A Guest of Honor* was a far more ambitious undertaking. The opera called for a cast of thirty and featured elaborate musical numbers, including "The Dude's Parade" and "Patriotic Patrol." Joplin booked a tour and made plans to play venues in Illinois, Kentucky, Missouri, and Nebraska. While advertisements never specified the exact subject of the show, probably because it was controversial, Berlin surmises that Joplin pulled his story straight from the headlines, of which there were so many.

Unfortunately, the opera disappeared forever at the height of its 1903 tour. Disaster struck in Pittsburgh, Kansas, according to Berlin. Someone stole Joplin's money and he was unable to pay either the company or his own expenses. His possessions, including the music and libretto for the opera, were seized by creditors. There was talk of a black trunk filled with music and mementos that never found its way back to Joplin. Only an entry at the U.S. Copyright Office (the opera itself was mailed, but never arrived) and a smattering of tour advertisements attested to *A Guest of Honor*'s existence.

In the spring of 1903, the dark clouds that seemed to follow Booker T. everywhere suddenly parted and revealed a shiny silver lining. Andrew Carnegie, one of the world's wealthiest men, decided that Booker T. was the "Modern Moses." He believed that "the serious race problem of the South" could be "solved wisely only through Mr. Washington's policy of education." The same man who gave Tuskegee a library endowed the school with an additional $600,000, the equivalent of $15 million today. Carnegie's gift came with only one stipulation: money was to be set aside to support Booker T. and his family for the rest of their lives. "I wish that great good man to be free to devote himself to his great mission," the philanthropist decreed.

After decades of pawning watches and knocking on doors, Booker T. had been given a generous measure of financial security. He vowed that the gift would inspire him to work harder than ever before, for his school, for his people, and for the election of Theodore Roosevelt, the man who could help him achieve his goals.

In the months leading up to the election on November 8, 1904, Booker T. was in constant contact with TR, giving him practical advice about racial issues and voting patterns in key states. He even wrote and distributed campaign materials endorsing Roosevelt's candidacy, although sometimes he insisted on remaining anonymous. In one lengthy editorial, he stated that "no man . . . ever went into the White House with a keener desire to be of real and permanent service to the former slave states than Mr. Roosevelt." TR, who was famously impulsive, benefited from Booker T.'s careful and often cautious advice, and came to depend on him. When considering an issue for the Republican convention, the President wrote to Booker T. to say that "the question is one of such importance that I should not be willing to discuss it without going over the whole subject with you. . . ."

The presidential election inspired a new wave of dinner propaganda. There were the usual malicious cartoons, including a billboard in Baltimore that showed an oversized Roosevelt extending his hand to a flashy, shifty-looking black man who was meant to be Booker T. The tagline was "He's good enough for me." But in the spring of 1904, racism and technology became odd bedfellows when veteran minstrel show performer Lew Dockstader experimented with a new way of playing dirty politics.

The portly king of "coon songs" set out to make a short film satirizing the Roosevelt-Washington dinner. In this turn-of-the-century comedy sketch, a black-faced Dockstader played Booker T., while another member of his acting troop portrayed TR. Their slapstick antics, performed on the steps of the Capitol building, were filmed by a man with a Kinetoscope, an early version of a movie camera. Spectators watched as Dockstader feigned falling to the ground and was helped up by a concerned TR look-alike. The fake president handed the "bogus Booker" a cigar and invited him to use his carriage.

When Patrolman Jones rode by on his bicycle and saw the crowd, he realized that one of the actors was meant to be TR and reported the suspicious incident to Major Sylvester at the White House. Acting on his orders, police hunted down Dockstader, held him for questioning, and seized his film. The impresario argued he was not trying to stir up "the race question" for political reasons (although rumor had it that his backers were Democrats who planned on using the finished product as a campaign tool). He was simply making an entertainment, he insisted. But his protests fell on deaf ears, especially after it was revealed that his longtime collaborator, composer Jean Havez (whose latest effort was the tune "Goodbye Booze"), was working on a new song for Dockstader called "Won't You Come and Dine with Me." Free speech was not a consideration when the film was handed over to an outraged President Roosevelt and destroyed before anyone else could see it.

Creative smear campaigns notwithstanding, 7,630,457 Americans voted for Roosevelt instead of Democrat Alton Parker, the lackluster candidate who was said to have *lost* the election by a landslide. For most people, casting a ballot in a presidential election was a routine matter, but for a black man in Alabama in 1904, it was a matter of life and death. Despite threats from a local Democratic congressman who hinted it would be no great loss if an anarchist were to blow up TR and his black dining companion, Booker T. proudly voted for President Roosevelt at the Tuskegee poll. Predictably, other Southerners preferred TR's opponent.

When TR received news of his victory on election night, he impulsively issued a statement that shocked his family and supporters. "Under no circumstances will I be a candidate for or accept another nomination," he said, explaining that he considered the first three and a half years of his inherited presidency to be an official term. He subscribed to the custom of restricting a president to two terms, although there was room for interpretation in his situation. Edith suspected that her husband would come to regret his hasty words.

Political insiders rushed to praise Booker T. for the part he played in the President's triumph. "You yourself must come in for congratulations, too," wrote lawyer Robert Terrell. "For your fame was constantly linked with the President's in the campaign . . . you were almost as much as issue as he was." But Booker T. did not presume to be a part of a parade, or any other inaugural celebrations. He requested two tickets for the reviewing stand, happy to watch TR from the safety of the sidelines.

Shortly before TR's inauguration, a student named Reginald Hodgson stepped up to the blackboard at the Western High School in Washington, DC. A vocabulary class was in session and he had been asked to use the word *debased* in a sentence. He thought for a moment before writing, "Roosevelt debased himself by eating with a nigger." Edith C. Wescott, the outraged principal, wanted to expel Hodgson immediately, but the superintendent of schools argued that such a move would "have a bad effect on public sentiment." Instead they came up with a fitting punishment. They decided to deprive him of the privilege of marching with his classmates in President Roosevelt's inaugural parade.

BLINDSIDED

———•◆•———

It was full speed ahead for TR in 1905. The second-term president knew that whatever he intended to accomplish had to be done in the next four years, so he moved quickly and decisively. Despite the fact that wealthy and powerful industrialists had contributed large sums of money to his campaign, TR wasted no time in proclaiming that Big Business was one of his targets for reform. "We bought the s.o.b. and then he didn't stay bought," financial titan Henry Clay Frick complained. TR godfathered the Hepburn Act to curb runaway pricing on the country's railroads and used the Pure Food and Drug Act to regulate dangerous patent medicines and other ingestibles. After reading *The Jungle*, Upton Sinclair's exposé of the meatpacking industry, TR instituted the Meat Inspection Act. And an ardent conservationist, he established national monuments, including the Grand Canyon, set up wildlife preserves, founded the U.S. Forest Service, and placed hundreds of thousands of acres of land under federal protection.

No problem was too large or too small for the energetic president. TR tackled the ongoing crisis of the war between Russia and Japan, inviting diplomats from those countries to meet with him on a yacht in Oyster Bay to discuss a treaty. He even found time to address a pressing problem involving college football. The sport was so dangerous (eighteen young men died in one season) that TR urged colleges to establish rules to make the gridiron safer. Thanks to him, gang tackling was banned, and other reforms were introduced that enabled the sport to flourish.

———— • ◆ • ————

THEN THERE WAS the matter of race. TR and Booker T. met frequently at the White House. TR eagerly sought Booker T.'s advice on upcoming speeches, legislation, appointments—anything that pertained to blacks in the South. Booker T. was so caught up in the success of their liaison—the smooth exchange of information, ideas, and opinions ("My dear Mr. Washington, Will you read the enclosed and send it back with any comments?"), the wildly complimentary letters, and the intoxicating feeling of power that came with unobstructed access to a dynamic world leader—that he didn't see trouble coming from unexpected directions.

After forty-eight years in the trenches, Booker T. was an old hand at deflecting assaults from the South. He knew how to deal with the racist rants of a Tillman or a Vardaman. He was a mastermind (with the help of Emmett Scott) at manipulating the black and white media. And he was a brilliant strategist who skillfully navigated the increasingly treacherous roads to racial uplift. Yet somehow, Booker T. underestimated one of the greatest threats to his work, and, ultimately, to his legacy: the enemy within.

W. E. B. Du Bois, who was born in relative comfort and freedom in the North, and Booker T., who famously pulled himself up from slavery, were never able to see the world from the same point of view. Nonetheless, they managed to maintain a cordial, if somewhat cautious, relationship until 1901, when Du Bois was one of the only critics to write a negative review of *Up from Slavery*. "Among the Negroes, Mr. Washington is still far from a popular leader," he wrote, oddly ignoring the fact that Booker T. had been the acknowledged "Moses" of his race for over fifteen years. Du Bois also made the condescending observation that "nature must needs make men a little narrow to give them force," meaning that if Booker T. succeeded in achieving his goals, it was because he didn't aim high enough.

His hostility seemed to intensify *after* Booker T. cemented his relationship with TR, and the White House dinner may have played a part in accelerating the rift. In Du Bois's mind, the dinner emphasized Booker T.'s worst flaws—his preoccupation with power, especially *white* power; his obsession with self-promotion; and his hypocrisy in dining at the President's table while urging other blacks to be satisfied with the scraps that came with social inequality. Perhaps Du Bois considered himself a better choice than the controversial wizard from Tuskegee for the role of presidential guest of honor.

In 1903, Du Bois posed a more overt challenge to Booker T.'s leadership in his book *The Souls of Black Folk*. His essay "On Mr. Booker T. Washington and Others" grudgingly acknowledged his subject's accomplishments at the same time that it berated him for standing in the way of progress. Booker T.'s "gospel of work and money" was "stunting the growth of Negro education" argued Du Bois, who believed that there was a black intelligentsia, the "talented tenth," he called them, who deserved a proper liberal arts education rather than mere technical training. Thanks to Booker T., he suggested, industrial schools such as Tuskegee were perceived as the *only* form of Negro education worth funding. But "Was there ever a nation on God's fair earth civilized from the bottom upward?" Du Bois asked. Where would the race's leaders come from if all blacks were busy making bricks and sowing fields?

It was a good question. But, brilliant as he was, Du Bois oversimplified and perhaps deliberately misrepresented his rival's philosophy. Booker T. focused on African Americans who were at the "bottom" because he believed it was more important for an emerging people to learn healthy practices and how to support themselves than to speak French or read Latin. But Booker T. never imposed limitations on blacks who aspired to accomplish *more,* and Du Bois knew that. The two men had solid ideological differences: Booker T. advocated patience, hard work, and even compromise in the interests of survival, while Du Bois called for activism and agitation at all costs. Both approaches were valid, and the men might have been twice as effective in building a future for African Americans if they had found a way to work together, with Booker T. leading blacks out of slavery and Du Bois ushering them into the new century.

The British writer and intellectual H. G. Wells offered an interesting analysis of the Washington/Du Bois dichotomy. "Mr. Washington has states craft," he said admiringly after visiting America in 1906. "He looks before and after, and plans and keeps his counsel with the scope and range of a statesman . . . his is a mind that can grasp the situation and destinies of a people." But Du Bois, he said, "conceals his passionate resentment all too thinly." Booker T. was not blameless, and Du Bois was right to criticize him for manipulating the black press and dispensing patronage through the "Tuskegee Machine." Yet there were times when Du Bois seemed more troubled by Booker T.'s celebrity than his machinations. With the formation of civil rights groups such as the Niagara Movement in 1905 and the National Association for the Advancement of Colored People in 1909, Du Bois and the like-minded African Americans who rallied to his side challenged Booker T.'s hegemony and set out to undermine his power.

In 1906, an incident in Brownsville, Texas, set off a chain of events that proved more harmful to Booker T. than anything Du Bois might say or do. On August 13, Brownsville residents were startled by the sound of gunfire. Under the cover of darkness, an unseen assailant killed a white bartender and injured a policeman. Racial tensions were high in the Southern town because Fort Brown, home of the Army's Twenty-Fifth Infantry, housed several companies of black soldiers. The locals didn't like having uniformed African Americans in their midst and treated them as outcasts. That very evening, black soldiers were blamed for the shootings, despite the fact that white officers insisted the soldiers were locked in their barracks at the time.

"Evidence" (a handful of bullet casings) was found or possibly planted at the crime scene. The black soldiers were ordered to name the wrongdoers in their company, but they refused to cooperate. When the incident was brought to the attention of President Roosevelt, he was so infuriated by their willful silence that he threatened all 167 men with dishonorable discharge, a punishment that would rob them of their jobs, their pensions, and their dignity. Despite TR's tirade, the black soldiers maintained their silence.

Booker T. watched apprehensively as the incident unfolded. He pleaded with TR not to do anything rash, hoping that his influence would work its usual magic. "There is some information which I must put before you before you take a final action," he wrote urgently. Perhaps Booker T. had consulted his own sources in Brownsville and had light to shed on the situation. Or he may have wanted to caution the President against making a move that was unfair and would alienate his black constituents. Even if a few soldiers were guilty, which seemed unlikely because the evidence was so sketchy, why would the President punish the entire company without benefit of a proper investigation or trial? TR refused to listen to him. "I could not possibly refrain from acting as regards those colored soldiers," he answered imperiously. "You can not have any information to give me privately to which I could pay heed."

Army officers who supported TR's actions condemned the black soldiers for behavior they described as out-and-out "cockiness." The reason for the men's insolence, they said, was "the luncheon given to Booker T. Washington by the President at the White House." Amazingly, six years after it took place, the White House meal was back in the headlines.

Ben Tillman agreed that the meal, whether lunch, dinner, or breakfast, was the root of this particular evil, and he expounded on his theory in a fiery speech he delivered to Congress. The episode in Brownsville was TR's fault from start to finish, because he pushed "Negroes"—in this case, those black soldiers—into places they didn't belong, just as he did with Booker T. "In recognizing Booker Washington socially, Mr. Roosevelt had offended 7,000,000 white people in the South and two-thirds of the people in the North," he reminded his listeners, exaggerating the numbers to make a point.

TR was astounded. That dinner again! The reservations he expressed in 1901 were turning into feelings of out-and-out regret. TR relished fighting battles that could be won, but it was becoming clear to him that no victory was forthcoming in the tired old race war in the South. Suddenly the international front presented more enticing challenges. He won the Nobel Peace Prize in 1906 for his efforts to bring peace to Russia and Japan, and he was the force behind the completion of the Panama Canal—"bully" endeavors that could change the world. The South, he feared, would never change.

As threatened, TR impulsively issued an order to dismiss the men, a move that won favor among Southern whites. However, he wisely delayed releasing the news until the day *after* the midterm elections of 1906. As Booker T. predicted, the Brownsville incident made TR extremely unpopular with blacks, and they would have expressed their hostility by voting against the Republican Party if they had known about TR's unfair treatment of the black soldiers.

African American ministers cried foul, insisting that the President would never treat white soldiers so unjustly. "The black man and woman do not want social equality, they want justice and equity," they insisted. As for that White House dinner, African Americans concurred that "the President might eat with a thousand Booker T. Washingtons and it would not hurt us as much as this action." In their minds, President Roosevelt was "our Judas." The black community in New York swore they would "seek revenge at the ballot box" next time around.

Booker T. tried to calm the waters by urging his people to stop carrying on about Brownsville. "Civilization soon tires of a race . . . that continually whines and complains . . . the country will not tolerate any element in the population abusing and cursing the Chief Executive," he advised. But blacks wondered why he was sidestepping the issue of TR's culpability. (Roosevelt's mistake was confirmed in 1970, when *The Brownsville Raid*, a book by John Downing Weaver, provoked an official investigation that revealed the evidence had been falsified. The Brownsville soldiers were exonerated.)

Booker T. refused to pass judgment because he was more concerned about preserving his relationship with TR than speaking out against him. He did not realize that TR was backing away from the very race issues that had brought them together, and had moved on to more achievable goals. By not taking a stand on Brownsville, and by not publicly opposing TR, he left himself vulnerable to the criticism Du Bois and other detractors had been making for quite some time. Perhaps Booker T. Washington was no longer the right man to lead nine million black Americans.

SLIPPING AWAY

———•◆•———

TR endorsed Secretary of War William Howard Taft as the Republican candidate in the upcoming 1908 presidential election. Taft was an affable man who seemed to be a good choice, although he was portly and far less energetic than TR, who advised him to spend less time on the golf course and more on politics. Thanks to the counsel and efforts of his popular "godfather," Taft won in November, and it was time for TR to step aside. He joked about his readiness to leave the White House, claiming that Americans were "sick of looking at my grin and they are sick of hearing what Alice had for breakfast," but he seemed a little melancholy about his impending retirement from public life. Alice wittily summed up TR's relationship with the presidential limelight when she observed, "My father always wanted to be the corpse at every funeral, the bride at every wedding, and the baby at every christening." If this were even somewhat true, how would the former chief executive fare in private life as "Colonel Roosevelt"?

Alice understood TR's conflicting emotions because she shared them. Improbably, given their frequent squabbles, father and daughter were becoming more and more alike. Both were strong-willed ("Alice and I are toughs," TR said proudly), outspoken, quick-witted, impulsive, imperious, and addicted to attention—all characteristics that made them inexhaustible fodder for reporters. Alice had emerged from her rocky adolescence as "Princess Alice," an international celebrity with adoring fans. A color fittingly called "Alice Blue" was named for her, and songs, including "Alice, Where Art Thou?" were written in her honor. Recognizing his daughter's star power, TR sent her as his emissary on a diplomatic cruise to Japan in 1905, during which time she was gifted with silks, pearls, and ultimately a husband. She enjoyed a shipboard romance with Republican congressman Nicholas Longworth, an older man with a reputation for being a playboy, and their White House wedding the following year was a national event.

Now that the Roosevelts were leaving the White House, Alice was nostalgic about her time there and resented the Taft takeover. Rumor had it that she buried a voodoo doll of Mrs. Taft on the grounds and perfected a wickedly funny impersonation of the new First Lady—pranks that prompted the Tafts to bar her from presidential events. Despite the fact that she was no longer the First Daughter, Princess Alice could always be counted on for a quip and a scandal.

TR needn't have worried about fading into obscurity after retirement. His reputation continued to grow after he left office, leading one admirer to describe him as a show-stopping one-man circus. "He is the whole three rings, ringmaster, and elephant," said the fan. His first post-presidency adventure was an African safari, a yearlong trek that took him to dangerous places such as the Congo and Khartoum. Accompanied by his son Kermit and a group of hunters and scientists, TR gathered thousands of specimens to ship home to the Smithsonian and the American Museum of Natural History. He killed his first lion and his first elephant, and slew hundreds of other "big game" animals, including rhinoceroses, buffaloes, hippopotamuses, zebras, and giraffes.

TR maintained his breakneck schedule when he returned to America in March 1910. He wrote a book about his trip, worked as contributing editor of the *Outlook,* served on Tuskegee's Board of Directors, and contemplated his next moves. Gradually, one thought supplanted all others: TR wanted to be president again. He was not happy with Taft and feared that, under his leadership, the Republican Party was becoming too conservative. While TR did not want to appear too eager to run, he prepared an answer for those who might wonder why he changed his mind about serving a third term. He was against the idea of a *consecutive* third term, he explained, but an additional term was acceptable. "Frequently, when asked to take another cup of coffee at breakfast, I say 'No thank you.' . . . This doesn't mean that I intend never to take another cup of coffee during my life." In his mind, the Taft interruption left him free to run again.

TR threw his hat into the political ring, but, much to his surprise, Republican party bosses threw it right back at him. They were determined to support the incumbent in 1912 and believed that TR's sudden bid for the nomination would divide and possibly destroy the GOP. Their opposition prompted TR to take his campaign to the people. He accused Taft of being a "fathead" and a "puzzlewit," while Taft branded him a "dangerous egoist" and even a "demagogue." At the convention in

Chicago, officials used loopholes to rob TR of the delegates he had amassed, enabling Taft to win the Republican nomination.

Roosevelt's outraged supporters retaliated by founding the National Progressive Party and naming him as their first presidential candidate. TR was so committed to winning that he refused to stop campaigning even when a crazed, would-be assassin shot him in the chest while he was en route to a political rally. "It takes more than that to kill a bull moose," TR proclaimed from the podium, the bullet still lodged in his sternum. TR and his "Bull Moose" Party performed admirably on Election Day of 1912, winning 4,119,538 votes—694,558 more than Taft—but 2,173,916 fewer than the Democratic candidate, Woodrow Wilson, whose 6,293,454 votes secured him four years in the White House.

A disappointed TR immediately turned his attention to a new adventure—a nine-month trip to South America with Kermit to explore the Amazon's treacherous and uncharted "River of Doubt." The expedition was far more arduous than he ever imagined, and after surviving hostile natives, tropical diseases, punishing terrain, deprivation, and every manner of physical hardship, TR emerged from the jungle with a tenuous hold on life. He was fifty-seven pounds lighter, weak from gastrointestinal ailments, virulent infections, and malaria, and happy to be reunited with Edith and his family at Sagamore Hill. TR told a friend that the trip had cut his life short by ten years. He recovered, but after South America, the legend of the rough-riding Bull Moose was much more powerful than the man himself.

Like TR, Booker T. was slipping from his former position of power. His decline began with the Brownsville incident in 1906 and TR's departure from the White House two years later. Taft invited him to continue in his role as advisor, but it was a hollow gesture. Ultimately the new president ignored Booker T., and on the rare occasion when he invoked him, he did more harm than good. Taft told a group of African Americans in California that Booker T. was "one of the greatest men of this and the last century, white or black, because he has the courage to tell you the truth" about "the one way by which you can earn your place in the community," meaning, stick to industrial education and don't aim too high—a message that sounded distinctly like the door of opportunity slamming shut.

In 1911, during one of his frequent trips to New York City, Booker T. found himself embroiled in a scandal that threatened to be his undoing. He claimed to be looking for an auditor who worked for Tuskegee when he studied the directory of an apartment building on Manhattan's Upper West Side. A resident named Henry Ulrich didn't like seeing a black man loitering in his vestibule, so he verbally abused Booker T. and beat him with a cane.

The police intervened, and once they established Booker T.'s identity, the incident seemed to be an open-and-shut case. The neighborhood was seedy, and his assailant was a man of questionable character. But Ulrich's girlfriend testified that Booker T. had the nerve to call her, a white woman he didn't know, "sweetheart." That indignity sparked the attack, she insisted.

Booker T. was an exceedingly polite man who was unlikely to speak to a man he didn't know, let alone a white woman. But the case started to become complicated when it was established that Tuskegee's auditor lived in New Jersey, not New York. Booker T. insisted he had been given the wrong address, but couldn't prove it or offer any other explanation. Ulrich was tried for the attack, but acquitted. The fact that one of the judges on the case may have been a career racist didn't alter the fact that Booker T.'s reputation was compromised. There were unsubstantiated rumors that he had been drunk, or visiting a prostitute, and Du Bois was quick to suggest that Booker T. was on his way to a clandestine tryst with a white woman of ill repute when the incident took place. There was not a shred of evidence to support this or any other theory; Booker T. seemed to be in the wrong place at the wrong time.

Booker T. was fifty-five years old, an esteemed educator, statesman, author, husband, father, grandfather (Portia married a black architect, had three children, and taught piano), and beloved role model for blacks everywhere. He had been so for decades. However, at the first accusation of impropriety from an aggrieved white woman and her hotheaded consort, his status was challenged. His mistake was to go someplace he wasn't invited. The scandal prompted the Hotel Manhattan, Booker T.'s preferred lodging in the city, to close its doors to him forever.

Yet Booker T. carried on. Clad in his simple suit and worn hat, his health failing, he continued to ride the rails, making one more speech against injustice, seeking one more donation for Tuskegee. He won a major victory for black education when he convinced Sears Roebuck magnate Julius Rosenwald to fund more than five thousand schools for African American students throughout the South. Rosenwald wanted to donate modern, prefabricated buildings made by Sears to house the classrooms, but Booker T. stuck to his Tuskegee philosophy of self-help: blacks would use Rosenwald's money to erect their own schools, and the buildings would be simple and serviceable. Otherwise white people might "have a feeling that the colored people are getting ahead of them," Booker T. explained.

He may have been his diplomatic self about the Rosenwald schools, but friends and foes observed that Booker T. was increasingly outspoken about racial prejudice. He publicly objected to the inequities African Americans endured when they tried to use public transportation, rent housing, obtain an education or a job, vote, or go about the business of daily life. "Is the Negro Having a Fair Chance?" he asked forthrightly in an article he wrote for *Century Magazine,* and the answer he offered was a resounding "No." If Booker T. had more to say about what was wrong, it was probably because his declining power left him with less to lose, suggests biographer Robert J. Norrell.

When Woodrow Wilson became president in 1912, he didn't even go through the motions of consulting Booker T. His administration had its own ideas about the country's race problem: the new president (who was endorsed by W. E. B. Du Bois during the election) believed that segregation was the solution. For the first time, applicants for federal jobs were required to submit photographs—an easy way to determine the race of prospective employees. It was for the black man's own good, Wilson maintained, as he separated whites from blacks in government workplaces, restrooms, and lunchrooms . . . even in the staff dining facilities at the White House, where Possum Jerry and Annie O'Rourke once sat at the same kitchen table.

Now the only images of whites and blacks sitting together at the White House were rude and satiric. An author named George Corbin Perine used the pseudonym "Mr. George Washington Dabney (A Gent'man ob Color)" when he published a work called *De Roosterfelt Book.* Perine was a poet and an art dealer who claimed George Washington as an ancestor and sympathized with the South. He was enraged by some ungallant remarks TR may or may not have made about Southern women (supposedly, he called them "anarchists"), so he decided to fight back with his pamphlet. A thousand copies were printed and sold for a penny each. But if Perrine refused to use his real name on this title, it was because the book was so offensive. The subject of *De Roosterfelt Book* was the Washington/ Roosevelt dinner, and in Perine's hands, the depiction of this event was more ribald and incendiary than ever. Its title page showed the two men sitting at the same small round table that had appeared in other cartoons memorializing the event. Five champagne bottles and a large roasted turkey covered the table. A huge napkin tucked around his substantial neck and a glass in his hand, "Booker T." (who actually did not resemble the man at all) looked very happy and more than a little bestial. An equally delighted "TR" (rendered perfectly) sat beside him, his glass raised in a toast.

The picture illustrated a poem titled "My Dinner at the White House." Three pages of verse described the details of the historic meal. But the most hateful rhyme in the odd little book was the one that invited readers to imagine "A Nigger President." With Negro-lovers like Roosevelt in force, the poem suggested, it was inevitable. To reinforce his point, Dabney included a cartoon that showed a well-dressed black woman— "De furs' one in de lan', A-standing' at de White House doo', A-waibin' her black han'!" The partnership that was meant to place Booker T. and TR in the constellation of great freedom fighters, alongside Abraham Lincoln and Frederick Douglass, had been reduced to two cartoon figures in a racist comic strip.

EULOGIES

———•◆•———

Booker T. Washington liked to say, "I was born in the South, have lived all my life in the South, and expect to die and be buried in the South." His wish came true on November 14, 1915, when he quietly passed away at Tuskegee. He had been ill for some months with indigestion, kidney trouble, headaches, and what was termed at the time a "nervous breakdown."

Newspapers all over the country reported his demise, and the profusion of headlines in the *Washington Post*, the *New York Herald Tribune*, the *New York Times*, the *Boston Globe*, the *Boston Herald*, the *Chicago Tribune*, and other outlets equaled the media storm that followed his controversial dinner with Theodore Roosevelt. Despite the flood of obituaries, the *Atlanta Constitution* was one of the only papers to mention that Booker T. was the first "Negro" to dine at the White House. Ironically, the story referred to the meal as "lunch," even though the *Constitution* had printed a detailed account of the dinner in its exclusive coverage only fourteen years earlier.

"Born a Slave, Dies a Celebrity," wrote the *Hartford Courant*. Northerners and Southerners alike paid homage to the man ordinary folk called "Booker T.," but his most eloquent admirer was his old friend TR. The former president was called upon to speak at Booker T.'s memorial service at Tuskegee. "Booker T. Washington," he said, "did justice, loved mercy, and walked humbly. His every step helped others." All fine sentiments, beautifully expressed by a great man. But the tribute Booker T. himself would have valued most was TR's public endorsement of their long-standing collaboration.

TR stated that he always trusted Dr. Washington's advice because he "knew that he would not give me one word based on a selfish motive." Instead, Booker T. "would state what in his best judgment was in the best interests of the people of the entire country." And while various memorials were in the works (including a $2 million endowment fund for Tuskegee), TR expressed the hope and belief that "his monument lies in the minds and memories of those whom he has served and uplifted."

Predictably, W. E. B. Du Bois refused to pay unadulterated tribute to the lost leader. In an article he wrote for the *Crisis*, Du Bois made it clear that he didn't consider death an excuse for Booker T. to escape censure. Yes, he deserved praise for being "the most distinguished man, white or black, who has come out of the South since the Civil War." And yes, there was no doubt that he helped blacks appreciate the "pressing necessity of economic development," that he "emphasized technical education," and that he promoted "understanding between the white and darker races."

But Du Bois also voiced disapproval. "In stern justice," he

wrote, "we must lay on the soul of this man, a heavy responsibility for the consummation of Negro disfranchisement, the
decline of the Negro college and public school and the firmer
establishment of color caste in this land." Perhaps recognizing
the cold-heartedness of his words at a time of eulogy, Du Bois
backpedaled. "What is done is done," he added. "This is no fit
time for recrimination or complaint," although he had just expressed both things.

Du Bois did not need to discredit a dead man to validate his
more militant solutions to the race problem. Booker T.'s cautious, "walk-before-you-run" philosophies were more meaningful to African Americans who experienced slavery than they
were to those who never witnessed it. It was time for blacks to
follow Du Bois, to fight the new indignities of segregation with
new strategies and new intensity. *His* moment arrived just as
Booker T.'s was passing.

It is interesting to consider what Booker T.'s posthumous
influence might have been if opera companies throughout the
land routinely performed *A Guest of Honor,* Scott Joplin's proud
ragtime tribute to Washington's groundbreaking dinner at the
White House. The lost work became a kind of Holy Grail for
Joplin scholars and fans, who searched for any scrap of information to illuminate the mythic score and its story. Joplin
biographer Ed Berlin has dedicated years to the pursuit. Occasionally, someone claims to have found a remnant of the opera,
but the rumors come and go.

Booker T.'s wife, Margaret, lived at Tuskegee until her death
in 1925. His youngest son, Ernest Davidson, died in 1938, while
his eldest son, Booker T. Jr., died in 1945. Portia, who endured a
rocky marriage, taught music at Tuskegee for twenty-five years

and lived to the age of ninety-four. In a twist of fate, Booker T.'s granddaughter, Nettie Washington, married Frederick Douglass's great-grandson, Frederick Douglass III. They met on the Tuskegee campus in 1940.

TR's final years were colored by deteriorating health, disappointment, and ultimately, heartbreak. He was his enthusiastic, "bully" self when America declared war on Germany in 1917, and tried to convince President Wilson to allow him to lead a new generation of Rough Riders into battle. TR was especially interested in heading a volunteer division of African American soldiers. Although the French were eager to work with the legendary warrior and implored Wilson to send him over, the President cruelly claimed that TR was "incompetent to lead a large military force" and denied his request to serve.

His sons, Ted, Kermit, Archie, and Quentin, eagerly went to war, and on July 14, 1918, twenty-year-old Quentin, the Roosevelts' "fine little bad boy," was killed in action. TR tried to be stoic about his son's death, but it was a harsh blow. On January 6, 1919, he suffered a fatal embolism at the age of sixty. "The funeral services for Colonel Theodore Roosevelt will be among the simplest ever held for a man who played so great a part in the world," reported the *New York Times*. TR's farewell ceremony was held at a simple church in Oyster Bay, and he was buried on a grassy hill overlooking the water.

Edith surprised her family after TR died by bravely moving forward. Her daughter Ethel was so concerned about her mother that she confided to her husband, "I almost believe she might die too." Not only did Edith *not* die, but she enjoyed a long and colorful life. The dutiful wife and mother who stayed home playing Penelope to TR's Odysseus traveled to exotic places such as China and Siberia. She outlived Kermit and Ted, and died in 1948. She was eighty-seven.

Alice, truly her father's daughter, became a veritable institution in Washington. She was an outspoken and eccentric political hostess who was famous for her wicked sense of humor. One of her oft-repeated sayings was "if you can't say anything good about someone . . . sit right here by me." At some point in her life, Alice became friendly with Portia Washington Pittman and invited her to her home without raising any eyebrows. "She's my contemporary, Booker T. Washington's daughter. She brings her grandchildren here," she mentioned in an interview in 1968.

TR's death initiated a wave of biographies and memoirs. But in the massive amount of coverage, surprisingly little was said about his invitation to Booker T. When people talked about the White House dinner, if they talked about it at all, they seemed more interested in debating whether it was dinner or lunch than in discussing the event's historical significance. In 1927, a black man named James Amos penned *Theodore Roosevelt: Hero to his Valet*. As the title implied, Amos was TR's loyal manservant, and this was his fond White House "tell-all." He suggested falsely that he was present when Booker T. was entertained. It made more sense for TR to have invited him to lunch, he argued, because it was unlikely that a Negro would have "Black Tie," the required outfit for a man dining at the White House in the evening. Amos admitted that Roosevelt himself told him he was wrong—Booker T. did indeed come for dinner, the colonel insisted—but his valet maintained that TR had a bad memory and *he* knew better. Actually, Amos's memory was suspect. He didn't start working at the White House until a few months *after* the Booker T. episode.

In 1931, the popular magazine *Collier's Weekly* ran a story titled "Dark Discretion," which professed to reveal the "simple" truth about that controversial meal. According to Dr. W. H. Frazier, president of Queens College in North Carolina, Booker T. himself admitted to eating lunch, not dinner, at the White House. "With his plate on his knee, Dr. Washington ate a sandwich and drank a cup of tea while the President refreshed himself similarly—at his desk. That was all there was to it," *Collier's* reported.

One week later, an editor at the *Afro-American*, a black newspaper in Baltimore, expressed outrage and disbelief, and set out to disprove the story with the zeal of a modern-day investigative reporter on the trail of a big exposé. A headline asked, "Would You Believe Booker T. Washington Or *Collier's Weekly*?" and ran quotes from Booker T.'s late-life autobiography, *My Larger Education*, alongside Dr. Frazier's account. In his book, Booker T. described the events leading up to *dinner*. When probed by the *Afro-American*, Dr. Frazier admitted that he had never discussed the matter with Dr. Washington, and may have read the anecdote in a newspaper several years earlier.

Determined to get to the bottom of the mystery, the persistent editor turned to the highest authority on the subject: Edith Roosevelt. "Was it lunch, or dinner?" he inquired in a letter. "My dear sir," Edith replied promptly. "An entry in my diary for Tuesday, October 16th, 1901, notes 'Mr. Booker Washington at dinner.' Believe me, Very truly yours, Edith Roosevelt." She had the wrong day of the week—it was Wednesday, not Tuesday—but the record stated clearly that Booker T. was a dinner guest.

Henry Pringle's 1931 biography of Roosevelt confirmed the

former First Lady's findings. Pringle had access to seventy-five thousand heretofore inaccessible personal and official letters belonging to the Roosevelt family. Among them was a note dated October 16, 1901. "My Dear Mr. President," it said. "I shall be very glad to accept your invitation for dinner this evening at seven-thirty." It was signed, Booker T. Washington.

With this letter, the debate over whether Booker T. was invited to lunch or dinner was solved once and for all. But a larger question remained. Why was it so important to relegate Booker T. Washington to the lesser meal?

Interestingly, the same question could be asked of Booker T.'s reduced standing in history. Why, when he had accomplished so much, and was a source of inspiration to so many people, was he dismissed as an accommodationist, or worse still, as an "Uncle Tom"?

In his recent book *Up from History: The Life of Booker T. Washington,* Robert J. Norrell argues persuasively that Booker T.'s compromised reputation was forged by scholars who perpetuated a sinister and simplistic portrait of a complicated man living in complicated times. He draws a line from Du Bois, who was a self-avowed expert on the subject of Booker T.'s flaws, to C. Vann Woodward, author of the 1951 history *Origins of the New South.* "DuBois's views reverberate through this work," says Norell, and Du Bois's legacy didn't stop there. Woodward, in turn, mentored Louis R. Harlan, who wrote the definitive, two-volume biography of Washington and edited *The Booker T. Washington Papers.* These books are substantial studies that have won serious prizes, yet their authors seemed to have closed their minds to *all* of Booker T.'s virtues. History wasn't unkind to Booker T.; historians were.

Perhaps Norrell's revisionist biography will inspire readers to take a closer look at a man, and a life, worth reconsidering. It is the story of a slave who became a teacher and a leader who extended a hand to the man farthest down. It is the story of Booker T. Washington, the first black man to fearlessly step over the color line to sit, in true equality, at the President's table.

EPILOGUE

———•◆•———

At 11:15 PM on Tuesday, November 4, 2008, Senator John McCain walked onto a stage in Phoenix, Arizona, to address his loyal supporters. The purpose of his speech was to concede victory to his opponent, Barack Obama, the newly elected president of the United States. "My friends, we have come to the end of a long journey. The American people have spoken, and they have spoken clearly," he said, acknowledging Obama's dramatic win. McCain said all the right things about mutual respect and putting aside differences to work together in the future. But one of his observations was so fresh and so sincere that it stood out from the usual post–election rhetoric.

"A century ago, President Theodore Roosevelt's invitation of Booker T. Washington to visit—to dine—at the White House was taken as an outrage in many quarters," McCain pointed out, reminding his audience of a long-forgotten moment in the country's history. "America today is a world away from the cruel and prideful bigotry of that time. There is no better evidence of this than the election of an African American to the presidency of the United States."

As Booker T. predicted to a journalist in 1899, a black man had attained the highest office in the land. It took more than a century for him to get there, but now he dines in the White House seven nights a week.

And he is no longer the guest.

He is the host.

ACKNOWLEDGMENTS

*A*gent is a word that usually connotes contracts and commissions. But my agent, Scott Waxman, is a constant source of inspiration and this book's best friend. Thank you, Scott, for always giving more than you take.

I benefited from the wisdom of experts, academics, and historians whose considerable knowledge about Booker T. Washington, Theodore Roosevelt, and their fascinating times enhanced the book immeasurably. Thank you Dana Chandler, Cheryl Ferguson, and Vester Marable at Tuskegee University; Dr. Clement Alexander Price at Rutgers University; Wallace Finley Dailey at the Houghton Library at Harvard University; William G. Allman at the White House; the New York Public Library; the Library of Congress; and the Smithsonian. I would also like to acknowledge writers who have made significant contributions to the subjects I researched, including Edmund Morris on Theodore Roosevelt, Robert J. Norrell and Louis Harlan on Booker T. Washington, and Edward Berlin on Scott Joplin.

At Atria Books, my thanks to my amiable and insightful editor, Peter Borland, and to Nick Simonds and Daniel Loedel.

At home, I appreciate the unwavering support of my dear mother, Jean Gatto, and my remarkable children, Oliver Davis-Urman and Cleo Davis-Urman. And I am beyond grateful to my multitalented and exceedingly good-humored husband, Mark Urman, to whom this book is dedicated.

NOTES

The Big House

9 Freedom, in his childish imagination: The recipe for Booker T.'s ginger cakes would have been similar to this: one quart of New Orleans molasses; one cupful of hot lard; one cupful of boiling water; one tablespoonful of soda dissolved in the hot water; one tablespoonful of ginger. Make a soft dough, stirring with a spoon, and mix overnight. In the morning, flour the pie board the least bit, roll dough less than one-half inch thick, cut into round cakes, and bake in a moderate oven.

9 "all their dreams and hopes of freedom": *New York Times,* February 7, 1909.

10 "parting with those": Booker T. Washington, *Up from Slavery* (New York: Dover, 1995), 10.

12 "grind the Southern troops to powder": Corinne Roosevelt Robinson, *My Brother Theodore Roosevelt* (New York: Charles Scribner's Sons, 1923), 17.

13 "New York showed its grief": *New York Times,* April 11, 1915.

13 Ultimately, it took an irate telegram: *New York Times,* April 25, 1865.

Strive and Succeed

16 One of the writer's biggest fans: H. W. Brands, *T.R.: The Last Romantic* (New York: Basic Books, 1997), 27.

17 "Now and then a friend": Hermann Hagedorn, *The Boy's Life of Theodore Roosevelt* (New York: Harper & Brothers, 1922), 29.

17 "I was sick of the Asthma": Ibid., 31.

19 "Some of our neighbors": Washington, *Up From Slavery,* 13.

22 "I was on fire": Ibid., 21.

22 nearly four hundred miles away: In his various memoirs, Washington described his journey as being somewhere between four hundred and five hundred miles.

22 In the fall of 1872: Washington also offered conflicting dates for his trip to Hampton. In *The Story of My Life and Work* he specified October 1, 1872, as the day he left home, but in another memoir he says that he arrived in Hampton on October 5.

23 "Obedience and even the semblance": Bertram Wyatt-Brown, *Southern Honor: Ethics and Behavior in the Old South* (Oxford: Oxford University Press, 1982), 406.

23 "clear vertical hierarchy": Ted Ownby, *Manners and Southern History* (Jackson: University Press of Mississippi, 2007), 29.

23 "This was my first experience": Washington, *Up from Slavery,* 23.

24 "one of the happiest souls on earth": Ibid., 25.

The Force That Wins

26 "the noblest, rarest human being": Ibid., 26.

27 From Lincoln, Booker T. learned: Louis R. Harlan, *Booker T. Washington: The Making of a Black Leader 1856–1901* (New York: Oxford University Press, 1983), 68.

27 "You literally took the school": Ibid., 69.

28 "presented with vigor": Ibid., 76.

32 Douglass diplomatically claimed: Frederick Douglass, *Autobiographies: Narrative of the Life of Frederick Douglass: An American Slave; My Bondage and My Freedom: Life and Times of Frederick Douglass* (New York: Literary Classics of the United States, 1994), 517.

33 "Washington is all ablaze": Lawrence Otis Graham, *The Senator and the Socialite* (New York: Harper Perennial, 2007), 89.

34 "They knew more about Latin": Washington, *Up from Slavery,* 42.

35 "The idea is": Louis Harlan et al., *The Booker T. Washington Papers,* vol. 2, 1860–1889 (Champaign: University of Illinois Press, 1972), 75.

35 "there are some graduates of Yale or Harvard": Ibid., 76.

36 "the best man we ever had here": Ibid., 127.

An Exemplary Young Gentleman

37 "I most sincerely wish": Carleton Putnam, *Theodore Roosevelt* (New York: Scribner, 1958), 136.

38 "He was everything to me": Ibid., 149.

38 "most faithful correspondent": Sylvia Jukes Morris, *Edith Kermit Roosevelt: Portrait of a First Lady* (New York: Modern Library, 2001), 22.

40 "saloonkeepers, horsecar conductors": Putnam, *Theodore Roosevelt,* 249.

41 "a splendid breeze": Ibid., 275.

41 "he has little tact": Ibid., 280.

Brick by Brick

46 "to be educated, not to work": Lyman Abbott, *Silhouettes of My Contemporaries* (Garden City, NY: Doubleday, 1921), 272.

Great Expectations

50 One of the speakers: Ibid., 389.

50 "He does not know": Morris, *Edith Kermit Roosevelt*, 74.

53 "You're talkin' like a fool": Putnam, *Theodore Roosevelt*, 528.

53 "comforts of a refined civilization": *Weekly Detroit Free Press*, July 7, 1886.

Let Me Keep Loving

57 "She was one of the most intelligent": Harlan, *Booker T. Washington: The Making of a Black Leader*, 155.

60 "hearty and strong": Putnam, *Theodore Roosevelt*, 530.

62 "Every day I went to the office": Stefan Lorant, *The Life and Times of Theodore Roosevelt* (Garden City, NY: Doubleday, 1959), 244.

Moving Up

69 "the burial forever of the old South": *Century Illustrated Monthly Magazine*, vol. 29, 1896, 470.

70 "[S]omehow I was expecting to see": Louis Harlan et al., *The Booker T. Washington Papers*, vol. 6, 1901–1902 (Champaign: University of Illinois Press, 1972), 309.

70–71 Booker T.'s eyes filled with tears: Washington, *Up from Slavery*, 144.

71 "I feel like a huckleberry": Harlan, *Booker T. Washington: The Making of a Black Leader*, 236.

Rough Riding

78 "All—Easterners and Westerners": Theodore Roosevelt, *The Rough Riders* (New York: Scribners, 1902), 27.

Rising Stars

79 On this occasion: *New York Tribune*, September 12, 1898.

80 "I am more than contented": Brands, *T. R.: The Last Romantic*, 369.

81 "grew up in an atmosphere of Victorian privilege": Thomas G. Dyer, *Theodore Roosevelt and the Idea of Race* (Baton Rouge: Louisiana State University Press, 1980), 2. Dyer's book offers a comprehensive study of TR and his conflicted (and often conflicting) attitudes about race.

81–82 Even the adventure sagas: Ibid.

82 As he matured: Ibid., 92.

83 "If he should do nothing more": Paul Laurence Dunbar, *The Life and Works of Paul Laurence Dunbar* (Naperville, IL: J. L. Nichols, 1907), 17.

86 "He held the big audience": *Boston Journal*, March 22, 1889.

Jump Jim Crow

96 "I am bound": Louis Harlan et al., *The Booker T. Washington Papers,* vol. 5, 1899–1900 (Champaign: University of Illinois Press, 1972), 68.

97 "I do not think I exaggerate": Booker T. Washington, *Some European Observations and Experiences* (Tuskegee, AL: Tuskegee Institute Press, 1899), 2.

97 "But hundreds are able": *New York Age,* July 20, 1899.

Pride and Prejudice

99 "If your head is in the lion's mouth": Michael Bieze, *Booker T. Washington and the Art of Self-Representation* (New York: Peter Lang, 2008), 27.

99 "A black man who overplayed": Joel Williamson, *A Rage for Order: Black-White Relations in the American South Since Emancipation* (New York: Oxford University Press, 1986), 56.

99 In private, behind a screen: Harlan, *Booker T. Washington: The Making of a Black Leader,* 297.

100 Bigots such as Mississippi politician James K. Vardaman complained: Norrell, *Up from History,* 179.

101 "I noticed a very large house": Harlan et al., *The Booker T. Washington Papers,* vol. 5, 1899–1900, 61.

102 "Do you think the time might ever come": Ibid., 279.

104 "Talk about yourself more": Ibid., 408.

104 "My general plan": Harlan, *Booker T. Washington: The Making of a Black Leader,* 247.

105 "historians, ministers, poets": Pauline E. Hopkins, *Contending Forces: A Romance Illustrative of Negro Life North and South* (New York: Oxford University Press, 1988), 13.

That Damned Cowboy

107 "They are peculiarly dependant": Roosevelt, *The Rough Riders,* 143.

108 TR subsequently softened his account: Dyer, *Theodore Roosevelt and the Idea of Race,* 101.

109 "My children sit in the same school": Nathan Miller, *Theodore Roosevelt: A Life* (New York: Morrow, 1992), 328.

111 "Now it is up to you to live": Lorant, *The Life and Times of Theodore Roosevelt,* 344.

Best Behavior

114 "There is no country": M. E. W. Sherwood, *Manners & Social Usages* (New York: Harper & Brothers, 1884), 256.

114 "more than the Muses": Ibid., 180.

115 "propriety of deportment": M. F. Armstrong, *On Habits and Manners* (Hampton, VA: Normal School, 1888), 80.

117 His book advised: E. M. Woods, *The Negro in Etiquette: A Novelty* (St. Louis: Buxton & Skinner, 1899), 29.
118 "Too many so-called intelligent": Ibid., 86.

Lazy Days

122 "beautiful spectacle": Walter Page, "The Pan American Exposition," *World's Work*, http://books.google.com/books?id=EUZYAAAAYAAJ&pg =PA1015&1pg=PA1015&dq=%22beautiful+spectacle%22+the+world's+w ork&source=bl&ots=fkN57RVPSD&sig=fEG8yNJCvsSVWwlPgQWWmL YxEWM&hl=en&ei=7RHoTpKKMKnh0QGHn6zuCQ&sa=X&oi=book_re sult&ct=result&resnum=1&ved=0CB4Q6AEwAA#v=onepage&q=%22be autiful%20spectacle%22%20the%20world's%20work&f=false.
123 Buildings of all sizes: Ibid.
125 "We . . . do assure the World": Hopkins, *Contending Forces*, viii.
125 "the number of authors": *Washington Post*, January 22, 1900.

A Wild Ride

129 "It seemed to me that my own heart": *Atlanta Constitution*, September 8, 1901.
130 "Just think": Ibid.
131 "a look of unmistakable anguish": *New York Times*, September 6, 1901.
131 "The man who occupies it": Brands, *T.R.*, 410.
131 "standing to-night in the shadow": *New York Times*, September 6, 1901.
132 "had saved President McKinley": *Atlanta Constitution*, September 13, 1901.
133 "it was the stunning blow": *Atlanta Constitution*, September 10, 1901.

The People's President

138 "It was not only that he was a great man": Robinson, *My Brother Theodore Roosevelt*, 160.
141 "You look anxious": John Logan, *Thirty Years in Washington: Or, Life and Scenes in Our National Capital* (Hartford, CT: A. D. Worthington, 1901), 175.
142 "In our country": George Juergens, "Theodore Roosevelt and the Press," *Daedalus* 111, no. 4 (Fall 1982): 113–33.
143 "You go into Roosevelt's presence": Mark Sullivan, *Our Times: The United States 1900–1925* (New York: Scribner's, 1935), 253.
145 "anyone attempting to take a picture": *Chicago Daily Tribune*, September 23, 1901.

The Family Circus

148 "I shall not have to count the pennies": Morris, *Edith Kermit Roosevelt*, 221.
150 "Let's go to the hotel": Ibid., 265.
151 "to let out the politicians": Belle Hagner, "Memoirs of Isabella Hagner 1901–1905," *White House History*, no. 26, 58.

152 "a sort of genteel secret police": William Seale, *The President's House,* vol. 1 (Baltimore: Johns Hopkins University Press, 1986), 682.

152 She actually complimented the President: Frank Carpenter, *North America* (New York: American, 1898), 26.

154 "the grey-haired, dignified colored person": *New York Times,* March 31, 1895.

154 "Tall and well-shaped": *Washington Post,* March 3, 1901.

155 "The Executive Mansion is overrun": *Washington Post,* October 14, 1889.

157 "Them the President's kids": *The World,* September 27, 1901.

158 "You can't think": Morris, *Edith Kermit Roosevelt,* 221.

158 TR was a firm believer: Hagner, "Memoirs," 56.

159 As far as she was concerned: Stacy A. Cordery, *Alice: Alice Roosevelt Longworth, from White House Princess to Washington Power Broker* (New York: Penguin, 2008), 44.

Behind Closed Doors

166 "my best living friend": Jennifer Fleischner, *Mrs. Lincoln and Mrs. Keckly: The Remarkable Story of the Friendship Between a First Lady and a Former Slave* (New York: Broadway, 2003), 315.

166 An early advertisement: *American Literary Gazette,* April 15, 1868.

167 "the backstairs gossip": Fleischner, *Mrs. Lincoln and Mrs. Keckly,* 317.

167 In his autobiography": Douglass, *Narrative,* 301.

170 A sharp-eyed correspondent: *Los Angeles Times,* September 29, 1901.

Fathers and Daughters

171 "a young wild animal": Morris, *Edith Kermit Roosevelt,* 273.

172 "We'd better be nice to Alice": Carol Felsenthal, *Princess Alice: The Life and Times of Alice Roosevelt Longworth* (New York: St. Martin's Griffin, 2003), 45.

172 "would have been bored": Alice Roosevelt Longworth and Michael Teague, *Mrs. L: Conversations with Alice Roosevelt Longworth* (New York: Doubleday, 1981), 37.

176 "there can be no graceful dancing": *Chicago Chronicle,* September 30, 1900.

176 "stifle the nostrils": Susan Curtis, *Dancing to a Black Man's Tune* (Columbia: University of Missouri Press, 1984), 174.

176 "symbolic of the primitive morality": Edward Berlin, *The King of Ragtime* (New York: Oxford University Press, 1995), 88.

176 If a young white person: Ibid.

177 An article that circulated: *Los Angeles Times,* September 24, 1901.

Bold Moves

185 Emmett Scott had arranged: Letter from Whitfield McKinlay to Emmett Scott, October 4, 1901.

187 TR acted on his impulse: TR described sending the invitation to Washington in the following letter: "When I asked Booker T. Washington to dinner I did not devote very much thought to the matter one way or the other. I

respect him greatly and believe in the work he has done. I have consulted so much with him it seemed to me that it was natural to ask him to dinner to talk over this work, and the very fact that I felt a moment's qualm on inviting him because of his color made me ashamed of myself and made me hasten to send the invitation. I did not think of its bearing one way or the other, either on my own future or on anything else. As things have turned out, I am very glad that I asked him, for the clamor aroused by the act makes me feel as if the act was necessary." Letter from Theodore Roosevelt to Albion Tourgee, November 8, 1901.

188 Though the invitation was addressed: Washington described his reaction to the invitation in a letter to Charles Waddell Chesnutt on July 7, 1903: "My dear Mr. Chesnutt . . . When I accepted the invitation to dine with the President of the United States and his family it was with my eyes open. The invitation was in my hands for a day and during that period I had ample time to discuss the whole matter with friends and to count the cost. Notwithstanding that I felt that in accepting the invitation I was not doing so as a personal matter but it was a recognition of the race and no matter what personal condemnation it brought upon my shoulders I had no right to refuse or even hesitate. I did my duty in the face of the opposition of the entire Southern press and at the risk of losing my own life."

Dinner Is Served

189 Would his daily uniform: *Afro-American*, January 6, 1931.

192 "a rabble": Poppy Cannon and Patricia Brooks, *The President's Cookbook: Practical Recipes from George Washington to the Present* (New York: Funk & Wagnalls, 1968), 128.

194 "Never have epicures so enjoyed themselves": Ibid., 235.

196 "I have seen two tremendous works": Gilson Willets, *Inside History of the White House: The Complete History of the Domestic and Official Life in Washington of the Nation's Presidents and Their Families* (New York: Christian Herald, 1908), 66.

196 the smaller one, though designated for family: Edna M. Colman, *White House Gossip* (Garden City, NY: Doubleday, 1927), 301.

200 TR was full of chatter: William B. Hale, *A Week in the White House with Theodore Roosevelt: A Study of the President at the Nation's Business* (New York: G. P. Putnam's Sons, 1908), 33.

200 "Theodore absorbed the conversation": Morris, *Edith Kermit Roosevelt*, 231.

201 "it is here": *Sunday Herald*, November 16, 1901.

202 But when Booker T. talked about the dinner: Booker T. Washington letter to Charles Waddell Chesnutt, July 7, 1903.

A Big Stink

210 The only exception to tabletop segregation: Ownby, *Manners and Southern History*, 169.

Sitting Ducks

221 Edgar Gardner Murphy: Louis Harlan et al., *The Booker T. Washington Papers,* vol. 6, 1901–1902 (Champaign: University of Illinois Press, 1977), 262.
223 "The storm that burst on us": Mark Twain, *Mark Twain in Eruption: Hitherto Unpublished Pages About Men and Events* (New York: Harper, 1940), 33.
226 "a woman whom all Americans": *Chicago Tribune,* October 28, 1901.
227 "The action of President Roosevelt": Dewey W. Grantham, "Dinner at the White House: Theodore Roosevelt, Booker T. Washington, and the South," *Tennessee Historical Quarterly* 17 (June 1958): 112–30. Grantham offers a detailed description of the White House dinner and its aftermath.
227 A year later: Lewis L. Gould, *The Most Exclusive Club: A History of the Modern United States Senate* (New York: Basic Books, 2005), 21.
231 He even had a title in mind: Discussed with Ed Berlin, Scott Joplin's biographer and the author of *The King of Ragtime,* in an email exchange on September 14, 2010.

Undercover

238 "so saturated": Robert J. Norrell, *Up from History* (Cambridge, MA: Belknap Press, 2009), 251.
239 "That ain't the kind of place": *New York Times,* January 18, 1903.
243 "I think that is": TR letter to Booker T. Washington, July 13, 1903.
247 Shortly before TR's inauguration: *New York Times,* March 11, 1905.

Blindsided

256 But blacks wondered: *New York Tribune,* January 15, 1907.

Slipping Away

257 "sick of looking at my grin": Cordery, *Alice,* 190.
259 He killed his first lion: Aida de Pace Donald, *Lion in the White House: A Life of Theodore Roosevelt* (New York: Basic Books, 2007), 234.
259 "Frequently, when asked to take": Brands, *T. R.,* 698.
262 There were unsubstantiated rumors: Norrell, *Up from History,* 401.
262 "have a feeling that the colored people": Ibid., 370.
263 If Booker T. had more to say: Ibid., 407.

Eulogies

266 "his monument lies in the minds": *New York Times,* December 13, 1915.
269 "She's my contemporary": Cordery, *Alice,* 463.
270 "An entry in my diary": *Afro-American,* September 4, 1948.
271 "DuBois's views reverberate": Norrell, *Up from History,* 434.

BIBLIOGRAPHY

Periodicals

NUMEROUS ISSUES OF nineteenth- and twentieth-century periodicals provided information about the White House Dinner. They include:

Afro-American
American Literary Gazette
Atlanta Constitution
Baltimore Herald
Boston Globe
Boston Guardian
Boston Journal
Boston Transcript
Brooklyn Eagle
Century
Charleston Messenger
Chicago Chronicle
Chicago Daily Tribune
Collier's Weekly

Colored American

Crisis

Detroit Free Press

Galveston Daily News

Geneva Reaper

Georgia Baptist

Indianapolis Freeman

Jackson Argus

Kansas Plaindealer

Kentucky Courier Journal

Life

Los Angeles Times

Macon Telegraph

Memphis Scimitar

Nashville Tennessee American

New Orleans Picayune

New York Age

New York Times

New York Tribune

Philadelphia North American

Raleigh Morning Post

Sunday Herald

Washington Post

Washington Star

Books and Articles

Abbott, Lyman. *Silhouettes of My Contemporaries*. Garden City, NY: Doubleday, Page, 1921.

Amos, James E. *Theodore Roosevelt: Hero to His Valet*. New York: John Day, 1927.

Armstrong, M. F. *On Habits and Manners*. Hampton, VA: Normal School, 1888.

Baker, Ray Stannard. *Following the Color Line: American Negro Citizenship in the Progressive Era*. New York: Harper & Row, 1964.

Batchelor, Bob. *The 1900s*. Westport, CT: Greenwood, 2002.

Benjamin, R. C. O., and J. C. Carter. *Don't: A Book for Girls*. San Francisco: Valleau & Peterson, 1891.

Berlin, Edward A. *King of Ragtime: Scott Joplin and His Era*. New York: Oxford University Press, 1995.

———. *Ragtime: A Musical and Cultural History*. Berkeley: University of California Press, 1980.

Bieze, Michael. *Booker T. Washington and the Art of Self-Representation*. New York: Peter Lang, 2008.

The Black Washingtonians: The Anacostia Museum Illustrated Chronology [300 Years of African American History]. Hoboken, NJ: Wiley, 2005.

Boller, Paul F. *Presidential Wives*. New York: Oxford University Press, 1998.

Bontemps, Arna. *Young Booker: Booker T. Washington's Early Days*. New York, 1972.

Booker T. Washington: An Appreciation of the Man and His Times. [Washington, DC]: National Park Service, U.S. Department of the Interior, 1972.

"Booker T. Washington Papers." *History Cooperative*, November 1, 2011, http://www.historycooperative.org/btw/.

Boren, Carter E. *Essays on the Gilded Age*. Austin: University of Texas Press, 1973.

Brands, H. W. *T. R.: The Last Romantic*. New York: Basic Books, 1997.

Brawley, Benjamin Griffith. *A Social History of the American Negro*. Mineola, NY: Dover, 2001.

Brinkley, Douglas. *The Wilderness Warrior: Theodore Roosevelt and the Crusade for America*. New York: HarperCollins, 2009.

Butt, Archie, and Lawrence F. Abbott. *The Letters of Archie Butt: Personal Aide to President Roosevelt*. Garden City, NY: Doubleday, Page, 1924.

Cable, Mary. *American Manners and Morals*. New York: American Heritage, 1969.

Cannon, Poppy, and Patricia Brooks. *The Presidents' Cookbook; Practical Recipes from George Washington to the Present.* [New York]: Funk & Wagnall's, 1968.

Caroli, Betty Boyd. *The Roosevelt Women.* New York: Basic Books, 1998.

Carroll, Rebecca, and Booker T. Washington. *Uncle Tom or New Negro? African Americans Reflect on Booker T. Washington and Up from Slavery One Hundred Years Later.* New York: Broadway/ Harlem Moon, 2006.

Chase, Henry. "Memorable Meetings: Classic White House Encounters." *American Visions,* February–March 1995.

Clark, Thomas Dionysius. *The Southern Country Editor.* Gloucester, MA: P. Smith, 1964.

Colman, Edna M. *White House Gossip, from Andrew Johnson to Calvin Coolidge.* Garden City, NY: Doubleday, Page, 1927.

Cooper, John Milton. *Pivotal Decades: The United States, 1900–1920.* New York: Norton, 1990.

Cordery, Stacy A. *Alice: Alice Roosevelt Longworth, American Princess and Washington Power Broker.* New York: Penguin, 2008.

Cowles, Virginia. *1913: An End and a Beginning.* New York: Harper & Row, 1968.

Crichton, Judy. *America 1900: The Turning Point.* New York: Henry Holt, 1998.

Curtis, Susan. *Dancing to a Black Man's Tune: A Life of Scott Joplin.* Columbia: University of Missouri Press, 1994.

Dagbovie, Pero G. "Exploring a Century of Historical Scholarship on Booker T. Washington." *Journal of African American History* (Spring 2007).

Dalton, Kathleen. *Theodore Roosevelt: A Strenuous Life.* New York: Knopf, 2002.

Davis-Horton, Paulette. *Death in 60 Days: Who Silenced Booker T. Washington? A Nurse's View.* Bloomington, IN: AuthorHouse, 2008.

Donald, Aïda DiPace. *Lion in the White House: A Life of Theodore Roosevelt.* New York: Basic Books, 2007.

Douglass, Frederick. *Autobiographies: Narrative of the Life of Frederick Douglass, an American Slave; My Bondage and My Freedom; Life and times of Frederick Douglass*. New York: Literary Classics of the United States, 1994.

Drinker, Frederick E. *Booker T. Washington: The Master Mind of a Child of Slavery*. Washington, DC: B. F. Johnson, 1915.

Dunbar, Paul Laurence, and Lida Keck Wiggins. *The Life and Works of Paul Laurence Dunbar; Containing His Complete Poetical Works, His Best Short Stories, Numerous Anecdotes and a Complete Biography of the Famous Poet*. Naperville, IL: J. L. Nichols, 1907.

Dyer, Thomas G. *Theodore Roosevelt and the Idea of Race*. Baton Rouge: Louisiana State University Press, 1980.

Felsenthal, Carol. *Princess Alice: The Life and Times of Alice Roosevelt Longworth*. New York: St. Martin's Griffin, 2003.

Fleischner, Jennifer. *Mrs. Lincoln and Mrs. Keckly: The Remarkable Story of the Friendship between a First Lady and a Former Slave*. New York: Broadway, 2003.

Fleming, Thomas. *Around the Capital with Uncle Hank*. New York: Nutshell, 1902.

Furman, Bess. *White House Profile: A Social History of the White House, Its Occupants and Its Festivities*. Indianapolis: Bobbs-Merrill, 1951.

Gates, Henry Louis, and Cornel West. *The African-American Century: How Black Americans Have Shaped Our Country*. New York: Free Press, 2000.

Gatewood, Willard B. *Aristocrats of Color: The Black Elite, 1880–1920*. Fayetteville: University of Arkansas Press, 2000.

———. *Theodore Roosevelt and the Art of Controversy: Episodes of the White House Years*. Baton Rouge: Louisiana State University Press, 1970.

Gould, Lewis L. *The Most Exclusive Club: A History of the Modern United States Senate*. New York: Basic Books, 2005.

Grantham, Dewey W., Jr. "Dinner at the White House: Theodore Roosevelt, Booker T. Washington, and the South." *Tennessee Historical Quarterly*, 2nd ser., 17 (June 1958): 112–30.

Grimké, Francis J. *The Roosevelt-Washington Episode, Or, Race Prejudice: Delivered October 27, 1901*. [Washington, DC]: Hayworth, 1901.

Hagedorn, Hermann. *The Boys' Life of Theodore Roosevelt*. New York: Harper & Brothers, 1922.

Hale, Annie Riley. *Rooseveltian Fact and Fable*. New York: Author, 1910.

Hale, William Bayard. *A Week in the White House with Theodore Roosevelt: A Study of the President at the Nation's Business*. New York: G.P. Putnam's Sons, 1908.

Haley, James T., and Booker T. Washington. *Afro-American Encyclopaedia: Or, the Thoughts, Doings, and Sayings of the Race, Embracing Addresses, Lectures, Biographical Sketches, Sermons, Poems, Names of Universities, Colleges, Seminaries, Newspapers, Books, and a History of the Denominations, Giving the Numerical Strength of Each. In Fact, It Teaches Every Subject of Interest to the Colored People, as Discussed by More than One Hundred of Their Wisest and Best Men and Women*. Nashville, TN: Winston-Derek, 1992.

Harlan, Louis R. *Booker T. Washington: The Making of a Black Leader, 1856–1901*. New York: Oxford University Press, 1972.

———. *Booker T. Washington: The Wizard of Tuskegee, 1901–1915*. New York: Oxford University Press, 1983.

Holland, Jesse J. *Black Men Built the Capitol: Discovering African-American History in and around Washington, D.C.* Guilford, CT: Globe Pequot, 2007.

Hoover, Irwin Hood. *Forty-two Years in the White House*. Boston: Houghton Mifflin, 1934.

Hopkins, Pauline E. *Contending Forces: A Romance Illustrative of Negro Life North and South*. New York: Oxford University Press, 1988.

Hughes, Langston, Milton Meltzer, Hugh H. Smythe, and Mabel M. Smythe. *A Pictorial History of the Negro in America*. New York: Crown, 1956.

Jacob, Kathryn Allamong. *Capital Elites: High Society in Washington, D.C., after the Civil War*. Washington, DC: Smithsonian Institution, 1995.

"James B. Parker Revisited—Illuminations: Revisiting the Buffalo Pan-American Exposition of 1901." *University at Buffalo Libraries,* November 2011, http://library.buffalo.edu/libraries/exhibits/panam/essays/rasuli/rasuli.html.

Jeffries, Ona Griffin. *In and Out of the White House from Washington to the Eisenhowers.* New York: Funk, 1960.

Johnson, Edward A. *History of Negro Soldiers in the Spanish-American War and Other Items of Interest.* Raleigh, NC: Capital Print Company, 1901.

Keckley, Elizabeth. *Behind the Scenes in the Lincoln White House: Memoirs of an African-American Seamstress.* Mineola, NY: Dover, 2006.

Kraft, Betsy Harvey. *Theodore Roosevelt: Champion of the American Spirit.* New York: Clarion, 2003.

Litwack, Leon F. *Trouble in Mind: Black Southerners in the Age of Jim Crow.* New York: Knopf, 1998.

Logan, John A. *Thirty Years in Washington: Or, Life and Scenes in Our National Capital.* Hartford, CT: A. D. Worthington, 1901.

Lorant, Stefan. *The Life and Times of Theodore Roosevelt.* Garden City, NY: Doubleday, 1959.

Mansfield, Stephen. *Then Darkness Fled: The Liberating Wisdom of Booker T. Washington.* Nashville, TN: Cumberland House, 1999.

McCaskill, Barbara, and Caroline Gebhard. *Post-bellum, Pre-Harlem: African American Literature and Culture, 1877–1919.* New York: New York University Press, 2006.

McCullough, David G. *Mornings on Horseback.* New York: Simon & Schuster, 2003.

Meier, August. *Negro Thought in America, 1880–1915: Racial Ideologies in the Age of Booker T. Washington.* Ann Arbor: University of Michigan Press, 1966.

Millard, Candice. *The River of Doubt: Theodore Roosevelt's Darkest Journey.* New York: Broadway, 2005.

Miller, Nathan. *Theodore Roosevelt: A Life.* New York: William Morrow, 1992.

Morris, Edmund. *The Rise of Theodore Roosevelt.* New York: Modern Library, 2001.

———. *Theodore Rex.* New York: Modern Library, 2002.

Morris, Sylvia Jukes. *Edith Kermit Roosevelt: Portrait of a First Lady.* New York: Modern Library, 2001.

Norrell, Robert J. *Up from History: The Life of Booker T. Washington.* Cambridge, MA: Belknap Press of Harvard University Press, 2009.

Ownby, Ted. *Manners and Southern History.* Jackson: University Press of Mississippi, 2007.

Pendel, Thomas F. *Thirty-six Years in the White House: Lincoln-Roosevelt.* Bedford, MA: Applewood, 2008.

Putnam, Carleton. *Theodore Roosevelt.* New York: Scribner, 1958.

Randolph, Mary. *Presidents and First Ladies.* New York: Appleton-Century, 1936.

Rijn, Guido Van. *Roosevelt's Blues: African-American Blues and Gospel Songs on FDR.* Jackson: University Press of Mississippi, 1997.

Robinson, Corinne Roosevelt. *My Brother Theodore Roosevelt.* New York: Charles Scribner's Sons, 1921.

Roosevelt, Priscilla. "Memoirs of Isabella Hagner 1901–1905." *White House History* 26, www.whha.org/whha . . ./whitehousehistory _26-hagner.pdf.

Roosevelt, Theodore. *Theodore Roosevelt's Diaries of Boyhood and Youth.* New York: Charles Scribner's Sons, 1928.

Scott, Emmett Jay, Lyman Beecher Stowe, and Booker Taliaferro Washington. *Booker T. Washington: Builder of a Civilization.* London: Unwin, 1916.

Seale, William. *The President's House: A History.* 2 vols. Washington, DC: White House Historical Association with the Cooperation of the National Geographic Society, 1986.

———. *White House History: Collection 1, Numbers 1 through 6.* Washington, DC: White House Historical Association, 2004.

———. *White House History: Collection 2, Numbers 7 through 12.* Washington, DC: White House Historical Association, 2004.

Sherwood, M. E. W. *Manners & Social Usages.* New York: Harper & Brothers, 1884.

Smith, Marie D. *Entertaining in the White House.* New York: Macfadden-Bartell, 1970.

Soriso, Carolyn. "Unmasking the Genteel Performer: Elizabeth Keckley's 'Behind the Scenes' and the Politics of Public Wrath." *African American Review* 34 (Spring 2000): 19–38.

Spencer, Samuel R., and Oscar Handlin. *Booker T. Washington and the Negro's Place in American Life.* Boston: Little, Brown, 1956.

Stewart, Ruth Ann. *Portia: The Life of Portia Washington Pittman, the Daughter of Booker T. Washington.* Garden City, NY: Doubleday, 1977.

Sullivan, Mark. *Our Times; the United States, 1900–1925.* New York: Charles Scribner's Sons, 1926.

Thayer, William Roscoe. *Theodore Roosevelt: An Intimate Biography.* Boston: Houghton Mifflin, 1919.

Theodore Roosevelt, Patriot and Statesman: The True Story of an Ideal American. Philadelphia and Chicago: P. W. Ziegler, 1902.

Thornbrough, E. L., Carter Godwin Woodson, H. M. Bond, and M. Curti. *Booker T. Washington.* Englewood Cliffs, NJ: Prentice-Hall, 1969.

"The 3 Wives of Booker T. Washington." *Ebony,* September 1982, pp. 29–34.

Tompkins, Vincent. *American Decades: 1910–1919.* New York: Gale Research, 1996.

Truman, Margaret. *The President's House: A First Daughter Shares the History and Secrets of the World's Most Famous Home.* New York: Ballantine, 2004.

Twain, Mark, and Bernard Augustine De Voto. *Mark Twain in Eruption: Hitherto Unpublished Pages about Men and Events.* New York: Harper, 1940.

Walker, Lee H., Diane Carol Bast, and T. S. Karnick. *Booker T. Washington: A Re-examination.* Chicago: Heartland Institute, 2008.

Washington, Booker T. *An Autobiography: The Story of My Life and Work.* S.l.: Dodo, 2008.

———. *My Larger Education.* Radford, VA: Wilder, 2008.

———. *Some European Observations and Experiences.* Tuskegee, AL, 1899.

———. *Up from Slavery.* New York: Dover, 1995.

———. *The Booker T. Washington Papers.* 14 vols. Edited by Louis R. Harlan et al. Champaign: University of Illinois Press, 1972–89.

Washington, Booker T., and Victoria Earle Matthews. *Black Diamonds: The Wisdom of Booker T. Washington: Originally Titled Blackbelt Diamonds: Gems from the Speeches, Addresses and Talks to Students of Booker T. Washington.* Deerfield Beach, FL: Health Communications, 1995.

Washington, Booker T., Fannie Barrier Williams, and Norman Barton Wood. *A New Negro for a New Century: An Accurate and Up-to-date Record of the Upward Struggles of the Negro Race; The Spanish-American War, Causes of It; Vivid Descriptions of Fierce Battles; Superb Heroism and Daring Deeds of the Negro Soldier . . . Education, Industrial Schools, Colleges, Universities and Their Relationship to the Race Problem.* Chicago: American, 1900.

"What Happened to Big Ben Parker," http://www.nsm.buffalo.edu/~sww/0history/parker_big.ben.html.

Whitcomb, John, and Claire Whitcomb. *Real Life at the White House: Two Hundred Years of Daily Life at America's Most Famous Residence.* New York: Routledge, 2002.

The White House: An Historic Guide. Washington, DC: White House Historical Association, 1962.

Willets, Gilson. *Inside History of the White House: The Complete History of the Domestic and Official Life in Washington of the Nation's Presidents and Their Families.* New York: Christian Herald, 1908.

Williamson, Joel. *The Crucible of Race: Black-White Relations in the American South Since Emancipation.* New York: Oxford University Press, 1984.

———. *A Rage for Order: Black-White Relations in the American South Since Emancipation.* New York: Oxford University Press, 1986.

Wilson, Dorothy Clarke. *Alice and Edith: The Two Wives of Teddy Roosevelt: A Biographical Novel.* New York: Doubleday, 1989.

Woods, E. M. *The Negro in Etiquette: A Novelty.* St. Louis: Buxton & Skinner, 1899.

Wyatt-Brown, Bertram. *Southern Honor: Ethics and Behavior in the Old South.* New York: Oxford University Press, 1982.

Young, Elizabeth. *Disarming the Nation: Women's Writing and the American Civil War.* Chicago: University of Chicago Press, 1999.

Young, Nathan B. *A Guest of Honor: A Re-creation, 1999 A.D.: Scott Joplin's "White-Black" Magic Years in Texarkana-Sedalia-Chicago & St. Louis, 1868–1908.* St. Louis: W. H. Green, 1986.

Ziemann, Hugo, and F. L. Gillette. *White House Cookbook.* Baltimore: Ottenheimer, 1999.

INDEX

———•◆•———